THE
CHARTIST MOVEMENT
IN SCOTLAND

ALEXANDER WILSON

MANCHESTER UNIVERSITY PRESS

Published by the University of Manchester at
THE UNIVERSITY PRESS
316–324 Oxford Road, Manchester M13 9NR

UK standard book number 7190 0411 X

Made and printed in Great Britain by
William Clowes and Sons, Limited, London and Beccles

Contents

Illustrations

Preface

The research on which this book is based was done more than twenty years ago, and of the many people who gave me valuable help, several are now dead. In particular my belated thanks are due to the late Dr James Handley, Mr Anthony Hepburn, Mr James A. Flanagan, Professor A. R. Schoyen and Professor G. D. H. Cole, who started it off with his question 'Why on earth were the Scottish people not ardent Chartists?'

Amongst the others to whom I am indebted are Mr H. L. Beales, Dr W. H. Chaloner, Mr W. H. Marwick, Mrs Dorothy Thompson and Mr Morris Pearl. Librarians are the salt of the earth for the researcher, and the list of librarians who helped me in Glasgow, Edinburgh, Paisley, London, Birmingham, Leeds, Manchester, Dundee, Ayr and elsewhere would be a long one. Of these I should like to thank especially Mr A. B. Paterson of Glasgow, Miss Catherine R. McEwan of Paisley, Mr A. Small of Dundee, and Mr F. G. B. Hutchings of Leeds.

For their help in locating illustrative material, I am grateful to Miss Alice Brown, Mr D. R. Shearer, Mr James Aitken and the Rev. J. W. Burnside of Paisley, Mr J. F. T. Thomson of Kilmarnock, Dr S. M. K. Henderson, Mr R. B. Wilkie, Mr James Hood and Mr W. A. G. Alison of Glasgow, Miss M. Deas, Mr R. E. Hutchison and Mr C. S. Minto of Edinburgh.

Finally I must thank my wife, Sophie Luise, for her persistence in urging the rescue of this work from oblivion, even at the neglect of more urgent but less important matters.

A.W.

To H. L. Beales, Asa Briggs
and the late G. D. H. Cole

CHAPTER ONE

The social background of Scottish Chartism

The rapid growth of industry and of population, and the urbanisation and concentration of that population, especially in the areas around the coalfields of central Scotland, were the outstanding features affecting the social and economic life of Scotland in the first half of the nineteenth century.

During the period 1801–41 there was a net increase in population of more than 60 per cent. Population rose from 1,608,420 in 1801, at the rate of 200,000–250,000 each succeeding decade, to 2,620,184 in 1841. In its composition there were two particularly remarkable features. In 1841 there were 10 per cent more females than males, but in Glasgow the female population was 50 per cent greater in the 20–30 age group than the male. There was also a large and increasing Irish immigration. By 1841 the Irish-born population was estimated at 4·8 per cent of the total. It was located chiefly in Lanarkshire, Renfrewshire, Dumbartonshire and Wigtownshire. In each of these counties it accounted for more than 10 per cent of the total population, while in Glasgow it amounted to 16 per cent.

This growth of population was accompanied by wide variations in the rate of increase in different parts of the country and by considerable changes in the geographical distribution of population. While there was an accelerated exodus from the Highlands, Renfrewshire, Ayrshire and Edinburghshire (as it was termed) increased their numbers by 100 per cent, 95 per cent and 80 per cent respectively. In the east of Scotland, during the period 1821–41, Forfarshire's population increased by 50 per cent and that of Dundee doubled. More remarkable still was the growth of population in Lanarkshire. It increased by 75 per cent in the twenty years following 1821, and by approximately 200 per cent over the period 1801–41. Here a complete transformation took place. Villages expanded rapidly into large towns at Airdrie, Blantyre, Bellshill,

THE CHARTIST MOVEMENT IN SCOTLAND

Bothwell, Cambuslang, Coatbridge, Hamilton, Lanark, Mother-well, Shotts and Wishaw. Above all, there emerged, at Glasgow, a great city whose population had increased by about 360 per cent, to 274,533, during the first forty years of the nineteenth century.[1] The outstanding feature of the truly revolutionary developments in industry in the first decades of the century was the growth of the textile industry. By 1812 there were 120 cotton mills, with an annual import of about 11 million lbs of raw cotton, and by then cotton had displaced linen as the most important branch of the industry. In 1834 there were 134 mills, almost all within a radius of twenty-five miles from Glasgow, and raw cotton imports had risen to 34.5 million lbs.

Almost the whole of this development took place in the Clyde valley. In 1834, in Lanarkshire, almost 18,000 operatives were em-ployed in 74 cotton mills, two woollen and two silk factories. Over forty of these mills and factories were in Glasgow itself, while Paisley had also become an important textile centre. Throughout the south-west of Scotland 47,000 looms, controlled by the manu-facturers of Paisley and Glasgow, were working for the Glasgow market. Of these, over 15,000 were steam looms and 13,400 were hand-looms in other towns. Bleaching, dyeing and calico printing were important subsidiary trades, largely localised in the Vale of Leven.[2]

At Paisley there was considerable development of the manufac-ture of fashionable and fancy cotton goods, and of specialisation in the production of cotton thread. At Darvel, lace weaving was introduced, and Darvel became the most important centre of this branch of textiles in Great Britain. The manufacture of carpets was introduced at Kilmarnock, where bonnet making remained important.

Outside the Clyde valley, there were cotton mills and linen fac-tories at Perth and Aberdeen, and between 1821 and 1841 there was considerable growth of the flax and linen industry in Dundee and Forfar. Meanwhile, in the country districts the textile industry developed mainly in small establishments, with concentration of labour in large factories occurring only in a few places. At Catrine, however, almost a thousand workers were employed in a single establishment, and at Kilbirnie, a power loom factory and a flax spinning mill employed 500 people. Elsewhere mules, jennies and the domestic system remained normal for many years.

2

One consequence of this rapid development was an ever-increasing strain on the domestic weaver, who struggled hard against the competition of the weaving shed, working long hours for constantly decreasing returns. Despite this, there was considerable resistance from native labour to working in the mills and weaving sheds. Antipathy to the cotton thread factories was less, but cotton spinners held a lower social status than the fancy weavers, despite the fact that they frequently earned much higher wages. As a result, the new industrial proletariat was largely drawn from the Lowland peasantry, evicted Highlanders and immigrant Irish.[3]

The first decade of the century saw a considerable improvement in communications, with the completion of the central Scotland canal system and increased road-making between the main towns. Dock and harbour development took place at Glasgow and the Clyde harbours in the west, and at Aberdeen, Arbroath, Dundee and Perth in the east. The following decade saw a tremendous development of heavy industry, accompanied by that of the Scottish banking system to meet the needs of the new industrialists, also helped by, and largely motivating, the rapid construction of railways in the 1830's and 1840's.

During the period 1830–60 the rise of heavy industry was centred on the Clyde valley, where great coal, iron and steel, engineering and shipbuilding industries emerged. By 1850 Lanarkshire had been completely transformed. About half the 350 Scottish collieries were in the county, and more than two-thirds of the miners were then Irish. The iron industry was also chiefly centred in Lanarkshire, mainly around Airdrie and Coatbridge. In 1835 there were estimated to be 29 blast furnaces in Scotland, with an annual output of 75,000 tons of pig iron. By the end of the 1830's there were 56 in operation, producing over 195,000 tons. All but five of these were in the neighbourhood of Glasgow. By 1853 output had more than trebled, with 114 furnaces producing 685,000 tons a year.

Elsewhere, industrial development was much less dramatic, though around Falkirk the old-established Carron Company controlled 3,500 acres of coalfields, besides the greatest ironworks in Europe, employing more than 2,000 men in 1814. By 1850, about eighty collieries existed in Ayrshire, which also had 24 blast furnaces at Ardeer, Dalmellington, Eglinton, Glengarnock, Galston, Lugar, Muirkirk and Portland. In West Lothian there was some

3

growth of the long-established coal industry, while shale was being utilised for the production of commercial paraffin.[4]

This industrial and commercial revolution, with its growth of large towns and greatly increased total population, created an increasing demand for farm produce, and it provided, with the improvements in communications, a convenient and accessible market for the recently regenerated Scottish agricultural system, which was so admired by William Cobbett. The new markets were largely supplied by the south-eastern Lowlands, chiefly Berwickshire, Roxburgh and the Lothians. In these counties the average arable farm was of about 300 acres. Many were over 600 acres, and occasionally there were groupings of three or four farms with 1,000 acres or more under a single control, which Cobbett regarded as great factories for producing corn and meat. Meanwhile, in the Highlands there was rapid extension of sheep farming and ruthless clearance of the peasantry, which deeply shocked Karl Marx.[5]

The need for rapid harvesting in the traditionally uncertain autumn weather involved the use of a large seasonal labour force. Until the early years of the nineteenth century this had been supplied mainly from the Highlands. After 1812, however, there was an increasing supply of labour from Glasgow, Edinburgh and Ireland. Much of it was drawn from the casual labour of the handloom weavers of the villages and new towns, but with the development of cheap cross-channel services in the 1820's, there was a swelling tide of Irish harvesters and potato pickers.

In the 1820's about 6,000 to 8,000 Irish people came across to Scotland for the harvest season. By the 1840's this figure had risen to around 25,000. Irish labour was usually hired at an hourly rate, about 2d or 3d, while local labour was often hired for the season. Wages were sometimes paid according to results, or according to the acreage covered. They depended greatly on the demand for labour. At different periods in the harvest, they could vary from 8d to 2s 6d a day. Women were normally paid 20 per cent less than men. Bargaining strength was usually weak, largely as a result of the influx of Irish, with their modest demands, but partly owing to the efforts of local magistrates to prevent combination. Despite this, attempts at combination were quite frequent and there was often barracking, or more, of blackleg labour.[6]

Despite the obvious growth in the capital wealth of the country between 1811 and 1841, there were few trades in which this increase

4

was reflected in nominal wages. Something in the nature of a hierarchy in the scale of industrial wages was emerging, but, within it, wage rates in many trades were subject to violent fluctuation. In normal years, wage rates tended to approach the level of 1810–12, and since there was a considerable drop in the cost of living, especially in the period following 1822, there was probably some improvement in real earnings during this period for those in steady employment. Real earnings, however, depended on the state of trade and the ability to maintain employment, even more than on fluctuations in food prices.

After the post-war depression, unemployment and wage reductions were caused by the frequent slumps and the even more frequent 'slackness' of trade. Years such as 1819, 1825–26, 1829, 1832, 1837 and 1840–43 brought tides of hopeless distress to the growing industrial towns. After 1824, strikes marked both boom and slump, with trade unions determined to share the prosperity of the good years, and avoid wage cuts and short time when trade was poor. Paisley was probably the worst affected town in the kingdom. With its heavy dependence on the market for fancy cloth, it was chronically affected by every recession in trade. From 1837 to 1843 the town suffered constant and severe distress. It not only affected all classes of workmen, but bankrupted a large proportion of the local traders and manufacturers. Sixty-seven out of 112 manufacturing firms failed between 1841 and 1843. With the decline of the Paisley shawl trade, each succeeding depression became almost intolerable for the locality.[7]

The most striking development in wage scales was the collapse of the earning power of the hand-loom weaver, who had been an aristocrat of the working classes at the turn of the century. In 1836–40, weavers' earnings tended to average 6s to 11s a week. With the help of a wife and one or two children, the spending power of the family might average 16s for a working week of about seventy hours. Many of the older weavers had experienced a decline of 50 per cent or more in their earnings since 1810, despite greatly increased hours. In the country districts, earnings from the loom were often supplemented at harvest time by casual employment on farms. From his inquiries for the Hand-loom Weavers Commission, J. C. Symons calculated that 30,075 out of 51,060 looms were employed on the worst-paid types of work, and that domestic weavers averaged little more than half the earnings of factory weavers.

Much higher wages could be earned by the cotton spinners, who were, however, often subject to short time and unemployment. In 1836 spinners might earn up to 25s a week, with adult male spinners averaging 16s to 21s a week. Before the 1837 recession and strike, Glasgow cotton spinners were earning 23s–24s a week. After the strike they resumed work at 15s–17s. Women's wages were very much lower, averaging 5s–8s in cotton mills in the west of Scotland, and rather less in the linen trade in Dundee and Arbroath. The most prosperous section of the weavers was the silk weavers; rather less well paid were the woollen weavers of the border districts, whose earnings, however, averaged 50–100 per cent more than cotton or linen weavers'.[8]

The miners were still considered a rather servile class, whose actual earnings often bore little resemblance to their nominal wage rates. Wages were generally assessed on a daily output basis, subject to 'offtakes', 'drawbacks' and other fines, and were paid monthly. Even after 1831 the truck system still operated, unchecked by legal theory in many coalfields, and real pay corresponded only slightly with nominal wages. Nominal wage rates fell from around 5s a day in 1811–12 to about 4s a day in the 1830's, with considerable fluctuations in the intervening period. Conditions of employment and return for labour, moreover, varied considerably between different collieries and iron mines, depending largely on the nature of the employer. Colliers and their families generally received better treatment in the west of Scotland than in the Lothians.[9]

Throughout this period the building trades were relatively prosperous, thanks to the growth of towns and industries. In 1836 carpenters could expect to earn over 20s a week in Glasgow and about two-thirds of that in Kirkcaldy, Forfar, Brechin and small towns. Bricklayers earned 18s–21s a week in the larger towns, with stone masons tending to earn rather more, but the wages of both groups were subject to considerable loss in wet or frosty weather. During the winter months this would amount to at least 3s–4s on average.

Among the worst paid groups were the shoemakers, who were generally poorer than tailors, dyers, bakers and smiths, who tended to average 10s–15s a week. At the other end of the wage scale were the growing numbers of steam-engine machine makers and other engineers. These were the new aristocrats of labour, and some could rent property worth £10 a year, and enjoy voting rights.[10]

The recurrent unemployment and social distress which accompanied the growth of industrialism were only slightly alleviated by the Scottish system of poor relief. From 1425 onwards, and especially during the seventeeth century, the Scottish poor laws were directed at the prevention of vagrancy rather than towards the relief of poverty. In 1535 the parish had been made liable for the support of its aged and infirm poor, but collections for this purpose remained voluntary. In 1579 the power to tax and assess the whole population of the parish according to substance was added. Birth, or seven years' residence in a parish, was the qualification for relief. Overseers of the poor and collectors were to be appointed, and recipients were to be directed to work. In 1597 the Kirk session, and secondarily the presbytery, became the sole administrators of the law for the relief of the aged and infirm poor.

These provisions were effective in preventing neither destitution nor widespread vagrancy. Yet, in theory at least, they remained in force until 1845. Despite the growing need for large amounts of periodic relief, especially for the able-bodied unemployed, the power of assessment was rarely used in the nineteenth century by Kirk sessions or the men of property, the 'heritors'. The attitude of the clergy and of the rising middle classes was one of encouraging 'self-respect' and private benevolence, while avoiding interference with the somewhat harsh laws of political economy. Amongst the respectable classes it was widely felt that the absence of a compulsory, universal assessment for the poor had been 'the pride of Scotland' and 'the envy of England'.

The strongest protagonist of the voluntary school of thought in this matter was Dr Thomas Chalmers, the foremost churchman of his day, leader of the movement for the freedom of the Kirk from the intrusion of the State in such matters as the appointment of parish ministers. He hoped

that by moral influences, by reviving the spirit of brotherhood, by stimulating Christian liberality through the Church, above all by so dividing the districts as to create a new and more vigorous personal interest in the work, the necessity for vast machinery of a statutory support of the poor might be avoided and the proud independence of the Scottish spirit be maintained.[11]

7

The weight of legal opinion was voiced by Lord Cockburn, who knew 'of no constitutional right any man has to ruin his own morality and pick my pocket at the same time'. Even in the 1820's Lord Cockburn had been lamenting the progress of 'these cursed poor rates'. If the plea were accepted that able-bodied people out of work had a legal right to be maintained, 'the result is that any human creature who is poor must be made rich'.[12]

Against this attitude, Sir Archibald Alison, Sheriff of Lanarkshire, argued that great injustice had been done to the poor by the decisions of the Court of Session which had made the ratepayers the judges in their own cases, and had left the poor of Scotland without any right of appeal. He believed that the 1579 Act had placed the subject

on a footing to which subsequent wisdom has been able to add nothing in the way of improvement ... The Scottish Poor Laws have now stood the test, not only of ages, in point of time, but of every possible change in point of society; they have been found equally efficacious in the relief of real suffering, and equally effective in checking the growth of fictitious pauperism ... among the weavers of Lanarkshire.

Reform of the Scottish poor law was long delayed by the deep division of public opinion along such lines. As a result, proposed measures such as the Poor Law Bill of Joseph Hume and Kennedy of Dunure in 1824 were attacked equally violently both by those who felt that fresh legislation was less necessary than the enforcement of the acts of 1579 and 1597, and by the supporters of Chalmers, who contended that low rates of relief for the deserving poor were calculated to foster self-respect and charity, and that it was nobler to struggle with difficulties than to submit to official inspection.

Increasingly, however, it was becoming clear that contributions in parish churches, donations in times of emergency by prominent citizens to special relief funds, and other forms of charity were failing to provide more than very meagre rates of relief, and that the raising of increased funds to meet the increasing needs depended on more systematic recourse to legal assessment, especially in the more populous parishes. By 1840 there were 236 assessed parishes against 643 non-assessed, with total populations of about 1·1 million in each.

Where there was regular assessment, as in Glasgow, this was

8

often considered an unequal and unjust burden, imposed on a haphazard basis. At all events, the fears of Lord Cockburn were never realised, and the poor were not made rich. Both the poor rates and Scottish charity were held well in check by Scottish prudence and morality. The amounts which were made available for relief in Scotland in the 1830's seldom approached, in proportion to population, even a quarter of the amounts raised in England. Even in 1841, when there were 55,340 'permanent paupers', there was only £205,550 available for relief, or less than 1s 8d raised per head of the population. Of this amount 62, 11 and 16 per cent came respectively from legal assessment, voluntary assessment and church collections.

In some sections of the population—especially the hand-loom weavers—the 'sturdily honest people' battled with destitution rather than receive the slightest help from charity. Great obloquy was attached to pauperism, and the Assistant Commissioner to the Hand-loom Weavers Commission reported that these people would rather sacrifice their living wants than endure the prospect of a pauper funeral and pauper grave. Amongst the hand-loom weavers the contrast between their present condition and past comfort was felt more bitterly than their actual destitution. Their book societies decayed, religious attendances fell off, and the only societies which were constantly maintained were the funeral societies.[13]

The educational system of Scotland, which in the eighteenth century had been considered a model for the rest of Europe, was also suffering from growing pains in a rapidly changing social structure. The parochial system had been one of the legacies of the presbyterian reformation in the sixteenth century. John Knox had formulated the ideal of 'a school in every parish, a higher school or college in cities and large towns, and University education'. In 1616 the establishment of a school in every parish was ordained by the Privy Council, and this was reinforced by Acts of 1633, 1645 and 1696. Although the provisions of the Acts were carried out somewhat slowly, in the face of objections and procrastination by the heritors, the goal was achieved fairly thoroughly in many parts of the country. By the end of the seventeenth century there were 907 schools for a population of about one million.

During the eighteenth century, despite the growth in population, there was little further establishment of parish schools, but foreign visitors, observing the relative excellence of the system, appear to

9

have believed that schools existed in almost all parishes. There was, however, often a gap between the observation and the reality —especially in the Highlands, where in 1758 there were 175 parishes without a school or a schoolmaster. Many of the schools in the Lowlands, also, lacked masters for long periods. Teachers' incomes remained on a very low level, and many of them were subjected to strict surveillance by officious ministers.

The merits of the system were increasingly strained by the growth of population, and ability to read and write came to depend increasingly on the services offered by private individuals. By 1831 the population had risen to 2,364,000 but the number of parish schools had risen only to 1,005. Private schools had become fairly common throughout the country and were approximately three times as numerous as the parochial schools. About a quarter of these non-parish schools taught Latin and mathematics, and a much smaller number taught Greek. Some achieved high standards, and the *Scotch Reformers' Gazette* went so far as to claim that generally they were far more efficient than those under the control of the Established Church. The quality of the private schools, however, seems to have been even more variable than that of the parish schools. The teachers included fishermen, retired soldiers, aged females, students and youths. Especially in the Highlands, the teachers were often said to be too incompetent to find other employment.

The experiments of Robert Owen, Wilderspin, the Andersonian University and the Stow Training School for Teachers attracted considerable attention in the newspapers. Several mechanics' institutes were founded in the 1820's, and their work was supplemented by the efforts of Lord Brougham's 'Society for the Diffusion of Useful Knowledge' after 1825. Nevertheless it was becoming clear, throughout the early part of the nineteenth century, that general education was deteriorating with a rapidity which alarmed both *The Scotsman* and the General Assembly of the Church of Scotland. The needs of the growing towns were not being met, and little temptation was being placed in the way of parents to send their children to school rather than put them out to work at a very early age. The allegations of poor quality of teaching in parish schools and of low salaries of the masters attracted some attention.

Confirmation for much of this criticism was to be found in the surveys produced by the education committee of the Church of

Scotland, which indicated that in Glasgow about 20,000 of the 46,000 children of school age were growing up untaught, and that in 143 Highland parishes, with a total population of 500,000, about 250,000 could not write, while 83,000 could neither read nor appeared to have any opportunity of learning to read. The education committee considered that about one-sixth of the population, mainly between the ages of 5 and 15, should be receiving education, but found that the proportion achieved fell far short of this, except in a few Lowland parishes. The rural parishes as well as the manufacturing ones were suffering a grave deterioration, and the state of the country was almost equally bad. In 132 parishes of Banff, Elgin and Aberdeen the average proportion at school was one in eleven. Parishes in Edinburgh, Galloway, Berwick and Dumbartonshire varied between one in eleven and one in fifteen. Dundee, Glasgow and Perth had between one in fourteen and one in sixteen. In Old Aberdeen the proportion fell to one in twenty-five, while in Paisley the children of about 3,000 families were completely untaught, whereas thirty years earlier all above the age of 9 could read or were at school.

The Church of Scotland education committee considered that where parish schools were successful, it was often due to the co-operation of an active and zealous clergyman. This opinion was supplemented by W. E. Hickson in his report on the condition of the hand-loom weavers in 1840. He found, however, that the parochial schoolmaster was normally subjected to the petty and annoying superintendence of the clergyman, to whom he was a slave and obsequious bondsman. He could have no opinion in politics, religion or philosophy which was not permitted by his superior. He could introduce no educational improvement without the clergyman's approval. He could appeal against this tyranny, but only to the presbytery, which was often a 'congress of tyrants'. A man of talent in the job of parish schoolmaster under the control of a clergyman of limited capacity and indifferent temper was 'like a soul in purgatory. No language can be strong enough to express his degradation and misery.'

That was, however, an old, familiar complaint, and since most of the parochial schoolmasters were originally aspirant ministers there would probably have been many more submissive slaves for this work if teachers' salaries had been higher. *The Scotsman* suggested that a proper salary scale for teachers would be from £60 to £120 a year. The education committee thought that teachers should have £40 a year plus accommodation. The actual position was very much worse, with a typical figure of £15-£25. Salaries of £25 and over were rare, while the rewards for private teachers were often considerably less, averaging about £13 in the Highlands and as little as £3 in the Shetlands. Over a quarter of parish school-masters, and probably a similar proportion of private school teachers, had an additional occupation or employment in 1838.

Yet despite its defects the parochial system was considered vastly superior to the charity schools of England. In Scotland the master was often a classical scholar, and always had 'some knowledge of books'. Since the parish school teachers were, however, attached to the Established Church, this created distrust and jealousy among the seceders, who often kept their children away from the parish schools lest they be converted to the State Church.[14]

Religion was also being deeply affected by the dynamic economic, political and social forces of the early nineteenth century. For over two and a half centuries, religion had been the strongest factor in Scottish life, and it still entered deeply into the life of the people in the 1830's and 1840's, even in the industrial areas. There were long services for the masses on Sundays, and although many of the churches were miserable buildings both the Church of Scotland and the dissenting Churches were concerned with church extension schemes.

Within the Established Church there had been a considerable relaxation of the earlier rigid presbyterian discipline. This older Covenanting tradition, however, was still held to some degree by the 'Evangelicals', who became very important under the leader-ship of Dr Chalmers after 1830. This faction had considerable sup-port from the middle classes. Their hatred of the interference of the State, by its preservation of the rights of patronage in the appointment of ministers, raised a great storm in Scottish religious politics during the 1830's, especially after the 1834 General Assembly had adopted Dr Chalmers' motion on the right to invalidate the presentation of the heritors, and with the disputes over presenta-tions at Auchterarder and Marnoch which began the 'Nine Years' Conflict' and ended with the 'Disruption' of the Established Church in 1843.

While the Established Church was still, before 1843, by far the largest, the flow of Irish immigrants was causing a rapid growth in the Roman Catholic section of the population, and even by 1816 the presbyterian dissenting Churches, though split into several distinct sects, had almost the same number of sittings in Glasgow and its suburbs as had the State Church. Most of these sects held rigid, doctrinaire views on theological matters, but many of their ministers showed a more genuine interest and sympathy for the working classes than did the Established clergy. Many dissenting ministers abstained rigidly from politics, but in the agitations for parliamentary reform and corn law repeal many more dissenting than Established clergy were to be found on 'the side of the people'. As political feeling heightened, many dissenters prided themselves on the democratic nature of their church government. In the administration of parish relief to 'the deserving poor' there tended to be discrimination against dissenters and Roman Catholics, but the meagre doles of poor relief probably did not deter many of the poorer classes from joining the ranks of the 'voluntaries'.[15]

All the signs of the economic progress and the growing social stresses of the age were to be seen in large measure in Glasgow, where industrial development and growth of population proceeded at a great pace. Many of the social and medical observers were appalled by the living conditions of the poorest classes of Glasgow, in the very centre of which they found an accumulated mass of squalid wretchedness. The situation was vividly portrayed to the British Association for the Advancement of Science in 1840 by Captain Miller, the Superintendent of Police:

There is concentrated everything that is wretched, dissolute, loathsome, and pestilential. These places are filled by a population of many thousands of miserable creatures. The houses in which they live are unfit even for sties ... dunghills lie in the vicinity of the dwellings; and from the extremely defective sewerages, filth of every kind constantly accumulates.

In his report on the hand-loom weavers, in the previous year, J. C. Symons had drawn an equally depressing picture:

I have seen human degradation in some of its worst places both in England and abroad, but ... I did not believe until I visited the wynds of Glasgow, that so large an amount of filth, crime, misery, and disease existed on any one spot in any civilised country ... In the lower lodging-houses, ten, twelve and sometimes twenty persons, of both sexes, and all ages, sleep promiscuously on the floor, in different degrees of nakedness. These places are generally, as regards dirt, damp, and decay, such as no person of common humanity ... would stable his horse in. Many of the worst houses are dilapidated, and in a dangerous state, and are condemned by the Dean of Guilds' Court—a sentence of which the execution appears to be generally postponed. The lower parts of most of these houses are spirit shops, pawn shops, or eating houses. The population of all these districts is probably 30,000; it certainly exceeds 20,000; they consist in great proportion of the Irish and of Highlanders. Many of the younger girls, and there are a multitude of them who frequent these places, appear to have been driven there from sheer want, and apply to Captain Miller, (head of the Glasgow police), to be rescued from misery, in great numbers. No efficient aid can be afforded them under existing institutions, and hundreds in a year become inured to crime, and pass through the rapid career of prostitution, drunkenness, and disease, to an early grave.[16]

The problem of public health in Glasgow attracted serious attention for the first time during the cholera epidemic of 1831–32. Some people saw the scourge as divine retribution, but to most intelligent observers it was merely the inevitable consequence of inadequate nourishment and even less adequate sewerage. An even greater scourge, however, was typhus fever, which, like drunkenness, never left Glasgow throughout the 1830's. In 1835 it affected 6,180. The figure rose in the following year to over 10,000, and in 1837, a year of industrial depression and social distress, the toll rose to 21,800. From 1835 to 1840 there were 68,621 cases of typhus, with 5,844 deaths.

Distress and despair were both aggravated and alleviated by drunkenness. In Glasgow in 1831 there was one public house for every thirteen families, and it was estimated by the Sheriff of Lanarkshire, Archibald Alison, that 10,000 people got drunk every Saturday night. Tippling houses remained open on Sundays, except during the hours of church service. A rapid increase in habitual intoxication was ascribed to the rise in population and the growth of factories, with the formation of clubs and parties within these. Lack of pastimes or means of open-air amusement and exercise probably contributed to a significant extent. The influx of immigrants from Ireland and the Highlands was generally blamed, and the often highly paid cotton spinner was singled out as the worst offender.

Since 1828, John Dunlop of Brockloch had been active in trying to organise working men into total abstinence societies. Such societies were formed in Greenock and Glasgow in 1829, and spread to many other parts of the country during the 1830's. Newspaper comment was at first sympathetic, recognising the connection between drink and squalor. But such efforts remained on an almost insignificant scale in relation to the magnitude of the task. A large proportion of wages was spent on drink. Sheriff Alison reckoned this to be at least one quarter, and Dr Dunlop estimated that over £450,000 was being spent annually on drink in Glasgow in the early 1830's. Despite the reduced duty on spirits, much whisky was still believed to be smuggled out of the Highlands.

Among the consequences of drinking habits were considered to be a decreasing observation of the sabbath and church attendance, a deteriorating interest and moral pride of parents in the education of their children, and clamorous demands in seasons of dull trade from Irish and dram-drinking parents for poor relief. The general moral deterioration also led to the tyranny of the credit-providing licensed grocer and provision dealer, and to the encouragement of the laudanum-dispensing chemist and the profiteering 'wee pawn' (or unlicensed) pawnbroker. The credit-providing services of the pawnbroker and the grocer were becoming essential parts of the social fabric of the new industrial, urbanised communities. The rates of interest and profit margins were often high, but in conditions of fluctuating trade the risks were great and the social need was urgent.[17]

Among the working classes the chief organs of mutual protection and self-help were the friendly societies, which survived mainly for their funeral benefits, and the trades unions. But by the 1830's, cooperation was beginning to make some impact. Even before the schemes of Robert Owen and the Orbiston plan, which had attracted considerable interest among the newspaper-reading public, co-operation had been practised in Scotland since the Fenwick weavers in 1761, and the Govan Victualling Society of 1777, which survived for over 130 years. There were retail co-operative societies at Bridgeton, Lennoxtown, Larkhall, Forfar, Parkhead, Cambuslang and several other places in the first quarter of the nineteenth century. Many small retail store societies were established in the 1820's and 1830's, but most of them were crippled for lack of working capital, and by the widespread indebtedness of working-class families to credit-giving grocers. Usually they failed to survive the onset of a depression, and despite the efforts of co-operative pioneers, such as Alexander Campbell, few working men showed much interest in co-operation, whether on a consumer or producer basis of organisation. Campbell's energies had been largely directed to the fostering of co-operative societies based on the principle of mutual exchange of labour, the value of which would be represented by a currency of their own, but in the 1820's he had encouraged the formation of several retail societies on the basis of paying dividends in relation to purchases. This system was disliked by other co-operators, such as William Thomson of Parkhead, who helped to establish about seventy societies in the west of Scotland in the early 1830's, mainly on the 'economical principle', which aimed at reducing retail gross margins to the minimum compatible with the growth of the trade and the capital of the society.[18]

Little interest was shown within any class for the welfare of the other classes of society. Only at times of acute depression or strike action were the conditions of the labouring classes mentioned in the average newspaper. The attitude of the liberal press, of magistrates and manufacturers, was that strikes were futile and that combination was dangerous to society, even when not actually illegal. Trades unions should be permitted freedom of action, according to the prevailing public opinion, only in so far as they did not interfere with the rights and freedom of action of others. Trade union activities should be designed for protection only against the few unprincipled masters. Violence was criminal, and a free trade in labour was vital to the welfare of the State. The amount of money available for wages was strictly dependent on the accumulation of capital, so that to demand higher wages than this made possible was liable to reduce total employment opportunities. The growing disharmony between employer and employed was considered to be due to the obstinacy, stupidity and acerbity of feeling which often characterised both parties. Eventually they must find that the interest of each was dependent on the other, and the sooner they came to a proper understanding the better for all.

Many trades became organised in the 1820's and 1830's. Workers in the more highly capitalised industries, and those who possessed special skills which complemented the new machinery, often derived considerable benefit from combination. Nevertheless, unions remained largely powerless against the main forces which were determining supply and demand. While in the booms they brought about more rapid increases in wages than would have otherwise occurred, in commercial crises they normally had to accept wage reductions or dissolve.

Throughout this period, the Operative Cotton Spinners was the strongest of the Scottish unions. Its organisation covered all the Glasgow and Paisley cotton spinners, and it provided the fine-cotton spinners, whose craft required much training, with the benefits of a 'very perfect system of combination' in forcing the masters to keep up wages. In the building trades, which were enjoying an increasing demand, there was strong combination among the Operative Stone Masons and the carpenters. The colliers were increasingly ready to adopt combination, and held a widespread strike in 1837, largely over the failure to enforce the 1831 Truck Act. This strike was greatly aggravated by the introduction of Irish strike breakers, a tactic which became normal in colliery disputes thereafter.

Even the impoverished hand-loom weavers still placed their hopes on efforts for mutual protection, and in Glasgow and the west of Scotland several General Protecting Unions of Weavers were established about 1833. These provided an efficient information service, largely through their own newspaper, the *Weavers' Journal* (1835–37), which enabled them to try to enforce standard rates for the same work throughout the area. Through such combination, they claimed, there had been success in allaying jealousies and suspicions between employers and employees, and in establishing uniformity of prices and confidence. These peaceful victories, claimed the *Weavers' Journal*, had restored some measure of hope to a class which had been 'dejected, degraded and disorganised'. Despite the harsh suppression of their strike in 1813, when they attempted to enforce previous favourable court decisions, the weavers still placed importance on legislative action by parliament. They established a national association mainly for this purpose which was largely responsible for getting the Hand-loom Weavers Commission appointed.[19]

The overall social picture of Glasgow and Paisley in the late 1830's was a grim one, especially in times of dull trade, epidemic fevers or even 'flitting days'. The dynamic economic changes and inventions of the age seemed to be bringing more than their fair share of misery, and far less than their promise of plenty for all. The benefits of the system to the common man seemed dubious, yet a great deal of shallow philosophy was being expounded to reconcile him to the new system. All he really asked for was 'a fair day's wage for a fair day's work', and beyond that a small measure of personal dignity. Yet the cheaper it became to produce the necessities of life, the longer he seemed to have to labour for bare existence, and the benefits seemed to accumulate in the hands of a few. These extremes of unrelieved poverty and opulence became more obvious to many people, and it was also becoming clear that Christianity was not coming unfailingly to the aid of the suffering portion of the people.

It was not only the suffering who became bitter with this state of society. All the social investigators, in their painstaking observations for parliamentary commissions and the like, found on the surface 'masses of squalid misery, destitution and crime sickening to contemplate'. It might admit of dispute, reported Edwin Chadwick, but 'on the whole it appeared to us that both the structural arrangements and the condition of the population of Glasgow was the worst of any we had seen in any part of Great Britain'. And when they looked below the surface they found 'a horrifying discontent', which boded ill for the social framework.

Yet the picture was by no means one of unrelieved gloom and despair. The recurrent catastrophes of Glasgow and Paisley had not overtaken the rest of Scotland. Many more people were being supported on higher standards of living than ever before. Increasing numbers of working men were engaged in trades unions, friendly societies, co-operative societies, working men's associations of both a political and an educational nature, as well as in religious and charitable societies. Many of them were well-educated, highly paid skilled craftsmen who found increasing opportunities for leadership and social prestige in the new industrial setting. Nor were all employers regarded as heartless tyrants. Several of them, such as the Maxwells of Pollock, William Morton of Kilmarnock and William Dixon of Govanhill, were admired as humane and philanthropic men who supported the people's cause in religion, education and politics.

Even amongst the hardest hit sections of the community, particularly the weavers, there lingered considerable pride, independence of character and dislike of charity, which enabled them to endure, 'with a degree of patience unexampled', suffering which the 1834 Select Committee on Hand-loom Weavers' Petitions found to be of 'an extent and extremity scarcely to be credited'. Amongst the weavers, J. C. Symons found the strongly held opinion that only the abolition of the corn laws could better their condition, while W. E. Hickson concluded that

amongst the foremost remedies proposed by the hand-loom weavers for their depressed condition, is universal suffrage; not because they consider that giving every man a vote in itself will benefit his condition, but because they believe, very generally, that without it, as a means to an end, the grievances, real or imaginary, of which they complain, will never be redressed.[20]

Nor were the weavers alone amongst the working classes in looking for relief through better government and from a legislature responsible to the people. In the agitation for the Reform Bill in 1830–32, many of the trades unions combined to play a prominent role in the politics of the Scottish reformers. During the twenty years which preceded the Chartist movement, mass discontent with the social conditions prevailing found expression in political action and demonstration. The discontent which arose from the shock of industrialisation and urbanisation on the social economy of Scotland was aggravated by growing awareness of distress and discomfort on the part of large sections of the people, with the result that periods of large-scale unemployment provided a mass basis for the Radical agitations of 1816–17, 1819–20, 1830–32, 1837–42 and 1847–48.

NOTES

1. Census of Great Britain of 1851, vol. ii (Scotland), pp. 2, 22–3.
   J. Handley, *The Irish in Scotland*, 1943, pp. 89–90.
2. H. Hamilton, *The Industrial Revolution in Scotland*, 1932, p. 7.
   H. Hamilton, *The Economic Evolution of Scotland in the Eighteenth and Nineteenth Centuries*, 1933, p. 10.
   W. H. Marwick, *Economic Developments in Victorian Scotland*, 1936, p. 18.
   J. Handley, pp. 18, 128.
3. J. H. Clapham, *An Economic History of Modern Britain*, vol, I, pp. 184, 425–6.
   Hamilton, p. 20.
   Handley, pp. 96–7.
4. Marwick, pp. 17, 70–2, 75–8, 96, 127.
   Handley, pp. 97, 99–101, 104–5, 118, 121.
   Clapham, pp. 6, 188.

5. Clapham, pp. 24–5, 30–1, 108.
   Handley, pp. 22–3, 36–7.
   Cobbett, *Rural Rides*, vol. III (1930 edn.), pp. 762–3.
   K. Marx, *Capital* (1912 edn.), 752–7.
6. Handley, pp. 38, 49–52.
7. Marwick, pp. 20, 125.
   Glasgow Chronicle, 15 December 1841.
8. Place, Add. MSS 34,245 B, pp. 276–303.
   Assistant Commissioners' *Report to the Hand-loom Weavers Commission*,
   1839, vol. I, pp. 6–9.
   Report of the Commission on Hand-loom Weavers, 1841, p. 5.
   Marwick, pp. 134, 143–5.
   Handley, pp. 51, 276.
9. Marwick, pp. 147–8.
   Clapham, pp. 216, 558–9.
   Add. MSS 34,245 B, pp. 276–303.
   *Seventh Report of the Commissioners' Inquiry into Organisations and
   Rules of Trade of Trade Unions and other Associations*, 1868, p. 41.
10. *Glasgow Argus*, 23 August 1833.
    Marwick, p. 146.
11. Sir G. Nicholls, *History of the Scotch Poor Law*, 1856, Introduction.
    H. G. Graham, *Social Life of Scotland in the Eighteenth Century*, 1899,
    p. 229 et seq.
    Sir H. Craik, *A Century of Scottish History*, 1911, p. 603.
12. Lord Cockburn, *Letters on the Affairs of Scotland*, 1874, pp. 35–6.
13. Sir A. Alison, *Essays*, 1850, p. 640.
    R. M. W. Cowan, *The Newspaper in Scotland, 1815–60*, 1946, pp. 118,
    120–1.
    Glasgow Saturday Post, 23 September 1843.
    Glasgow Argus, 18 April 1839.
    Assistant Commissioners' *Report to the Hand-loom Weavers Commis-
    sion*, 1839, pp. 18–20.
14. H. W. Meikle, *Scotland and the French Revolution*, 1912, p. 65.
    H. G. Graham, pp. 418–47.
    R. M. W. Cowan, pp. 121–3.
    Glasgow Argus, 30 June 1834.
    Scotsman, 13 December 1828; 17, 20, 31 December 1828; 7 January 1829.
    Glasgow Chronicle, 27 October 1841.
    True Scotsman, 20 February 1840.
    Glasgow Examiner, 11 February 1854.
    W. E. Hickson, *Report on the Condition of the Hand-loom Weavers*,
    1840, pp. 15, 65.
    Place Add. MSS 34,245 A., p. 256.
15. Cleland, *Annals of Glasgow*, 1816, pp. 145–51.
    H. G. Graham, p. 380.
    Lord Cockburn, *Journal of Henry Cockburn*, vol. I, pp. 56–62 et seq.
    Handley, p. 177.
    R. M. W. Cowan, pp. 106–7, 225–6, 230, 234–5.

16. *Proceedings of the British Association*, 1840, p. 170.
   Report of the Assistant Commissioners to the Hand-loom Weavers Commission, 1839, p. 55.
17. J. B. Russell, *Public Health Administration in Glasgow*, 1905, p. 4.
   Handley, pp. 250–1, 256–7.
   Select Committee of Inquiry into Drunkenness, 1834, Q. 2905, 2908, 2924, 2929, 2948, 2972, 2992, 2995.
   Select Committee on Combinations of Workmen, 1838, Q. 1986.
   R. M. W. Cowan, pp. 35, 124–5.
   J. C. Symons, *Arts and Artisans at Home and Abroad*, 1839, pp. 125–6.
   J. Dunlop, Artificial Drinking Usages of North Britain, 1836.
18. R. M. W. Cowan, pp. 99–100.
   G. J. Holyoake, *History of Co-operation*, 1906, pp. 478–9, 236.
   G. D. Cole, *A Century of Co-operation*, 1944, pp. 14, 21–2.
   Marwick, pp. 23–4.
   Glasgow Argus, 14 August 1834.
   Weavers' Journal, 1 February 1837.
   Glasgow Sentinel, 20 December 1862.
19. Cowan, p. 99.
   Glasgow Argus, 19 August 1833, 28 May 1834, 24 July 1834, 30 October 1834.
   Cockburn, *Journal*, vol. I, pp. 160–1.
   Cockburn, *Letters*, pp. 84–5.
   A. B. Richmond, *Narrative of the Condition of the Manufacturing Population and the Proceedings of the Government, etc.*, 1824, pp. 13–17, 29–33, 38–44.
   Marwick, pp. 132, 185–8.
   Seventh Report of the Commissioners' Inquiry on Organisation and Rules of Trade Unions and other Associations, 1868, p. 53.
   Weavers' Journal, 2 May 1836, 1 February 1837, etc.
   Select Committee of Inquiry into Drunkenness, 1834, Q. 2984.
   Select Committee on Combination of Workmen, 1838, Q. 1841.
20. *Glasgow Argus*, 18 April 1839.
   Select Committee on Hand-loom Weavers' Petitions, 1834 (X), p. iii.
   Report of the Assistant Commissioners to the Hand-loom Weavers Commission, 1839, vol. I, p. 69.
   Report on the Condition of the Hand-loom Weavers, 1840, p. 71.

CHAPTER TWO

The political antecedents of Scottish Chartism

While the fundamental basis for the Chartist agitation in Scotland must be found in the prevailing social, and the underlying economic, conditions of the period, the shaping and direction of the movement was conditioned to a great extent by its political antecedents in the reform struggles since 1790, and particularly by the political background of the period 1830–37. In Scotland, the appeals of the Radicals were made to the spirit of men whose forefathers had fought against their kings for religious freedom, and whose burghs and small towns had struggled against the encroachments of feudal lords. This spirit had been rekindled in the days of the French revolution, and had been silenced only by severe repression. In 1816–17 and 1819–20 it had flared up again, only to be suppressed by military force, transportation and execution.

Among the immediate causes for the acceptance of the Chartist programme in Scotland were to be found the disillusionment of the working classes with the results of the Reform Act of 1832 and the spectacle of a largely enfranchised middle class legislating in its own interests, with the harsh treatment meted out by the law to trades unions, as well as the deliberate pursuit of fresh excitement by dissatisfied or ambitious political leaders. The older traditions and patterns of political action were considerably modified by the course of Scottish politics in the 1830's, but they still remained strong.

Throughout most of the eighteenth century, apart from the malt tax and Porteous riots of 1713 and 1736, there had been little to suggest that an active interest was taken in political affairs by the middle or working classes. Dr Meikle suggests that

while industrially and intellectually Scotland by 1780 was ... an awakened country, politically it was still asleep ... The Scottish Parliament . . . remained to the end of its existence a feudal assembly. It had little influence on the national history . . . [The Act of 1469] rendered impossible any healthy political life in the towns, since even the Scottish burgh representatives at Westminster were chosen by delegates from the town councils. In the counties, the franchise was of such a restricted nature that in 1788 there were only 2,662 voters on the freeholders' roll. The issue at stake in the elections was mainly personal.

Even the somewhat belated spread to Scotland of the English movement, of 1780–84, for constitutional reform did not produce any remarkable change in the attitude of the people to politics.

By 1787 only a few of the gentry and the middle classes had begun to be sensible of their bondage. The people generally remained outside the influence of politics. The county movement was strictly limited in its appeal, and the burgh reformers had expressly condemned such proposals as universal suffrage and the ballot, whereby advanced reformers in England had sought to enlist 'the people at large' in their cause. The masses in Scotland had no opportunity to develop an interest in politics.[1]

Active participation by the middle and working classes in politics, however, was delayed only a few years after that date. The catalytic agent was the French revolution, the influence of which was spread by the emergence of ardent Scottish reformers and by the growth of a newspaper-reading public. A less noticeable, but increasingly important, influence in the background was the rapidly changing economic environment, which was beginning to break down the traditional modes of Scottish life.

The fall of the Bastille was celebrated widely—in Edinburgh, Dundee, Glasgow and other towns. At Dundee, in July 1791, the Revolution Society pledged itself to struggle for the rights of man, an equal representation of the people, the speedy abolition of the slave trade and the abolition of all religious tests for civil offices. In Perth, Aberdeen, Dundee and almost every village in the north of Scotland, the effigy of Lord Dundas, the Secretary of State, was burnt in 1792, and the Riot Act was read when workmen tried to do likewise in George Square in Edinburgh.[2]

The suggestion that the Scots had long enjoyed a considerable measure of democracy in their social relations is somewhat borne out by the composition of even the early societies of the 'Friends of the People'. Rates of subscription were fixed which would not prevent the admission of the 'lower orders of society'. In the towns these societies were largely recruited from tradesmen and shop-keepers, while in the country districts there was normally a greater proportion of working class men, drawn chiefly from the hand-loom weavers and the shoemakers. Working class participation in the agitation became more important, and at the second convention of the societies of the Friends of the People, in April 1793, it was observed of the 116 delegates from 28 towns and villages that these were 'as a whole . . . of a lower type than their predecessors' at the first convention, five months previously.

It was apparently this introduction of the working classes into politics which most disturbed Lord Braxfield later that year at the trial of Thomas Muir. Braxfield left it to the jury to judge whether

it was perfectly innocent in Mr Muir, at such a time, to go about among ignorant country people, and among the lower classes of people, mak-ing them leave off their work, and inducing them to believe that a reform was absolutely necessary to preserve their safety and liberty, which had it not been for him, they would never have suspected to have been in danger.

From 1792, concludes Dr Meikle of this formative period, there was no complete break in the life of the nation. 'The lower classes, irritated by repressive and harsh laws, still based their hopes on Universal Suffrage and Annual Parliaments, which to them at least, were the legacy of the French Revolution.' Nevertheless, except for the United Scotsmen Society, before its suppression in 1798, little, if anything, of the real leadership of the reform move-ment rested in the hands of working class men. Possibly as a result of this awakened dissension, however, the working classes were more ready to act on their own initiative, as in their resistance to the Militia Act in 1797, and in the meal riots of 1800–01.[3]

A further wave of popular political agitation swept over Scotland in 1816. A tour by Major Cartwright saw the formation of little Hampden Societies in many towns, inspired by the belief that much of the post-war depression was attributable to class admini-stration and partisan legislation. The writings of William Cobbett and T. J. Wooler became widely disseminated in the west of Scot-land, and throughout the manufacturing districts there were demands for universal suffrage and repeal of the 'iniquitous corn laws'. Public meetings were held during the autumn of 1816 to petition support for Sir Francis Burdett's motion in the House of

Commons and for the adoption of measures to alleviate the prevailing distress.

The most important of these took place in a field at Thrushgrove, near Glasgow, after the civic authorities had refused permission for the meeting to be held on Glasgow Green or in the town hall. At this demonstration, on 29 October 1816, about 40,000 people under the leadership of James Turner, a tobacconist, who had provided the field, protested against

the late, unnecessary, ruinous, and sanguinary war, the re-establishment of the despicable family of Bourbon, the restoration of the Pope in Italy and of the Jesuits, and the Inquisition, in Spain; the extravagance of the Government, the increase of the Civil List, the exorbitant salaries of public officers, the burdens of pensions and sinecures and of the Standing Army, and the corrupt state of Parliamentary representation in Scotland.

Following this meeting, petitions for parliamentary reform were 'numerously subscribed' in every suburb and village around Glasgow. The leaders of these suburban activities, mostly working class men, met weekly in Glasgow during December 1816 and January 1817. Despite the petitioning basis of their organisation, the Lord Advocate was convinced that these reformers were revolutionaries. Amidst them were sent spies, including Alexander Richmond and George Biggar, who were soon to do their utmost to confirm the suspicions of the Lord Advocate. The members of the secret committees, he was informed, were being initiated by taking an oath which bound them 'to try by all means in their power, moral and physical, to endeavour to obtain universal suffrage and annual parliaments'.

In February 1817, twenty-two members of the central committee were arrested as being involved in a plot to overturn the government. The principal trial was that of Andrew McKinlay, who was alleged to be the leader of a phalanx of operative weavers who had conspired to overthrow the constitution, and to establish annual parliaments and universal suffrage. The charge was at first one of treason, but eventually the indictment was under the statute 52 George III for administering unlawful oaths. When it was revealed at the trial that the law authorities had attempted to bribe one of the witnesses the case collapsed, and the administration decided against proceeding with the remaining prosecutions. By then discontent appeared to be less rife, and for some time the agitation for reform was stifled.[4]

When trade depression was causing severe unemployment in the autumn of 1819, the Radicals became active again. Despite the example of the Manchester authorities at Peterloo and the Six Acts of December 1819, large open-air meetings continued to be held throughout the manufacturing districts of the west of Scotland. Wooler's *Gazette* and *Black Dwarf* and the pamphlets of Hunt and Cobbett increased substantially in circulation, and in October a new Radical paper, *The Spirit of the Union*, was published in Glasgow. Apart from a riot in Paisley, in September, when the authorities interfered with a Radical demonstration, and some minor disturbances in Glasgow, gatherings were conducted with scrupulous orderliness, and the reformers generally disapproved of violence and moved with great caution. There was no military training nor 'arming in general' and the Glasgow Radicals decided to further their objects by abstaining from the consumption of tea and alcohol.

The discomfort and anxiety of the government, however, once again resulted in a crop of arrests. Amongst the victims were George Kinloch, a Forfarshire proprietor who was popular with the Dundee Radicals, and Gilbert McLeod, the editor of *The Spirit of the Union*. Kinloch had denounced Peterloo as unprovoked murder, and accused Sidmouth of committing treason against the people. There was no remedy, he claimed, for the horrors of the people's situation except radical reform, including annual parliaments, universal suffrage and vote by ballot. All this had been spoken in an 'inflammatory tone' at a meeting 'composed of the lower orders of the people, by a person whose station gave him influence over them'.

Kinloch fled to France, where he remained for seven years. McLeod died in transportation, and a number of lesser known local leaders were prosecuted. Among them was John McCrae of Cumnock, a schoolteacher, who fled to Canada.[5]

1819 ended with *The Scotsman* ridiculing the anti-Radical scare 'invented' by the Tory press, but the new year saw no diminution of the alarm of the authorities and upper classes. Considerable troop movements were arranged to forestall rebellious moves from disaffected working class radicals. The early months of 1820 were marked by increased activity on the part of Tory-paid and government-employed informers, and by increasing confusion over rumours of rebellion, emanating in part at least from these spies.

In February 1820, twenty-seven members of the Glasgow central committee were arrested. This was followed by a call for a four-day strike to start on 1 April, covering most manufacturing industry in central and south-western Scotland. The strikers were left in great uncertainty about the intentions of their leaders, who constantly warned them against spies and *agents provocateurs*. Many believed that they were waiting for news of rebellion from England, while others believed that an address published by a 'Committee for forming a Provisional Government' must be the work of spies. One or two groups were less cautious, and obeyed the summons to take up arms and assemble on Cathkin Braes and at Bonnymuir, and the strike ended with a bloodless encounter between a handful of armed Radicals and dragoons at Bonnymuir, and with reports of disorder in several other localities.

Judicial commissions were then set up in Edinburgh, Glasgow, Dumbarton, Paisley and Ayr, and forty-seven working class men were placed on trial for treason. Three of these who had openly taken up arms were executed and became political martyrs— Baird, Hardie and Wilson, 'They were all guilty of high treason,' commented Lord Cockburn, 'as any old woman is who chooses to charge a regiment of cavalry.' Eighteen others were transported for life, but several of the special commissions decided that the Solicitor-General, in his attempt to implicate the accused in treason, had stretched the definition of treason so far that it became almost meaningless. As a result most of the accused were acquitted, including John Fraser, a Johnstone schoolmaster, who had been imprisoned for four months.

The Whigs poured scorn on the alarm of the Tory government over the 'Radical War' and the 'Battle of Bonnymuir'. 'The whole affair was composed of three nearly equal parts,' concluded Cockburn, 'popular discontent, Government exaggeration and public craze.' In Edinburgh 17,000 adult males signed a petition to the King for the dismissal of the Ministry, and the year ended with a big Whig meeting in the Pantheon, under the leadership of Lords Jeffrey and Moncrieff. This meeting resolved

That they [his Majesty's advisers] have struck an alarming blow at the morale of the people, and have invaded the private security of every

class of subjects, by employing, encouraging, and protecting an unprecedented number of spies and informers who are proved in many
cases to have been themselves the instigators of those disorders for
which others have been exposed to prosecution and punishment.[6]

Ten years later, when the Whigs came to power, Lord Cockburn, by then Solicitor-General, observed of the period:

There is a good deal of Radicalism in the country, founded on long
and absurdly defended abuses—excited by recent triumphs, and exaggerated by distress. But tho' the alarm that many people feel may be
useful, I cannot say that I as yet discern anything that reasonable concession and a firm government may not overcome.

Twelve months later he still felt optimistic, and wrote:

The whole country is still in a most excited and uncomfortable state,
but disgraced by no violence. Political unions have been very generally
formed ... and people are everywhere familiarised to great meetings
in the open air, guided by men banded together and organised in
associations ... to hear things discussed—such as the use of bishops, the
refusing to pay taxes, and the propriety of arming, which till now, they
would have started at even thinking of. As yet the Unions are composed of the poorer classes or wilder spirits. They are useful at present,
because whenever they have been established the peace has been preserved; but they are most dangerous engines. If their force be once
experienced they may easily be applied to all other questions. But I
suspect that all that well-disposed men can do at present is to try to
manage, not to attempt to suppress them.[7]

Cockburn was referring to the strong political unions, largely
modelled on the Birmingham Political Union, which had grown up
in 1830 and 1831 in Glasgow, Edinburgh, Dundee, Leith and
several other towns. Their programmes normally included extension of the suffrage, triennial parliaments and vote by ballot.
Leadership within these unions was confined mainly to middle class
Radicals, merchants and journalists of liberal newspapers, but they
were dependent for their larger meetings, processions and demonstrations on the collaboration of joint committees of the trades
unions, and welcomed the support of the working classes.

A significant step was taken by the Glasgow trades in July 1830
when they decided to sponsor the establishment of a newspaper to
be called the *Trades Advocate*. This was to be the medium of
communication for the working classes in the west of Scotland,

and would provide 'the sum and substance of every information—not of a political kind only, but on historical, literary and scientific subjects'. While efforts were being made to raise share capital for this venture, it was decided to publish a twopenny unstamped paper, the *Herald to the Trades Advocate (and Co-operative Journal)*. For eight months, from September 1830, this paper voiced fairly orthodox liberal-reformist views on political topics in addition to more radical views on the functions of trades unions, on co-operation, on truck, on temperance and on the education of women. Its political idol was Joseph Hume, who sent addresses to the 'Operatives of Glasgow' on the desirability of gradual reform. 'Reform is out of the hands of the Radicals,' he wrote to Alexander Campbell. 'Let us take what we can get, and look for more.'

Meanwhile missionaries were sent out to neighbouring towns and villages to promote the sale of shares in the *Trades Advocate*. By February 1831, 1,110 shares worth £277 10s. had been bought, and when the Solicitor of Stamps eventually suppressed the *Herald to the Trades Advocate* its place was taken by the *Trades Advocate*, which was published through much of 1831 and 1832 by John Tait and the other leading members of the sponsoring committee, Alexander Campbell, George Donald, George Rodger and Daniel McAulay.[8]

During 1831, in accordance with the advice of Joseph Hume and other Radical leaders, numerous public meetings were held in Scotland to petition in support of the ministerial plan of reform. The country was 'thoroughly roused, and there was an almost universal demand for the Bill, the whole Bill, and nothing but the Bill!' Enormous multitudes of about 150,000 people were estimated to have assembled on Glasgow Green on 8 September 1831, on coronation day and on 12 May 1832 to demonstrate in favour of the Bill, and against the actions of the House of Lords. Lord Cockburn was constantly noting in his journal the peaceful nature of the agitation, and the 'safe and constitutional opinions of the great majority of the lower orders here'. The passing of the Reform Act was followed by several weeks of celebration all over the country. In Edinburgh, a 'most impressive' reform jubilee was organised by the Trades Union Council. This included a procession of the trades, with numerous banners and insignia to the memory of Muir, Gerrald and other reform martyrs.[9]

The Reform Act wrought a considerable transformation in the

size and composition of the Scottish electorate. About twenty times the previous total of privileged persons became entitled to vote. The new franchise qualifications created a new privileged class, admitting many of the small shopkeepers but excluding most of the skilled craftsmen, who constituted the real middle class in many Scottish burghs. Some working class men were enfranchised, but in relation to the total number of working class leaders of political, friendly, trades and other societies their number was small. Many of them held misgivings about settling for what they regarded as little more than a half-measure.

The relief of the Whigs that the political excitement was now safely over was expressed by Lord Cockburn, who was delighted by

the limited effect of the Reform Act in promoting that rise of low radicals with which we were threatened . . . I suppose we shan't have above two or three more Hunts, but a houseful of good sound aristocratic Whigs . . . It is quite clear that Toryism is over, that Radicalism is on the rise; and that but for the Reform Bill they would have taken all the institutions of the country by storm. Whether they are to be permanently repressed remains to be seen.[10]

The period immediately following the great reform agitation of 1830–32 was marked by several features which were of importance in relation to later agitations. These included the growth of the newspaper press, the development of political unions as permanent features of Scottish political life, the emergence of the trades unions as an important political factor, and the growing strength of the anti-corn law movement. The period was also marked by a growing distrust felt by many of those reformers who had seen the 1832 Act merely as the first step in the thorough reform of the constitution, towards their erstwhile Whig allies. This relationship did not improve as the attitude of the Ministry towards the feasibility and desirability of further reform became clearer.

Nor was impatience with Whig policy confined to the more extreme Radicals. It was soon widely expressed in the Liberal press, which criticised the slowness of the government to initiate reforms in local government, in sinecures, in tithes and in repeal of the corn laws. Much of the popularity which the Whigs had enjoyed in previous years was forfeited by their measures in 1833 to deal with Ireland. The suspension of Habeas Corpus was bitterly criticised, and petitions against the 'Irish Coercion Bill' were presented from public meetings in Dunfermline, Kilmarnock, Irvine, Leslie, Kilbirnie, Dundee and Renfrewshire, and from several political unions. Discontented newspapers in Aberdeen, Dundee, Montrose, Dumfries, Dunfermline and Glasgow were once again calling for household suffrage, triennial parliaments and vote by ballot. The *Glasgow Argus* was soon followed by other newspapers, towards the end of 1833, in giving prominence to corn law repeal, and in giving encouragement to anti-corn law associations. In March 1834, the Glasgow Anti-Corn Law Association organised a petition for repeal which was signed by 60,000 people.

Generally, in this period, the trades unions were more concerned with the development of industrial organisation and action than with further political action. Their progress in this field was noted with disquiet by formerly sympathetic liberal editors, who were becoming alarmed at the recourse by many unions to strike action and to violent methods for the intimidation of blacklegs and non-unionists. 'Scarcely a branch of trade exists in the West of Scotland that is not now in a state of Union,' reported the *Glasgow Argus* in December 1833, at which time the calico printers, the engineers, the cabinet makers, the operative stone masons and, until recently, the operative cotton spinners were all on strike.[11]

Nevertheless, the trades committees, especially that of the Glasgow trades unions, had no intention of quitting the political scene, and they continued to play a prominent role in local political activities. In November 1832 the Glasgow trades founded the *Liberator*, which took the place of the *Trades Advocate* and was aimed at a somewhat wider public. The venture was successful, and the *Liberator* became the most important medium and the spokesman for the Radicals and trade unionists for the next six years. In 1833 the unions found much to criticise in Lord Althrop's amendment to Lord Ashley's factory Bill, which excluded young persons aged 13–18 from the protection of the ten hour limitation. This criticism was voiced strongly at public meetings and in the Glasgow Political Union, where the chief spokesman for the trades, Abram Duncan, was called to order for 'an over-severe attack' on the Ministry. Duncan had argued that the trades must now decide on their hours of work themselves, and that the authority of the legislature should be displaced if it continued to act so foolishly.[12]

The political highlights of the period, however, were the triumphal tours and meetings of Lord Durham and Daniel O'Connell. Great demonstrations, estimated at over 100,000, were held on Glasgow Green for Durham in October 1834, and for O'Connell in September 1835. Processions were organised by the trades, and addresses were presented to the Radical leaders from political unions, trades unions, and the trades committees of Edinburgh, Greenock and Glasgow. On each occasion working men presided over the meetings. Meanwhile the somewhat shaky desire for unity which lingered among reformers of all classes had been greatly reinforced by the return to office, in November 1834, of the Duke of Wellington and the Tories. Surprise, dismay and indignation resulted in a call to action which was eagerly obeyed throughout much of Scotland. The aristocracy had 'thrown down the gauntlet' and the people would 'pick it up'.

Led by 'the Trades', the reformers of Glasgow and Edinburgh met to declare their 'hatred of a military government', and their determination to oppose it by every constitutional means. Within a few days, at least thirty-five Scottish towns had addressed the King, urging him not to 'hazard the peace and property of the nation' in this way. This advice was usually coupled with the more familiar demands for shorter parliaments, vote by ballot and extension of the franchise. At these events a prominent part was often played by Abram Duncan, who contended that the working classes ought to remain content no longer with a purely nominal recognition of their influence as 'the people'. They must insist on being given a share in the franchise and in the 'substance of the constitution'.

Along with Duncan, several other individuals who later played important roles in the Chartist movement achieved some prominence through these events. Among these was Bailie Hugh Craig, a Kilmarnock draper, who represented the local political union at the Durham demonstration and who made 'eloquent' speeches during the Duke of Wellington crisis. Another was the Rev. Patrick Brewster, of Paisley Abbey parish, who was becoming well known locally for his activities in the anti-slavery movement, for the relief of his poor parishioners, and for his lectures on the 'Rights of subjects and the duties of rulers' and on 'Passive obedience'. For his presence at the Glasgow dinner given in honour of Daniel O'Connell, the 'great Popish leader', he was required to stand trial

32

before the Synod of Glasgow and Ayr, censured by his presbytery, and praised by his congregation.[13]

In the larger towns the political unions provided an arena for the personal rivalries and ambitions of local politicians. To some extent they existed as mutual admiration societies, but most served as the main focus of local political life, encouraging the acceptance of growing social responsibilities under the reformed local government system, as well as being a training ground for aspirants to political leadership. Their main purpose, however, remained that of preserving the unity of reformers against the Tories. Largely they pursued this aim by attention to parliamentary and municipal electoral registration, but their activities also included the commemoration of Muir and the reform martyrs, appeals to the Lord Advocate on behalf of the Bonnymuir victims, motions for the impeachment of the Duke of Wellington, denunciations of the spy system and the parts played in it by Kirkham Finlay and Alexander Richmond, and celebrations of the 1816 Thrushgrove meeting.[14]

Two trends had been outstanding in the 1792–1829 and the later reform struggles. There had been both a readiness to co-operate between the middle and working classes, and an increasing tendency towards political action on purely working class initiative. During the 1833–38 period a further trend became noticeable: a growing tension between the Whigs and Radicals, and, further, between the middle and working class reformers. These tensions derived mainly from the divergent opinions held on the need for and feasibility of further measures of constitutional reform. Despite the absence of any well defined Radical or Whig policy, there was a marked crystallisation in the division of the reform parties, with the Tory-hating 'moderate reformers' becoming increasingly fearful of a Tory–Radical alliance, and alarmed by the vehement anti-Whig denunciations of the working class Radicals.

The turning point in the pre-Chartist period came with the quarrel which developed amongst the Glasgow reformers, in February 1836, over the election of Lord William Bentinck. Here arose a marked division between those inclined to support the Whig Ministry, out of fear of a Tory revival, and the more radically inclined leaders, who succeeded in eliminating Bentinck as the choice of the Political Union. This rift deepened with the death, in October 1836, of John Tait of the *Liberator*, with his succession as editor by Dr John Taylor, and with the Scottish tour in December of Feargus O'Connor at Taylor's invitation.

Dr John Taylor had already established quite a reputation as one of the foremost Radicals in the west of Scotland before joining the *Liberator* as assistant editor in July 1836. On Tait's death, Taylor was appointed editor, and proudly announced that he had been 'thrown by an all-wise Providence' upon his new responsibilities. Within a month Taylor had become the sole proprietor and had changed the name of the paper to the *New Liberator*. This he also regarded as an act of God and an important stage in his career towards a glorious destiny, which he had unremittingly pursued almost since his birth, in Newark Castle, near Ayr, in September 1805.

Fired by the ideal of political liberty and 'those principles which are dearer to me than life', Taylor had spent a large part of a substantial fortune in fitting out a ship to help in the fight for Greek independence, and had been a confidant of French republicans. In 1832 and 1834 he stood as the Radical candidate for Ayr Burghs. He was imprisoned for challenging the victor, Kennedy of Dunure, to a duel, and his newspaper, *The Ayrshire Reformer and Kilmarnock Gazette*, was terminated after he lost a libel action raised by Kennedy. Noted for the strength of his advocacy of corn law repeal, Taylor was one of the Glasgow representatives on the London Anti-Corn Law Association in 1836, and was regarded as the leader of the 'advanced Radicals'. Esteemed by his middle class Radical colleagues, such as Hedderwick, Turner and Ure, Taylor was on much closer terms than any of these with the leaders of the trades unions.*

* His statue stands in the Wallacetown cemetery, Newton on Ayr (see plate 6). The inscription on the column reads: To / JOHN TAYLOR, ESQ.,/ OF BLACKHOUSE, M.D., / BORN AT NEWARK CASTLE, / AYRSHIRE, IOTH SEP., 1805, / DIED AT LARNE, IRELAND, / 4TH DEC., 1842 / HE CONTESTED THE AYR BURGHS / IN 1832, AND AGAIN IN 1834, / ON RADICAL PRINCIPLES; / AND REPRESENTED PAISLEY, ETC, / AT THE CHARTIST CONVENTION / IN 1839. / This Statue / WAS ERECTED BY / PUBLIC SUBSCRIPTION, / IN COMMEMORATION OF HIS / VIRTUES AS A MAN, AND HIS / SERVICES AS A REFORMER. / PROFESSIONALLY, HE WAS ALIKE THE / POOR MAN'S GENEROUS FRIEND AND / PHYSICIAN; POLITICALLY, HE WAS THE / ELOQUENT AND UNFLINCHING / ADVOCATE OF THE / People's Cause, / FREELY SACRIFICING HEALTH, / MEANS, SOCIAL STATUS, AND EVEN / PERSONAL LIBERTY, TO THE / ADVANCEMENT OF MEASURES / THEN CONSIDERED EXTREME, / BUT NOW ACKNOWLEDGED / TO BE ESSENTIAL TO THE / WELL-BEING OF THE STATE. / *"Requiescat in pace."*

It was largely out of this alliance that a new Radical association was formed in December 1836. It was named the Scottish Radical Association and, with Taylor as president, it adopted four principles as its rules—universal suffrage, annual parliaments, vote by ballot and a voluntary church system. At Taylor's proposal, the new body agreed to arrange a torchlight procession for the public entry in Glasgow a week later of Feargus O'Connor. This event, despite a hundred torchbearers, several bands of music and a procession, was somewhat marred by wet and stormy weather. Nevertheless, out of O'Connor's visit to Scotland emerged a long-enduring partnership between Taylor and O'Connor.

As a result of O'Connor's tour, Radical associations were established or strengthened in Edinburgh, Dunfermline, Paisley, Kilmarnock, Leith and several other towns. Some of these associations established branches in neighbouring districts. Yet the tour was not an unqualified success, for O'Connor aroused suspicion and antagonism among many of the 'more respectable' Radicals, whom he found to be 'at sea between the Durham and the O'Connell humbug', and who found him to be disturbing because of the vehemence of feeling which his presence and colourful language excited. Amongst the working classes, however, O'Connor had no lack of admirers, and some of his meetings were large and enthusiastic.[15]

Another event which was to have long term repercussions was the attempt in 1836 by the Tory press in Glasgow—particularly by the Church of Scotland newspaper, the *Scottish Guardian*—to give prominence to the local association of 'Conservative Operatives'. The association never possessed any effective strength, but the installation of Sir Robert Peel as Lord Rector of Glasgow University, in January 1837, was made the occasion for the publication of an address signed by 2,000 operatives. The new Radical Association deemed it necessary, as one of its first tasks, to repudiate any connection between it and the Tory Democracy campaign. The Radicals called a public meeting of Glasgow operatives to dissociate the operatives of Glasgow from the Peel celebration, and on 6 January 1837 this meeting decided to establish a standing committee of trades delegates which would serve as 'a nucleus round which the trades of Glasgow may rally on any future public emergency.[16]

More immediately important in the political atmosphere, in which reform dinners were being held in many parts of Britain, was the increasing severity with which the working classes were being hit by trade depression. In March 1837 the unemployed of Glasgow and Paisley petitioned Parliament for assistance. Throughout April and May there was a daily increase in the number of unemployed, and 'harrowing details of working class distress' were reported from all parts of the country. Reductions in wages, imposed by the cotton spinning masters without notice, led to strikes in the Glasgow neighbourhood which closed nearly all the works. In May, when snow was still on the ground, public meetings were held to raise relief for unemployed weavers, and in June the Glasgow weavers petitioned Parliament for aid, as a result of which a commission was appointed to inquire into the conditions of the hand-loom weavers. During this period, considerable tensions had been created in Glasgow as a result of the widespread unemployment and the hopeless prospects of the numerous strikes which were in progress. The *Glasgow Argus* reported 'some trifling disturbances' at a few of the cotton spinning mills, but the Sheriff of Lanarkshire later declared that at times during the strike Glasgow had been in a state of 'insurrectionary fever'.

Relations between the middle class Radicals of Glasgow and the working class and 'ultra-Radicals' came close to breaking point in the latter part of July. First there came a last-minute decision from Dr Taylor to stand as a candidate for Glasgow in the general election of 1837. Before he eventually withdrew to maintain the 'unity of the Reformers', he had been howled down with accusations of being bribed with 'Tory gold'. Almost simultaneously, an even more serious shadow was cast over Radical politics by the arrest, at the end of July, of eighteen committee members of the Operative Cotton Spinners' Union on suspicion of murder and arson.[17]

Strenuous efforts were made by Taylor and the Glasgow trades unions to exculpate the accused cotton spinners. A committee of inquiry was appointed by the standing committee of the united trades to investigate the conduct of the cotton spinners and of the authorities. Their findings, which accused the Sheriff of Lanarkshire and his advisers of 'partial, cruel and uncalled-for conduct', were published and circulated throughout all manufacturing districts of Great Britain, and financial support and protest meetings were called for.

Throughout the months of postponement before the trial finally took place in Edinburgh, in January 1838, the agitation on behalf of the accused men heightened considerably, especially around Glasgow and in the north of England. The cotton spinners were alleged to be the victims of an attempt by the authorities, urged on by Daniel O'Connell, to repress trade unionism. O'Connell now became one of the best hated men to the Scottish working class Radicals, who had so recently been his fervent admirers. In Glasgow, John Taylor was fighting a losing battle for the vindication of trade unionism in general, and of the cotton spinners in particular, against the prejudices of the middle class liberals and moderate Radicals, who were shocked by the alleged atrocities. Some were even more shocked by the flood of intemperate language which was let loose, supposedly on behalf of the cotton spinners, by Augustus Beaumont, the Rev. J. R. Stephens and Feargus O'Connor at excited meetings in Glasgow and Edinburgh.

'Oh that the time was come for a fight with the aristocracy, that we might show how ready we are to shed our blood,' cried Beaumont at a meeting of Glasgow workmen on 9 November. He was surprised not to find barricades in the streets, and that the people of Scotland had not followed the example of their ancestors. At another Glasgow meeting he declared that civil war was preferable to submission to slavery. Rather than submit to a middle class government, the working classes would 'have the streets of the cities running with blood'. By comparison, the Rev. Joseph Stephens was almost temperate in his advocacy of the propriety of merely burning the mills of 'the cotton tyrants'.[18]

Dr Taylor, who had used his influence before and during the strike to moderate violent feeling, and whose newspaper, formerly subsidised by the Cotton Spinners' Association, had advocated the pursuance of strictly peaceful policies, was apparently not to be outdone by the flamboyant utterances of his English and Irish demagogue partners. He was now reported in the Scottish press as becoming increasingly violent in his language, and in O'Connor's *Northern Star* he was reported to be making humorous addresses at Radical meetings in the north of England. At a dinner in Leeds, on 9 January 1838, he declared

the time for physical force had arrived, and he would maintain it ... As the law stood they had all of them committed treason and nothing but the damnable cowardice of the Whigs prevented their being arrested

...It was high time to lay down the spade and take up the sword... He knew he was talking what was called treason, he had been in the habit of doing so for some time... He should not object to stand in the Dock of the Cotton Spinners—not that he was much enamoured of martyrdom but it would give such an impulse to his principles that he should not object to sacrifice himself.[19]

In Edinburgh, according to Lord Cockburn, one of the judges during the first five days of the court proceedings, 'there has been nothing talked of for a fortnight except the trial of the cotton spinners'.

The workmen of this trade have for above twenty years had an association which has been the real mover of all the combinations and strikes of workmen in the manufacturing districts of Scotland... It contained about 1,000 names but these influenced all the other spinners, and when ... their demands were not complied with, their staff of president, secretary, treasurer, and committee ordered a general strike. Those who obeyed and required aid were paid out of a fund which had been accumulated during the years of prosperity. Those who disobeyed were proclaimed 'nobs', and were insulted, obstructed and punished. They were watched and marked by spies employed by the guard committee and attempted to be seduced by arguments and bribes; and this failing they were threatened, assaulted, scalded with vitriol and shot, and their masters' works attempted to be burned. All this was done systematically by the directions of the secret committee, and was persevered in for years... After [1826] they had only a few detached outbreaks till April 1837, when another general strike was ordered and the secret committee was revived. The old atrocities were renewed, and, among others, on the 22nd July, a poor man called Smith was murdered by being shot on the public street. This led to the detection and apprehension of the whole leaders... and this was followed by the trial of five of them, who were accused of Smith's murder, of sending threatening letters, of fire-raising, and of assault, and especially of conspiracy to compel the keeping up of wages by these things, murder included.

Cockburn was a staunch upholder of the legality of peaceful combination amongst workmen, but both he and Sheriff Alison feared the use of violence and any form of intimidation as a menace to the rights of property and workmen. Alison was apparently well informed about current trade union practices, but there appeared to be some degree of exaggeration in his evidence before the Select Committee on Combinations of Workmen in 1838. His claim that Glasgow had been living in a state of terror and 'insurrectionary fever' during the summer of 1837 could hardly be borne out by contemporary reports in the Glasgow newspapers. Fear and prejudice tended to bias the opinions of the sheriff and the judge on the use of violence by the trade union leaders. Cockburn had no doubt about the guilt of the cotton spinners on the count of murder. Their acquittal was due to a 'bad jury' and to the doubts of the justice-clerk, who took fourteen hours to sum up. From the voluminous evidence, it would seem that the qualms of the justice-clerk were more soundly based than Cockburn's judgment. No distinct connection could be shown between the murder of Smith and at least four of the prisoners, and even in the case of McLean, where circumstantial evidence pointed strongly against him, the connection was not proved, nor was it proved that he had been acting about this time under the instructions of the executive committee of the association. While it was shown that illegal assaults and coercion had been prompted and paid for by the union, it had not been shown that murder had ever been included in these coercive measures. Nor was it even clear that Smith was a transgressor against the union rules, for he had declared that he did not believe himself to be a marked man. Then, despite the opportunities apparently afforded to the Crown witnesses, through free access to each other in gaol, to concoct a coherent story, their evidence did not prove any distinct relationship between the prisoners and the 'riots', nor even between the union and the 'riots'.

The trial ended with the conviction of the cotton spinners for 'illegal conspiracy to keep up wages' and for instigating 'disturbances' at Oakbank and Mile End, and with sentences of seven years' transportation. The agitation conducted by their defence committee, however, continued for at least three months in protest against this conviction and the severity of the sentence in relation to the dramatically reduced charges. In London and throughout the manufacturing areas of England, a tour was made by a delegation of Glasgow trades. Public meetings took place at Ashton, Dewsbury, Hull, Rotherham, London, Edinburgh, Paisley, Glasgow and many other towns, at which the prosecution was denounced as an attempt by the Whig government to oppress free workmen, in response to the demands of vindictive master manufacturers. Petitions were sent from these meetings to Parliament; one of them contained 20,000 signatures. In the House of Lords, on 9 February 1838, Lord Brougham presented petitions and complained that the original diet had been deserted, with the cotton spinners being acquitted on ten counts of the original indictment.

From acts of incendiarism, arson and murder itself, the counsel for the prosecution proceeded to arraign these men of offences, which instead of being the worst, turned out to be of the very slightest import—of a combination to threaten, but with threats of a very inferior description, such as vexation, insult, annoyance, none amounting to arson or murder, or any attempt tending that way being preferred.[20]

The petition adopted by an Edinburgh meeting expressed the current feelings of the working class Radicals of Scotland:

Your Honourable House [it declared to the House of Commons] has been awfully deficient in the discharge of its highest duties, providing for the education of the whole people, giving equal rights and equal protection to all, and feeding the hungry, and clothing the naked by a well-regulated system of commerce and agriculture. The millions feel they have a right to live comfortably by the modest labour of their hands, and by the produce of the common property of man, the earth, with its never-failing abundance to satisfy the wants of every living thing. They feel themselves robbed by misgovernment of a just share of the blessings of nature...and discontent everywhere prevails. In the air they breathe, in the light that shines, in their food and their clothing, they feel the iron hand of tremendously heavy taxation, bearing a hundred times more oppressively on the labouring man than on the rich...The power of the capitalists for whose benefit all the institutions of the country are so much formed, will ever press down and endeavour to destroy the interests of unrepresented labour.[21]

Yet while the continued excitement over the trial of the cotton spinners overshadowed all other agitation, it neither eliminated nor was completely divorced from agitation for reform of the suffrage qualifications and repeal of the corn laws. J. C. Symons reported of this period that

the only measures desired by the weavers, or advocated by the manufacturers, as a sufficient remedy for the existing depression, is the repeal of the Corn Laws. They view the continuance of a tax which increases the price of food and diminishes the amount of employment, as grievous and intolerable...Such, though expressed in terms less mild, was the feeling I found among the weaving body south of the Forth, and I may safely say that their opinions on this point are the same as those held by nine-tenths of the population.[21]

There was renewed activity on the part of the Glasgow Anti-Corn Law Association at the end of 1837, and following Lord Brougham's declaration in favour of the extension of the suffrage, the Glasgow Reform Association decided to support this demand. Further impetus was given by the Address of the Birmingham Reformers of 7 December, which demanded universal suffrage, vote by ballot and triennial parliaments. At a meeting on 29 December the directors of the Reform Association, alarmed by the falling off of Liberal strength in the county elections in Lanarkshire, Renfrewshire, Ayrshire and Stirlingshire, declared their policy of seeking the ballot and an extension of the suffrage. This step was said to be in line with the policy of the Sheffield and Westminster reformers, but it was considered too cautious by the more radical of the Glasgow reformers, headed by John Taylor, George Ross, James Moir and Alexander Campbell. Refusing to be impressed by the plea not to embarrass the question with mere differences of opinion on the degree of extension required, they demanded that the meeting should petition for vote by ballot and universal suffrage. When this was adopted, the spokesman of the Reform Association intimated that the matter had now been taken out of the hands of his association, and the division between the Glasgow radicals and reformers became more distinct than ever.[22]

NOTES

1. W. L. Mathieson, *The Awakening of Scotland*, 1910, pp. 22, 92, 99–109.
   E. Porritt, *The Unreformed House of Commons*, vol. II, pp. 6, 180.
   H. W. Meikle, *Scotland and the French Revolution*, 1912, pp. xvi, xvii, 33.
2. Meikle, pp. 70, 73, 81, 96.
3. Meikle, pp. 93, 125, 134, 180–2, 215.
4. Meikle, pp. 220–2.
   Glasgow Examiner, 22 December 1849; 6, 13, 20 and 27 May 1854; 29 May 1858.
   A. B. Richmond, *Narrative of the Condition of the Manufacturing Population, etc.*, 1824, pp. 51–3, 60–2.
   Henry Cockburn, *Memorials of his Times*, 1856, pp. 331–5.
   Sir Henry Craik, *A Century of Scottish History*, 1901, pp. 507–9.
5. Craik, pp. 508–9.
   Meikle, pp. 226–7.
   Cowan, pp. 52–4.
   Cockburn, *Trials of Sedition*, vol. II, pp. 204–6, 207–19.
   J. R. Fraser, *Memoir of John Fraser*, 1879, pp. 20–9.

6. Cowan, pp. 55, 99.
   Cockburn, *Memorials of his Times*, p. 366.
   Meikle, p. 229.
   Green, *Trials for High Treason in Scotland*, 1825, vol. III, pp. 10–21.
7. Cockburn, *Letters on the Affairs of Scotland*, 1874, p. 271.
   Cockburn, *Journal of Henry Cockburn*, vol. I, pp. 25–8.
8. *Herald to the Trades Advocate*, 5 and 12 March 1831.
9. Meikle, pp. 236–8.
   McDowall, *The People's History of Glasgow*, 1899, pp. 83–4.
   Cockburn, p. 28.
10. Cockburn, *Letters, etc.*, p. 418.
11. Cowan, p. 117.
    Place, Add. MSS 27,796, p. 239.
    Argus, 28 December 1833.
12. *Argus*, 6 June 1833, 5 August 1833.
13. *Argus*, 30 October 1834; 6, 20 and 24 November 1834; 1 December 1834;
    16 May 1836.
    Glasgow Herald, 7 November 1834.
    Scots Times, 23 September 1835; 3 and 21 October 1835.
14. *Scots Times*, 3 February 1835, 20 June 1835, 31 October 1835, 4 November
    1835.
    Loyal Reformers' Gazette, 2 May 1835, 31 October 1835.
15. *Loyal Reformers' Gazette*, vol. VI, pp. 152, 166, 199, 309, 329, 409, etc.
    Weavers' Journal, 1 November 1836.
    Argus, 20 and 27 October 1836; 8, 15 and 26 December 1836.
    Liberator, 26 October 1836.
16. Cowan, pp. 186–7.
    Argus, 9 January 1837.
    The Champion, vol. I, p. 151.
17. *Argus*, 9 January 1837; 23 March; 6 and 17 April; 1, 4 and 22 May; 22
    June; 6, 17, 27 and 31 July; 14 August 1837.
18. *The Champion*, 4 and 11 November 1837; 2 December 1837.
    Argus, 13 and 30 November 1837.
19. *Northern Star*, 13 January 1838.
20. Cockburn, *Journal*, pp. 155–61.
    Select Committee on Combinations of Workmen, 1838, Q. 1841, 1851–2.
    A. Swinton, *Report of the Trial of the Cotton Spinners*, Edinburgh,
    1838.
    J. Marshall, *Report of the Trial of the Cotton Spinners*, Glasgow, 1838.
    Northern Star, 3 and 10 February 1838; 17 March 1838; 28 January
    1838
    Birmingham Journal, 17 February 1838.
21. *Northern Star*, 17 March 1838.
22. *Report* of the Assistant Commissioners to the Hand-loom Weavers Com-
    mission, vol. I, p. 69.
    Argus, 4 and 31 December 1837.

CHAPTER THREE

The men of Birmingham

Meanwhile, in the Midlands of England, the political temperature was being gauged weekly by that band of cautious conspirators, the council of the Birmingham Political Union. 'Must we again make all the great sacrifices political agitation requires?' asked T. Clutton Salt in April 1837. 'Manchester, Glasgow, Paisley, Coventry reply —"Our population wanders about without employment and without bread . . . The unions must meet."'

Eight months later the Birmingham Political Union came forward

not hastily nor inconsiderately . . . once more to demand for the people . . . a full and fair representation . . . We demand Universal Suffrage . . . We demand an absolute protection for the voter . . . the Ballot . . . We demand a recurrence to the old and wise rule by which the duration of Parliament was limited to three years . . . Agitate! Associate! Let every district have its union . . . The men of Birmingham will either lead or follow.

From Scotland came news of reform meetings in Glasgow and Dumfries, where resolutions in favour of universal suffrage had been adopted. From the Galashiels reformers came an address on the necessity of 'making the representative system co-extensive with the adult population. . . Reformers of Birmingham! . . . It is for you to pronounce that the day and the hour have even now arrived!' And from Edinburgh came news of the trial of the Glasgow cotton spinners.[1]

Progress in the formation of political unions to follow the leadership of the Birmingham reformers was not, however, rapid. At the beginning of February 1838, John Collins could report to the union only that they had political unions in Bradford, Coventry, and in Scotland, but soon they would have unions in all the important towns. With the treasurer, R. K. Douglas, able to announce a credit balance of £194, and with his own plan of action at their disposal, there was 'nothing now to stop them', T. C. Salt told the council on 20 February.

The basis of this plan of campaign was a 'holy and peaceful pilgrimage' throughout the country by a deputation from Birmingham. The same petition, embodying demands for 'universal suffrage, vote by ballot, short parliaments, abolition of property qualifications in members, and wages of attendance', should receive the sanction of great public meetings and be sent to Parliament. Having thus concentrated, and given unity to, the efforts of the people, a day of solemn observance would then be held on which

all the people should meet and enter into a covenant to abstain from all taxed and exciseable articles, from spirits, beer, sugar, teas etc. until their full rights were restored ... It was wild and wicked to talk of fighting, while they had the power, by a little and brief self-control, to stop twenty millions of taxes ... He was always disgusted with any allusions to physical force, while moral means were left them by which their object could be accomplished ... But where virtue failed he would depend upon excitement, and ... its contagious nature.

P. H. Muntz saw difficulties in Salt's plan. There must be other steps taken to ensure respect from the House of Commons. If they abstained at all, it must be

until the House of Commons entertained their petitions and granted their just claims. They must first proceed to arouse the large towns ... These towns must elect by universal suffrage, delegates to meet at a certain place on a certain day. These delegates must fix upon the day upon which the abstinence should commence, and when it should terminate, and the will of this delegated body, being known, would ... be obeyed. They must also have simultaneous meetings, and cessations from work ... Before, however, they proceeded at all, they must clearly establish the legality of their plans ... They possessed ... means by moral force to obtain justice ... and having moral means they ought not to resort to any other.

A week later, the council deliberated the crucial question: where should the campaign begin? If they were not able to obtain massive support at the opening demonstration, there could be little hope for the further implementation of their plan. Salt was convinced that Glasgow was 'the most favourable place to begin their opera-

tions'. With good arrangements, they could get up a meeting of
100,000 there. Glasgow was 'one of the most northern points of our
great commercial population'. Its people were suffering the most
severe distress, and there was also a 'peculiar excitement in the
public mind there which would render it especially disposed to
listen to the voice of the Birmingham men'. He was alluding to the
'recent persecution' of the Glasgow 'weavers'. The men of Glasgow
in their present suffering and excited state, were particularly entitled
to the advice and sympathy of the men of Birmingham. Then
there was another reason why he looked 'with most confidence to
Glasgow and neighbourhood. During the struggle for Reform in
1832, it was there that the northern cloud gathered, and that three
hundred thousand men stood ready to give aid in their need to the
men of Birmingham'. He earnestly desired to select, therefore, his
old friends as the first whose sanction and assistance he would ask
for their renewed efforts. The council had delayed their operations
from the 'difficulty of knowing whom to communicate with'. In
many parts of England, the exertions of reformers had not been
continuous:

They blazed as meteors and then went out again ... In this way they
had lost sight of many excellent Reformers at a distance; and as the
success of their efforts would mainly depend on the perfect execution
of its details, he proposed to send to Glasgow a missionary, a sort of
St. John, to prepare the way to gather the best reformers ... Measures
would be adopted which shall ensure the attendance of the whole mass
of the population on the day fixed for the beginning of this great work;
the fame of which spreading southwards, will prepare all minds for our
advent.[2]

On 10 April R. K. Douglas was able to report that the news
from Scotland was 'exceedingly gratifying'. Their emissary, John
Collins, Birmingham shoemaker and union councillor, had already
held meetings at Glasgow, Paisley and Barrhead. He had been well
received everywhere, and bailies had presided at his meetings. In
Dr Taylor's *Liberator* he had been the subject of three leading
articles, all of which approved his conduct and ability. Collins had
found that the people of Scotland considered it important that
'their friend Mr Attwood should go down to the north and preside
at a great public meeting. His appearance on such an occasion
would produce a sensation much greater than Lord Durham caused
by his visit to Glasgow'.

On the same day a meeting of Glasgow reformers was held in the town hall to approve the Birmingham plan of campaign. Many of the leading middle class reformers were absent, but James Moir felt that the working classes had much in their power to rectify this deficiency. James Turner, of Thrushgrove, thought that the former 12,000 members of the Glasgow Political Union could be enrolled in the new cause, and a committee to organise a demonstration, to which Attwood and the Birmingham leaders would be invited, was appointed. This contained many of the well known members of the Union in previous years, including Hedderwick, Birkmyre, Moir, Purdie, and Dr Walker. Resolutions were passed in favour of universal suffrage, annual parliaments, the ballot, and abolition of the corn laws.

A warning note was voiced on behalf of the absent reformers by Peter Mackenzie, of the *Scotch Reformers' Gazette*, who cautioned the working classes against becoming the tools of Tory Radicals. The agitation could only delight the Tories; in the present state of the House of Commons, and frame of mind of the working classes, it was 'extremely unwise even to moot the question of universal suffrage'. The wild and reckless conduct of the cotton spinners could not be forgotten, and the man who thought universal suffrage could now be carried by 'physical force' was 'worse than a knave'.[3]

After several weeks more of constant activity, John Collins reported that Dundee was certain, Edinburgh was being prepared, and that the Glasgow central committee had placarded the city to great effect. Nevertheless, the requisition for the Birmingham deputation would not be sent until the committee were certain of success. Meanwhile 'large meetings' and 'glorious meetings' had been held for him in Kilbarchan, Strathaven, Johnstone, Beith, Kilbirnie, Houston, Lochwinnoch, Parkhead, Bridgeton, Newmilns, Kilmarnock, Ayr, Mauchline and Cumnock, as well as at Paisley, Glasgow and Edinburgh, where the chair had been taken by a brother of the Lord Provost. There had been escorts by bands of music, and soirées had been held.

At Bridgeton the meeting was announced from the pulpit by the Rev. Mr Edwards, and 300 ladies who had been 'especially invited to attend' heard the prophet from Birmingham, whose main themes on the suffrage, the ballot and annual parliaments were coupled with condemnation of Daniel O'Connell and praise of the value of abstinence. In Ayrshire, Bailie Hugh Craig, the Kilmarnock draper and leader of the political union, had taken charge of him. On 18 April, Collins addressed 'the largest assemblage I had yet seen, since I had reached Scotland'. He was then driven on the same day to three other meetings by the erstwhile host of William Cobbett. The energetic bailie collected the crowds, chaired the meetings, spoke with 'great power and eloquence' and then drove furiously in his gig to the next place, until Collins was worn out. When they left Cumnock, they were 'preceded and surrounded by flaming torches, a band of music, splendid flags and thousands of inhabitants'.

From Edinburgh, John Fraser, the secretary of the Radical Committee, held out assurances of magnificent demonstrations in Dundee, Dunfermline and Cupar. They would do their best to rouse the north—even Aberdeen and Inverness. They could not yet count on Perth, but

We must not let the West of Scotland take all the glory from us . . . We want the glory and the blessedness of a peaceful triumph; we want to strike terror to the foe, and yet not touch a hair of their heads . . . Eternal thanks are due to the Birmingham Political Union for this movement, so opportunely commenced . . .[4]

In Glasgow, on 24 April, an important meeting of the central committee was held. More than 200 delegates from 'different trades, shops, factories and districts' met in the Session House, East Regent Street, and unanimously resolved to come forward with their flags, banners and music. The Grand Demonstration would take place on Glasgow Green on 21 May, and this would be followed in the evening by a soirée in Ducrow's Arena. Most of the trades were already actively preparing new flags and banners with appropriate devices, and 'not a town within 20 miles of Glasgow but will send a quota of honest men'.

Alexander Purdie, the secretary of the central committee, wrote on the following day to invite Thomas Attwood and 'other friends from Birmingham' to attend the demonstration 'in favour of universal suffrage, annual parliaments, and vote by ballot', on Monday 21 May 1838. The 'cool, cautious, yet firm and determined adherence to principle' of John Collins had won their confidence and esteem. There were many prejudices to be dissipated, 'but the masses are with us, and we therefore feel confident that you will be more cordially received, more heartily responded to, and by a larger assemblage, than ever congregated on the Green of Glasgow for a similar purpose'.

Thomas Attwood eventually replied on 5 May accepting the invitation. He emphasised that it was of the highest importance that the meeting should be memorable in the history of Scotland and England, and adjured the men of Glasgow to remember that their

GRAND RADICAL DEMONSTRATION.

———

Mr. T. Attwood, M.P. for Birmingham has ac-cepted the invitation sent him to meet with the Radicals of Glasgow on the 21st inst. The following is a copy of his letter on the occasion:—

London, May 5. 1838.

Sir,—Before I returned a reply to your letter of the 25th ultimo, I was desirous of consulting my friends in Birming-ham. This has occasioned some delay, which I trust that you and the men of Glasgow will excuse.

Sir, I accept with plasure the invitation which you have done me the honour to send me, and will not fail to attend the Grand Meeting at Glasgow, *on Monday the 21st inst.*, ac-companied by four or five of my Birmingham friends, who will be appointed at a town's meeting, which will be held in a few days. Pray have the goodness to inform me, as early as you can, *at what hour of Monday* on the 21st instant, and *at what place*, it will be convenient to the men of Glasgow to receive us. It is of high importance that this meeting should be a day memorable in the history of Scotland and of England. We come to you with no base pride to gratify; but we come as the representatives of millions of our coun-trymen, determined to unite in the great work of restoring the prosperity and vindicating the liberty of our country—our long oppressed, misgoverned, and exasperated country. It is this great and holy cause, therefore, which we shall represent; and in our humble persons I doubt not that the men of Glasgow will take care that this glorious cause shall be gloriously vindicated.

Remember PEACE, LAW, ORDER. LOYALTY, AND UNION, these are our Mottos—under these ban-ners we will gather the strength of the people—under these banners the people possess a giant's strength; but if they once abandon them, they become but as an infant in a giant's hand.

I am, with respect,

Sir,

Your faithful servant,

THOMAS ATTWOOD.

Mr. A. Purdie.

———

Printed in the Glasgow Chronicle Office.

Leaflet announcing the Attwood demonstration,
21 May 1838

motto was 'Peace, law, order, loyalty and union'. Under these banners 'the people possess a giant's strength. But if they once abandon them, they become but as an infant in a giant's hand'.[5]

At this stage the men of Birmingham were still dithering about their tactics. The intention of the council was to have their National Petition signed in Birmingham on 7 May by the men, and on 8 May by the women, before carrying it to Glasgow. Attwood, however, objected to having any Birmingham meeting until after the Glasgow demonstration, lest its success might be prejudiced. Douglas thought that to ensure greater acceptability on Glasgow Green the petition drafted by the council must receive public sanction, and that only the great principles of radical reform—universal suffrage and the ballot—should be included in the National Petition. Annual parliaments might be injurious rather than beneficial. P. H. Muntz was beginning to have doubts that a deputation from the Birmingham Political Union might be an illegal body. It would be desirable to go to Glasgow as representatives of the people of Birmingham rather than merely as private individuals. Douglas thought that all except Attwood required to be appointed. At length, at a meeting in the town hall, on 14 May, the Birmingham delegates were appointed. The deputation was to consist of the two MP's, Thomas Attwood and Joshua Scholefield, along with P. H. Muntz, Benjamin Hadley, George Edmonds, Thomas Clutton Salt and Robert Kellie Douglas. J. A. Roebuck and Colonel Perronet Thompson had notified their intention of visiting Scotland along with the deputation. Douglas moved his draft of the National Petition—which now demanded universal suffrage, the ballot and annual parliaments—and this was adopted.

On the eve of the Glasgow demonstration, a delighted Thomas Attwood wrote from Hamilton about his reception in Scotland:

I find all is enthusiasm in Scotland, having already received invitations from all the chief towns. But you need not fear that I shall be led astray into visiting other towns. Many gentlemen from Glasgow are come over to meet us, 11 miles, and they give us a grand account of our reception tomorrow.

Monday 21 May turned out to be a dismal, rainy day. Despite this, the 'important gathering of the people, on behalf of their favourite measures ... came off ... with much greater *éclat* than was generally expected. Had the weather been favourable, the complexion of the whole business would have surpassed anything of a similar kind that has yet occurred in this quarter of the century'. The numbers in the processions were reported to be as great as those of the Reform Bill period. All public works were at a standstill. Seventy trades unions marched in a procession stretching for more than two miles. Forty-three 'bands of music, all in uniform', met Attwood at Parkhead, and about 300 banners were in the field, including a Covenanting flag from Strathaven, and many anti-corn law banners. Large bodies of reformers from Lanarkshire and Renfrewshire villages and towns marched into Glasgow. A great multitude, variously estimated at between 30,000 and 100,000 by the Whig and Tory press, and between 100,000 and 200,000 by the Radical press, assembled on Glasgow Green to try to hear their new political redeemers, Messrs Attwood, Douglas, Salt, Edmonds, Muntz and Collins.

James Turner of Thrushgrove, being the most highly esteemed of the Glasgow reformers, was as usual elected to the chair, from which he reminded the assembly of the 1816 meeting which had given 'the correct mode of behaviour to all reform meetings since then'. Thomas Gillespie, James Proudfoot, and W. C. Pattison moved resolutions condemning the Reform Bill, calling for the extension of the suffrage, and for the adoption of a petition based on these resolutions. Pattison called on the multitude to remember that the meeting had been organised by the working classes alone.

Attwood declared that 'the men of Birmingham were willing either to assist or to lead them on . . . In the cause of peace, loyalty and order, the men of Birmingham would not shrink from assisting them even to the death'. The Reform Bill had produced thorns, not grapes. He was no revolutionist, and he was doing all in his power to prevent revolution. Against them were arrayed all the aristocracy, nine-tenths of the gentry, all placemen and pensioners. They had no strength on their side but the justice of their cause. They could not afford discord. There must be unanimity. 'Master and man must unite and compel the Government to give them justice'. The men of Glasgow had now met and he knew forty-eight other towns which would follow suit. Once the forty-nine delegates of these towns had met in London, he would like to see the House of Commons that would reject their petition. But if God made them mad, then another and another petition would be sent. They would then make a general strike.

1. Glasgow Green in 1848

2. Princes Street, Edinburgh, from the west

3. John Fraser, 1794–1879

4 The Rev. Patrick Brewster, 1788–1859

5. Bailie Hugh Craig, 1795–1858

6. John Taylor, 1805–42

Such a strike as that of the Romans, who, whenever they were oppressed and had a grievance to be redressed, retired in a body to the Aventine Hill and would not return till their wrongs were removed; and in every case they succeeded.

Dr Wade and Mr Murphy of the London Working Men's Association were present to introduce 'the People's Charter', but this part of the proceedings went almost unnoticed in the newspaper reports, as had happened with the publication of the charter earlier that month.

The limelight was fixed entirely on the Birmingham guests, particularly Attwood, Collins and Douglas, to whom toasts were drunk at the banquet in the evening, and in whose honour a long programme of similar speeches was got through. On this occasion James Moir, the Radical tea merchant, acted as chairman, and ex-bailie James Turner represented the magistrates of Glasgow. One of the principal toasts was to 'Free Trade—a Speedy Repeal of the Corn Laws and all Commercial Restrictions'.

On the following day, Attwood was met 'on the sacred field of Elderslie (William Wallace)' by twenty bands of music and by another great multitude of people, which he somewhat optimistically estimated at 50,000. This gathering escorted him four miles, in a constant downpour of rain, to Paisley, where a county demonstration was held. 'All is enthusiasm and devotion to the cause,' reported Attwood, who refused to let his spirit be damped by the unkind Scottish weather and who was highly gratified to be told by 'all men . . . that my reception in Scotland has far exceeded that of Lord Durham, or of O'Connell'.[6]

During the next ten days, Scotland—especially the west and midlands—was in a ferment of excitement. Attwood, the Messiah, returned home on 23 May, but his apostles made triumphant visits to Kilmarnock, Stirling, Dundee, Cupar and Edinburgh. At a meeting at Dunfermline, Salt addressed 300 women, one of whom took the chair. In Edinburgh, there had been some dissension amongst the various groups of reformers, but Dr Wade indignantly denied that the demonstration, with 15,000 people on Calton Hill, could be considered a failure. At the Kilmarnock meeting Dr John Taylor, who had not been invited to play any part in the Glasgow meetings, appeared on behalf of the Radical reformers of Ayr and made an address to the Birmingham deputation.

NATIONAL REFORM PETITION

" Unto the Honourable the Commons of the United Kingdom of Great Britain and Ireland in Parliament assembled, the Petition of the undersigned, their suffering Countrymen,

" Humbly Sheweth

" THAT We your petitioners, dwell in a land whose merchants are noted for enterprise—whose manufacturers are very skilful—and whose workmen are proverbial for their industry.

" The land itself is goodly, the soil rich, and the temperature wholesome ; it is abundantly furnished with the materials of commerce and trade ; it has numerous and convenient harbours ; in facility of internal communication it exceeds all others.

" For three-and-twenty years we have enjoyed a profound peace.

" Yet, with all these elements of national prosperity, and with every disposition and capacity to take advantage of them, we find ourselves overwhelmed with public and private suffering.

" We are bowed down under a load of taxes ; which, notwithstanding, fall greatly short of the wants of our rulers ; our traders are trembling on the verge of bankruptcy ; our workmen are starving ; capital brings no profit, and labour no remuneration ; the home of the artificer is desolate, and the warehouse of the pawnbroker is full ; the workhouse is crowded, and the manufactory is deserted.

" We have looked on every side, we have searched diligently, in order to find out the causes of a distress so sore and so long continued.

" We can discover none in nature, or in providence.

" Heaven has dealt graciously by the people ; nor have the the people abused its grace.

" But the foolishness of our rulers has made the goodness of God of none effect.

" The energies of a mighty kingdom have been wasted in building up the power of selfish and ignorant men, and its resources squandered for their aggrandisement.

" The good of a party has been advanced to the sacrifice of the good of the nation ; the few have governed for the interest of the few ; while the interest of the many has been sottishly neglected, or insolently and tyrannously trampled upon.

" It was the fond expectation of the friends of the people that a remedy for the greater part, if not for the whole, of their grievances would be found in the Reform Act, of 1832.

" They regarded that act as a wise means to a worthy end : as the machinery of an improved legislation, where the will of the masses would be at length potential.

" They have been bitterly and basely deceived.

" The fruit which looked so fair to the eye, has turned to dust and ashes when gathered.

" The Reform Act has effected a transfer of power from one domineering faction to another, and left the people as helpless as before.

" Our slavery has been exchanged for an apprenticeship to liberty, which has aggravated the painful feelings of our social degradation, by adding to them the sickening of still deferred hope.

" We come before your honourable house to tell you, with all humility, that this state of things must not be permitted to continue ; that it cannot long continue without very seriously endangering the stability of the throne and the peace of the kingdom ; and that if by Gods help and all lawful and constitutional appliances, an end can be put to it, we are fully resolved that it shall speedily come to an end.

" We tell your honourable house that the capital of the master must no longer be deprived of its due profit, that the labour of the workman must no longer be deprived of its due reward ; that the laws which make food dear, and the laws which make money scarce, must be abolished ; that taxation must be made to fall on property, not on industry ; that the good of the many, as it is the only legitimate end so must it be the sole study of the government.

" As a preliminary essential to these and other requisite changes ; as the means by which alone the interests of the people can be effectually vindicated and secured, we demand that those interests be confided to the keeping of the people.

" When the state calls for defenders, when it calls for money, no consideration of poverty or ignorance can be pleaded in refusal or delay of the call.

" Required as we are, universally, to support and to obey the laws, nature and reason entitle us to demand, that, in the making of the laws, the universal voice shall be implicitly listened to.

" We perform the duties of freemen ; we must have the privileges of freemen. Therefore—

" We demand Universal Suffrage.

" The suffrage to be exempt from the corruption of the wealthy, and the violence of the powerful, must be secret.

" The assertion of our right necessarily involves the power of its uncontrolled exercise.

" We ask for the reality of a good, not for its semblance. Therefore—

" We demand the Ballot.

" The connection between the representatives and the people, to be beneficial, must be intimate.

" The legislative and constituent powers, for correction and for instruction, ought to be brought into frequent contact.

" Errors, which are comparatively light when susceptible of a speedy popular remedy, may produce the most disastrous effects when permitted to grow inveterate through years of compulsory endurance.

" To public safety, as well as public confidence, frequent elections are essential. Therefore—

" We demand Annual Parliaments.

" With power to choose, and freedom in choosing, the range of our choice must be unrestricted.

" We are compelled, by the existing laws, to take for our representatives men, who are incapable of appreciating our difficulties, or who have little sympathy with them ; merchants who have retired from trade, and no longer feel its harassings ; proprietors of land, who are alike ignorant of its evils and their cure ; lawyers, by whom the notoriety of the senate is courted only as a means of obtaining notice in the courts.

" The labours of a representative, who is sedulous in the discharge of his duty, are numerous and burdensome.

" It is neither just, nor reasonable, nor safe, that they should continue to be gratuitously rendered.

" We demand that in the future election of members of your honourable house, the approbation of the constituency shall be the sole qualification : and that, to every representative so chosen shall be assigned, out of the public taxes, a fair and adequate remuneration for the time which he was called upon to devote to the public service.

" The management of this mighty kingdom has hitherto been a subject for contending factions to try their selfish experiments upon.

" We have felt the consequences, in our sorrowful experience—short glimmerings of uncertain enjoyment swallowed up by long and dark seasons of suffering.

" If the self-government of the people should not remove their distresses, it will at least remove their repinings.

" Universal suffrage will, and it alone, can bring true and lasting peace to the nation ; we firmly believe that it will also bring prosperity.

" May it, therefore, please your honourable house to take this our petition into your most serious consideration ; and to use your utmost endeavours, by all constitutional means, to have a law passed granting to every male of lawful age, sane mind, and unconvicted of crime, the right of voting for members of Parliament ; and directing all future elections of members of Parliament to be in the way of secret ballot ; and ordaining that the duration of Parliaments so chosen shall in no case exceed one year ; and abolishing all property qualifications in the members ; and providing for their due remuneration while in attendance on their Parliamentary duties.

" And your petitioners, &c."

GLASGOW :—Printed and Published by W. & W. MILLER, 90, Bell Street ; Sold by JOHN CUMMING, 16, Hucheson Street ; and by several other Booksellers.

GLASGOW, June 13, 1838.

Before the men of Birmingham left Scotland, a great mass of the
working classes had been introduced to the National Petition.
However imperfectly they may have understood its political content, they had warmly acclaimed it as their political creed and their
hope of social salvation. By the beginning of June it had been
adopted in Glasgow, Edinburgh, Dundee, Perth, Dunfermline and
at county meetings in Renfrewshire, Ayrshire and Fifeshire.
Several of the working men's associations and a few of the surviving political unions espoused the new, but very familiar, programme. Although 'The People's Charter' had been published by
the London Working Men's Association on 8 May, remarkably
little notice had been taken of it, and as yet the agitation was hardly
identified with it. Some of the Radical associations formed under
the spell of Taylor and O'Connor in December 1836 renamed themselves Universal Suffrage Associations, but those who regarded
such a technicality as unnecessary were no less ardent in the cause.[7]

Despite all the excitement and activity, it was still unpredictable
whether this campaign would outlast the visit of the Birmingham
reformers. Several of the most popular political leaders had
received resounding welcomes from the Scottish reformers, but
within a few weeks little had been left behind except the
memory of their visits. Nor had any of the political agitations
under working class leadership lasted more than a few months.
Invariably their strength had faded with industrial recovery. Nor
was it at all clear that the movement had won the support from the
middle classes which Thomas Attwood claimed to have observed.
It was not the middle class leaders—merchants, printers, brewers,
editors and shopkeepers—who had figured most prominently in the
meetings, but trade union and other working class leaders.

The prospects that local political leaders would be forthcoming
and that political associations would continue to function were not
in fact very promising. Very largely they depended on the progress
of the National Petition campaign in England. Nevertheless, a
most encouraging beginning had been made and there were several
factors which argued well for the Scottish agitation. There was
emerging increasingly a vocal working class newspaper-reading
public, many of whom had begun to take an active interest in
schemes of social reform, in trade unionism, in temperance, in

---

The National Petition, as printed in the *Liberator*

co-operation, and more recently many of these group leaders had begun to assert themselves in politics. Many of them regarded the extension of the suffrage as the only practical road to the abolition of the corn laws. In addition, there were small groups of local politicians who were sufficiently impatient with the Whigs to accept a share in the reflected glory of Thomas Attwood and his movement. They had enjoyed the feeling of responsibility derived from their minor roles in the political unions, and—working class and middle class alike—they felt they could win still greater reputation as the office-bearers of the new political associations.

During the summer months of 1838 most of the Radical excitement subsided. Apart from a large meeting on Calton Hill, in Edinburgh, on coronation day, 28 June, there were no more large demonstrations or processions, and few of the meetings which took place attracted much attention from a generally unsympathetic press. In Glasgow the *Scots Times* had been won over to universal suffrage, but paid little attention to the movement, except in Glasgow. Increasingly the universal suffragists had to depend on the *Northern Star* for information on the progress of the movement. John Taylor's *New Liberator* was by now dead. It had lacked appeal for the more respectable of the Radicals, and after 1837 it no longer received adequate support from the Glasgow trades, who had established it in 1832. It ceased publication in May, while its undaunted proprietor was engaged in an attempt to rally his ultra-Radical supporters and prevent the agitation from falling completely under the sway of the respectable 'moderate party'.

On coronation day a public supper was given in honour of 'that stern Republican, Dr John Taylor'. A committee, with Taylor as convenor, was appointed for the formation of a Republican Society. The memories of Benjamin Franklin, George Washington and Augustus Beaumont were honoured. Eulogies were paid to Taylor, Feargus O'Connor, 'Bronterre', Stephens, Fraser and Robert Owen, but no mention was made of the reformers of London or the men of Birmingham.

A fortnight later, Feargus O'Connor arrived in the west of Scotland to assist Taylor in 'reproving' the more timid of the Scottish Radicals. Recently these people had been showing 'increasing kindness' to the 'Whig trimmers' under the pretence of 'fearing a revolution'. He and his friend 'John Taylor, the most abused man in Scotland . . . [sought] not the subversion of the constitution but the whole constitution and nothing but the constitution; as it was, as it ought to be, aye, and as it yet shall be'. For almost three weeks O'Connor and Taylor toured the west of Scotland. They appeared, they assured their audiences, 'to ensure that union was not frittered away by each section adopting some particular crotchet forgetful of national purposes'. A great national movement was now taking shape. Already their enemies trembled, but before long attempts would be made to divide the Radicals. They had already been taunted with advocating physical violence. Enemies used the word 'revolution' as synonymous with all that was dreadful. But the revolution that he, Feargus O'Connor, advocated was not one of riot and bloodshed, and his language had merely been that of O'Connell, Fielden, Brougham and Thomas Attwood.[8]

Ever since Attwood's speeches at Glasgow, O'Connor had been insistent on the similarity of the sentiments expressed and the language used by both of them. Attwood's words 'even to the death' accorded perfectly with the sentiments expressed in the objects of the Great Northern Union—'physical force shall be resorted to if necessary'. Moral power, the Radicals of Glasgow and Ayrshire were constantly reminded, was but a shadow. By itself, it had never been productive of any good. Their oppressors would not heed moral force unless they were aware that physical force was behind. Taylor's language tended to be less guarded, in his allusions to violence, than that of O'Connor; but in the reporting, at least, it could generally be presented as the expression of some other Radical, e.g.:

He approved of what O'Connell said, that moral force could produce no result except to make the people think. They had thought long enough and what better were they if they only thought themselves worse off than before. If a revolution got by blood, and after twenty battles, were good in 1688, it could not be bad in 1838.

Such efforts were clearly designed to win the Scottish Radicals over to the O'Connor–Great Northern Union axis of the movement. But despite the vitality of the Taylor–O'Connor *détente*, the leadership of Attwood and the men of Birmingham remained virtually unshaken. The most successful of their meetings had been held mainly in that part of Ayrshire where Taylor was regarded as a local hero, and even there they found it expedient to appear anxious to avoid provoking any irreconcilable schism within the movement. They demonstrated their loyalty to the national movement by recommending co-operation with the Birmingham Political Union as well as with the Great Northern Union. Thomas Attwood was 'honest and straightforward in his principles'. O'Connor had sat with him in Parliament for three years, and had 'great confidence in him'.

By the end of July, Taylor had gone into temporary retirement at Ayr, and O'Connor was southward bound for the Birmingham demonstration without the gratification of having been entrusted with the task of representing Glasgow at this important occasion, despite the kind offer of his services. At a meeting in the Bazaar on 23 July the men of Glasgow had instead decided to rely on James Moir and Alexander Purdie, and their main concern was obtaining further batches of signatures to the National Petition, which had already received over 70,000 signatures in Glasgow.

The most important activity of these months, however, was a less ostentatious but far more widespread tour by John Fraser of Edinburgh and Abram Duncan of Glasgow throughout the eastern, midland and southern counties of Scotland. To many of the small towns and villages to which Collins and his associates had not penetrated, Fraser and Duncan carried the new faith and introduced the National Petition. In three months, they claimed, they had addressed almost a million working men, urging them to form universal suffrage societies to obtain their political rights and to form teetotal societies for their moral regeneration.

Both Fraser and Duncan were known to be 'thorough-going Radicals'. Within recent months Fraser had been closely allied with O'Connor and Duncan with Taylor. Duncan was a pirn maker who had played a prominent part in the Glasgow Political Union, and had often acted as spokesman for the Glasgow trades. He was also well known in the Voluntary Church movement (which wanted Church disestablishment). With Fraser he had recently been active in the agitation on behalf of the cotton spinners. John Fraser had been a schoolteacher in Johnstone and had been imprisoned for his part in the 1819–20 Radical troubles. He had settled in Edinburgh in 1836, where he helped to found the Radical Association and the Teetotal Society. He was an advocate of hygeism and an agent for Morison's (Vegetable) Pills. For O'Connor's *Northern Star* he had reported the cotton spinners' trial.

In their peregrinations Fraser and Duncan discovered a decided bias against violent language and a great reliance on the Birmingham party. They found their fellow Scotsmen—in Aberdeen, Alloa, Arbroath, Auchtermuchty, Barrhead, Ceres, Dalkeith, Dysart, Hamilton, Leven, Musselburgh, Tillicoultry, Whitburn and numerous other places—extremely cautious on the question of physical force, and they denied that they came to advocate such a policy. There were great moral means which must be totally exhausted before any others were tried. They must obey the laws. 'But if soldiers or the armed police were to come amongst them and to break the laws' then it would be for the people of Scotland to say what they would do.[9]

At the Birmingham demonstration, on 6 August, Scotland was represented by Moir, Purdie and Duncan. They were accorded a place of honour, which they filled without achieving any distinction or prominence. They could, however, report that solid progress had been made since May, and that the agitation was now firmly established in Scotland. The work of establishing local associations and converting the existing working men's associations was continuing, with satisfactory results, especially on the east coast. Two newspapers devoted to universal suffrage had begun publication in July. In Kilmarnock there was now the weekly *Ayrshire Examiner* and in Edinburgh there was *The Edinburgh Monthly and Total Abstinence Advocate*. The latter was a two-penny unstamped paper published by John Fraser, 'one of the best Radicals in the Empire', to detail the progress of 'Radical democracy' throughout the villages of Scotland, in combination with 'the enforcement of the principles of total abstinence'.

The period closed with John Fraser reporting progress to the London demonstration on 17 September. Scotland was in 'a high state of preparedness', declared Fraser, who, along with Duncan, had been appointed to represent Edinburgh at the metropolitan demonstration by a meeting of 15,000 Radicals on Calton Hill, on 10 September. The movement was now strong in Dumfries, Hawick, Forfar, Arbroath, Montrose, Aberdeen, Hamilton and all the important towns between Glasgow and Edinburgh. In Ayrshire the principal towns and villages were organised; universal suffrage was advocated everywhere in Renfrewshire, except Greenock, by the Renfrewshire Political Union—a powerful organisation with more than 3,000 members, formed in July. In the east of Scotland, where the voice of reform had scarcely penetrated in the past, 20,000 had already signed the National Petition in

Fifeshire. They still lacked an adequate press to cover their activities and expound their doctrines, but they were determined to carry on their proceedings 'in sober seriousness'.

'The men of Scotland, when once in the field,' declared Fraser, 'were like their native oaks—stubborn, strong and unbending—and would be the last to turn their backs upon the common foe.' While the Scottish people were slow to warm, the warmth took long to pass away. The mass of the people would 'now struggle for one thing and one thing only—Universal Suffrage'. To which Abram Duncan added that the Radicals of Edinburgh were now resolved to 'attend every meeting held in Scotland, and whatever the nature of the meeting may be, to move as an amendment to their resolutions, Universal Suffrage'.[10]

NOTES

1. *Birmingham Journal*, 15 April 1837; 11 November 1837; 13, 20 and 27 January 1838; 3 February 1838.
   Glasgow Argus, 14 December 1837.
2. *Birmingham Journal*, 24 February 1838; 3 March 1838.
3. *Birmingham Journal*, 14 April 1838; 21 April 1838.
   Scotch Reformers' Gazette, 14 April 1838.
4. *Birmingham Journal*, 28 April 1838; 12 May 1838.
   Add MSS 27,820, pp. 72–8.
5. *Birmingham Journal*, 28 April 1838.
   C. M. Wakefield, *Life of Thomas Attwood*, pp. 333–4.
   Add. MSS 27,820, pp. 78, 85.
6. *Birmingham Journal*, 19 May 1838; 26 May 1838.
   Wakefield, pp. 335–7.
   Northern Star, 2 June 1838.
   Add. MSS 27,820, pp. 83, 109–23.
   Monthly Liberator, 13 June 1838.
7. *Birmingham Journal*, 2 and 9 June 1838.
   Northern Star, 2 and 9 June 1838.
   Wakefield, p. 337.
   Add. MSS 27,820, 125–6, 176.
8. *Birmingham Journal*, 23 June 1838; 14 July 1838.
   Northern Star, 2 June 1838; 7, 21 and 28 July 1838.
   Monthly Liberator, 13 June; 7 July 1838.
9. *Northern Star*, 28 July 1838; 4 August 1838; 22 September 1838.
   Edinburgh Monthly Democrat, July, August and September 1838.
   R. M. W. Cowan, p. 189.
10. *Birmingham Journal*, 11 August 1838.
    Northern Star, 11 August 1838; 15 and 22 September 1838.
    Add. MSS 27,820, p. 213–4.

CHAPTER FOUR

The battle of Calton Hill

For many parts of Scotland, October was a month of considerable Radical activity. In Glasgow the Universal Suffrage Association, which had been formed at the end of August, had now enrolled more than 2,000 members. Fraser and Duncan turned their campaign to the Border districts, where they met with ready support in Hawick, Selkirk, Jedburgh and Galashiels in 'vanquishing Whig (Corn Law) Repealers'. On 20 October the *Monthly Democrat and Total Abstinence Advocate* was superseded by the more ambitious weekly stamped newspaper *The True Scotsman*, owned and edited by John Fraser. There was no difficulty in finding news for this large scale publication. Preparations were being made in many places for the election of delegates to the 'General Convention of the Industrious Classes', and within a few weeks the *True Scotsman* was claiming a circulation of over 2,500 a week.[1]

At Alloa on 24 October Alexander Halley, a working man of Dunfermline noted for moderation, mild language and sound sense, was elected member of Convention for Stirlingshire. A few days later another working class Radical, W. G. Burns, a shoemaker and newsagent of Dundee with a rather more fiery temperament than Halley, was elected as member for Forfarshire. In Perthshire Patrick Matthew, a prosperous grain dealer and landed proprietor, was elected. He was a person of the most equable demeanour and behaviour, a well educated man with decidedly Radical opinions on social and educational reform. In Stirling, the election of Halley was confirmed, while at Edinburgh the ranks of the middle class members of the Convention were further augmented by the election of W. S. Villiers Sankey, a Greek scholar, philologist, mathematician, astronomist, medical theorist and graduate of Dublin and Cambridge. Among his published works were pamphlets on the rights of labour, and on universal suffrage.

In Ayrshire the stern voice of Dr John Taylor was again to be heard as he emerged from his retirement. He lectured his friends on the need to send only trustworthy men as delegates to the Convention—men 'whose principles are so defined that they cannot be mistaken—who are prepared to risk everything, even life itself, in supporting them'. Taylor denied the rumour that he would decline nomination, and was deeply disturbed at the conduct of many of his former friends, who were 'tampering with the Whigs' in the vain hope of conciliating them. Such men had become 'Modernists with Expediency for their motto'. They would spout ultra-Radicalism for the sake of public notice, and then spend the rest of their time in 'private recantation of their public expressions'.

The *Northern Star* noted with great pleasure the reappearance of 'this veteran defender of liberty' in the field, and prophesied that the Ayrshire Radicals would now 'prove their sense of obligation by resting on him the greatest amount of confidence, and conferring on him the greatest honour which it is in their power to bestow'. But although Taylor was called upon, 'by the unexpected kindness of the men of Cumnock and Ayr', to take part in 'the great drama about to be acted', he was not the only popular Radical in Ayrshire. At the county election, on 3 November, he found himself confronted by another candidate from Cumnock, schoolmaster John McCrae, and—more seriously—by Bailie Hugh Craig, the prosperous Kilmarnock draper and the most popular man in north Ayrshire. The working-class member of the trio was quickly eliminated, but the middle-class candidate won a clear majority over his aristocratic colleague, and amidst great enthusiasm Bailie Craig was declared elected.[2]

In Glasgow the trades met to pledge support for the Convention and the National Rent, while in Paisley, where political feeling had been 'repressed of late by the briskness of the textile trade', the Renfrewshire Political Union held a soirée, attended by the provost and other distinguished guests, in honour of the Rev. Patrick Brewster of Paisley Abbey. The accession to the cause of this clergyman, whose political opinions in recent years had been considered unorthodox and repugnant among his colleagues in the Established Church, was now considered the most important event since the visit of Thomas Attwood.

Meanwhile, 'Father Abram' Duncan, who had been scrupulously attending all elections for membership of the Convention to ensure the return of the most worthy candidates, but who was still without a seat of his own in the Convention, saw fit to keep himself in the public eye by administering a rebuke to Feargus O'Connor for his injudicious language and his increasing use of allusions to physical force. Partly this appears to have been prompted by the prejudice being stirred up against the movement by its identification, in the non-Radical press, with the language of O'Connor, Stephens and Oastler. In part, however, it was due to the quarrel then in progress between O'Connor and the leaders of the Birmingham Political Union.

Abram Duncan and John Fraser felt it necessary that the minds of the Scottish Radicals should be decided unmistakably on the question of physical and moral force, and in order to establish the purity of intention of the Scottish movement they decided to convene a delegate meeting of local Radical and universal suffrage associations. Draft resolutions, affirming the unqualifiedly peaceful nature of the means of agitation to which they would ever resort, were circulated in Duncan's name. 'The men of Scotland, at least, will never appeal to physical force at any time, or upon any occasion whatever,' was the key resolution proposed, and associations were invited to send delegates to a conference in Edinburgh to voice approval of the policy of 'moral, constitutional agitation', which had been advocated by the Birmingham Political Union.[3]

Several associations were perturbed by the nature of the proposed conference. This was regarded as 'an uncalled-for interference', and as 'more likely to cause dissension than to promote the interests of the cause'. Amongst these were the Radical Associations of Alva, Tillicoultry, Newmilns and Greenholm, and even of Irvine, which several weeks earlier had offered 'its heartfelt acknowledgements for this grand movement' to the Radical reformers of Birmingham. The secretary of the Working Men's Association of Ayr replied, on 27 November, that the proposal to call this delegate meeting was 'completely at variance with the principles of honest Radicals'. The men of Ayr

cannot view the proposed national resolution to use nothing but moral means in any other light than an unconditional surrender; for, if we cannot speak to the fears of our oppressors ... we shall never be able to speak with any good effect to their feelings, and we would ask you what good you can calculate upon obtaining, after having proclaimed to them that they have nothing to fear from physical force?

Elsewhere, however, the tide of Radical opinion was generally strong in favour of Duncan and Fraser. The Dundee Political Union passed a resolution condemning the incendiary language of Oastler and Stephens in their agitation against the new poor law. 'We are glad to see that the Radicals of Scotland have raised the Birmingham standard of "Peace, Law and Order", instead of the insane "war to the knife" injunctions of Oastler and Stephens', commented the *Bolton Free Press,* which drew attention to the much better organisation of the Scottish than of the English Radicals.

None of the replies from the local associations was published by Fraser in the *True Scotsman,* but on 1 December he claimed to have received favourable replies from thirty-seven associations. This quick and substantial response was considered to be highly gratifying, and the delegate conference was called for 5 December 1838.

When the Edinburgh conference duly took place, it was attended by about fifty delegates. They represented little more than a dozen local associations, but Fraser was able to claim that, of sixty letters which he had received from local associations, all but seven had 'warmly concurred with the proposed objects'. He wished it to be understood that although he and Abram Duncan had been instrumental in arranging the conference, they had not wished to act as dictators. They had merely made a suggestion which they believed to correspond closely to the opinion of the Scottish Radicals. At 100 meetings during six months, they had found decided support for denunciation of any appeal to physical force. So long as he had control over the *True Scotsman* it would advocate the great principles of the National Petition and the People's Charter, and its weapons would be 'reason, not violence . . . persuasion, not arms'.

The Rev. Patrick Brewster was not an official delegate, but he was encouraged to take a leading part in the proceedings. A series of resolutions disavowing physical force was adopted by the delegates, who included several of the elected members of the Convention. Amongst the proposers was W. G. Burns of Dundee, who thought the time might come when there ought to be resort to physical force. This, however, could never be until all other expedients had failed, so, above all things, they should repudiate every appeal to physical force.

It was very easy to talk of physical force when warming our toes before the fire. Even if we succeeded in wresting our rights from the ruling powers by its means, the demoralizing influence of the struggle would disqualify us from enjoying their beneficial influence.

James Hamilton of Stonehouse held that newspapers were the 'book of God's providence' which all men ought to read, to study what God was doing in their country and in the world. It was the doctrine of physical force that had made the blood of Wilson flow on the scaffold, that had deprived the country of the services of a Hardy, and that had retarded the progress of reform. 'Let the banner of universal suffrage be unstained with one drop of human blood,' declared John Mitchell of Aberdeen.

The resolutions were piloted to unanimous adoption by Brewster, who presided over the torchlit public meeting on Calton Hill that evening, to which they were submitted in order to be given a more authoritative send-off as the policy of the Radicals in Scotland. This gentleman, well known for his 'deep interest in the cause of human happiness, human improvement, and universal liberty', declared that there was no Tory Radicalism in Scotland. Bad as the Whigs were, they were not as bad as the Tories. They must, however, be compelled to set free the white slaves as they had been compelled to do with the black slaves. With the moral artillery of their resolutions they would sweep from the field 'the physical forcemen, the Stephenses and the Oastlers'; but he would not say Feargus O'Connor, for he was an honest man, and they could not spare one honest man from so good a cause.[4]

All things were now favouring the movement, declared the Chartist newspaper, the *Ayrshire Examiner*:

We hail the accession of Mr Brewster to be an active agent in the cause as another good man. The Working Men's Association of London ... has forced O'Connell to a distinct declaration of approval of the movement. The advances in the course of being made to Lord Durham, and the fearful anxiety to get a Reform Party together, on the principles of the Glasgow declaration, which at one time none but the Radicals would have anything to do with, prove what an impetus has been given by the movement of the masses to those above them ... The effects of the Universal Suffrage Movement are now beginning to tell upon the middle classes ... and they are all looking upon Lord Durham as the man they will take as their leader ... It is evident that unless he comes forward, the moderate Reformers will not make any move at all, till ... they join the national movement. The faster the people make that movement ahead, the sooner will they get the aid of those who are now hanging back.

The Edinburgh delegate conference and the Calton Hill resolution, however, did little either to promote the unity of the movement or to enlist the aid of those 'hanging back', and produced few, if any, of the beneficial results for which Fraser and Duncan had hoped. The non-Radical press refused to be impressed with the information, advanced at torchlit meetings, that the Scottish Radicals would restrict themselves to peaceful agitation. Few of the associations which had taken part in the conference were able to generate any enthusiasm on behalf of the moral force resolutions. Others which had acquiesced in, or shown little interest in, Fraser's proposals began to doubt the wisdom of the *'coup de main'*. Only Hawick, Dunfermline, Elie and Paisley showed the slightest enthusiasm. In Glasgow the Universal Suffrage Association at last took some interest in these Edinburgh events. Alexander Purdie complained that Stephens ought to have been given a hearing before being condemned, and objected to resolutions which denounced those counselling physical violence as unfit associates. The Glasgow Universal Suffrage Association then rejected a mild censure on the participants of the Edinburgh conference, without giving the slightest approval to the proceedings. Ayr, Irvine, Tillicoultry and Newmilns, which had voiced misgivings about holding the conference, now 'entirely disapproved' of it, denouncing the resolutions and the 'pretensions' of their protagonists.

The Calton Hill attack on physical force appears to have been timed to coincide with that of Birmingham. Rather, it followed in the wake of Daniel O'Connell's reply to the 'Radical Reformers of England, Scotland and Wales':

What can be more foolish than your miserable threats of armed violence and bloodshed ... Why do you not disclaim and disown the men who thus wickedly and foolishly injure the cause of Reform ... You have a strong case for the extension of the suffrage, and above all for the vote by ballot, if you will but allow the cause to be conducted within the bounds of law, order and commonsense.

By the time it was made, O'Connor had been making a truce with the Birmingham leaders. Even while the *Birmingham Journal* was applauding the Scottish meeting, which was of 'very great importance', it was reporting that 'the great meeting [with O'Connor] has been held. . . . The good genius of the Charter has conquered'.

This left O'Connor in a much stronger position to counter the Scottish offensive—which had been directed mainly against his anti-new poor law associates, Stephens and Oastler—and attack the allies of the Birmingham Political Union, whose leaders had left them in an exposed position. The counter-attack came swiftly and almost spontaneously. Expressions of confidence in O'Connor were quickly forthcoming from Ayrshire associations. Cumnock Working Men's Association looked on O'Connor as the man who had originated the national movement and who lived in their 'hearts and affections'. They would sacrifice their 'own lives to save a hair of his head'. The heartless hypocrites who denounced the Rev. Joseph Rayner Stephens, the undaunted advocate of the rights of the poor and of labour, as a visionary, incendiary or devil' were unworthy of the Democratic movement.[5]

From London, on 11 December, George Julian Harney wrote to convey the verdict of the London Democratic Association on the Calton Hill resolutions. These were denounced 'with feelings of the strongest indignation' as being 'most insulting to the people of England' and framed 'to create disunion in the ranks of Democracy'. Its unbounded confidence in O'Connor, Stephens and Oastler was coupled with a 'solemn determination to effect the salvation of our fatherland, at all hazards, or sacrifices—peaceably if we can, forcibly if we must'. The Newmilns Radical Association found it 'highly improper and calculated to raise contention amongst Radicals' for individuals or particular associations to lay down specific plans, or dictate certain measures for conducting the movement. 'All these matters ought to be left to the management of the Convention, whose directions the people, to have any chance of success, must implicitly obey.'

Feargus O'Connor added his own voice to the fray:

[He] had always taught the men of the North to depend on moral force alone. But by moral force he did not mean the moral power of the Scotch Philosophers nor their chippings of the Excise and their attacks upon the Teapot.

Many of these attacks were directed against Salt and Muntz for their overtures to O'Connell, as much as against Fraser and Duncan. While abuse of O'Connell was unqualified, Brewster was not mentioned in the denunciations. He was still little known. One of the few voices raised in support of 'the Edinburgh Radicals' was that of William Lovett:

As Feargus O'Connor found fault with the friends of the cause in Edinburgh, he at once denounced them as enemies, and that merely because they had deprecated language such as he had read ... They were deeply injuring their cause by using or approving such language; indeed he thought they ought to deprecate it. They were doing much harm to the cause by condemning all classes. There was not a class in which they had not thousands of friends; then why try to alienate them by denouncing them wholesale.[6]

John Taylor, now the member of Convention for Carlisle, found no difficulty in deciding that the Brewster–Fraser attack on his ally Feargus must be avenged, and that the honour of the Chartists of Scotland was at stake. At this time Taylor was trying to convince the Ayrshire Chartists that the advocates of moral force would destroy the movement unless they could put forward some plan which offered real prospects of success. 'Hope deferred maketh the heart sick,' declared Taylor—who was willing to agree, however, that a fair trial must be given to any promising moral force remedy. Such a remedy might be found in his own plan for a nation-wide federation of 'D'hurna' (or abstinence) societies. Simply by 'stopping supplies', by refusing to use heavily taxed luxury articles, he claimed, this method had been used successfully, without recourse to arms, on one occasion in India, and on two occasions by the American colonists. On 17 December Taylor was elected president of the Ayr D'hurna Society, and its members pledged themselves not to purchase, accept, offer or use intoxicating liquors, tea or tobacco for a period of at least six months, 'and generally to abstain from the use of such articles as paid a high duty to the Government'. In Cumnock a few faithful followers hastened to follow suit, but no D'hurna campaign materialised. More exciting things were distracting Taylor's attention.

In Paisley, Brewster had succeeded in persuading the Renfrewshire Political Union to adopt the Edinburgh resolutions, and at the same meeting it was decided that Bailie John Henderson, and not Dr John Taylor, should be the nominee of the Union at the forthcoming election of the county representative to the Convention. Taylor had already been nominated by Sandholes before the Edinburgh conference, but his prospects in the stronghold of 'Parson'

7. High Street, Edinburgh

8. High Street, Glasgow

MAY THE
People awake to the
Recognition of their Rights;
HAVE THE
Fortitude to demand them;
The Fortune to obtain them,
AND HENCEFORTH
Sufficient Wisdom and Vigour to
DEFEND THEM;

9. Reform demonstration banner, carried to Chartist demonstrations by James Caldwell, who became county clerk of Renfrewshire

Brewster seemed unpromising. For several years his opponent, Bailie Henderson, had been a Radical leader in Paisley politics. He was a working class man who had become editor of the local Radical newspaper, *The Glasgow Saturday Post and Paisley and Renfrewshire Reformer*, and was chairman of the Renfrewshire Political Union. Then, on the eve of the election, Brewster persuaded the Union to adopt once more his moral force resolutions, and had himself substituted for Henderson as the rival candidate to Taylor.[7]

For the next fortnight everything went wrong for Brewster. At the election, on new year's day, 1839, a storm raged over Thornhill, where the demonstration was held. The candidates could not be heard. Brewster failed to carry his ubiquitous moral force resolutions, lost his head and withdrew with his supporters in furious indignation—leaving Taylor in possession of the hill and the votes of the small rump of the meeting. On Glasgow Green the following day, an assembly which rejoiced with Dr Taylor in his victory over 'Parson' Brewster elected as member of Convention for Lanarkshire Brewster's erstwhile friend, James Moir, the 'moderate' Gallowgate tea merchant, who was quietly executing a somersault in his attitude towards Taylor and Brewster. Moir's rival candidate, ex-bailie Alexander Hedderwick, Gorbals brewer and printer of the *Glasgow Argus* and the *Scots Times*, lost the election by refusing to commit himself to no movement other than that for universal suffrage.

Then Feargus O'Connor, who had been loudly announcing his intention 'to deal with Brewster', came roaring across Scotland, packing meetings with his admirers in Edinburgh, Glasgow and even Paisley. At the latter meetings Brewster was able to muster only a handful of supporters and met with humiliating treatment. Brewster refused to admit that he had been fairly defeated, attributing his failure to the 'supineness' of his supporters, and challenged O'Connor to a further series of public debates. But O'Connor lacked the time and gracefully declined. He had achieved his purpose, for Brewster was almost totally eclipsed. A few more soirées were yet to be given in his honour, but his spell was broken and there was an increasing tendency to discount him as an 'uncompromising priest' who drew £300 a year from the Church of whose principles he disapproved but was ready to sacrifice the unity of the movement for the sake of his dogmatism.[8]

John Fraser did his best in the *True Scotsman* to discount the remarkable transformation which had been achieved by Taylor and

O'Connor. From Dunfermline, Airdrie, Elie, Largo, Kirkcaldy, Crossgates, Hawick, Perth and Paisley he garnered reaffirmations of the Calton Hill resolutions. In Paisley the council of the Renfrewshire Political Union decided to repudiate Taylor for constantly infringing their rule 'Peace, law and order' by stating his determination to use physical force. But on 14 January the members of the Union rejected the advice of their president, secretary and council. Instead of unseating Taylor, they confirmed the validity of his election. The president, secretary and most of the council members thereupon resigned, and later formed the 'Paisley New Political Union', while John Taylor was awarded a salary of £25 per month.

Fraser's own position in Edinburgh had been largely undermined, with the Universal Suffrage Association (into which Fraser's Radical Association had been merged in May 1838) disavowing all connection with its patron and with Abram Duncan. Duncan, meanwhile, had somewhat surreptitiously achieved his aim of being elected as a member of the Convention—at Dumfries, where, contrary to the normal procedure, he had been nominated and elected in a single day. But neither this nor the final confirmation of the peace-loving Alexander Halley as member for Stirlingshire—after Alva and Tillicoultry had waged a minor civil war in the county to disavow Halley, the Calton Hill resolutions and eventually the rest of Stirlingshire and Clackmannan—could minimise the magnitude of the defeat for the Fraser–Duncan–Brewster wing of Scottish Chartism.[9]

The Edinburgh conference had become an embarrassing episode for its authors. Even their personal alliance was beginning to fall apart, and much of their prestige had been sacrificed. Instead of outlawing a handful of 'physical force extremists' they had provoked a splintering of the movement in which it was the 'moral force extremists' who became the outcasts. In many districts the action had resulted in a closer union than ever before between the 'moderates 'and the 'ultra-radicals'. The leadership of the Scottish movement, which for several months had rested largely in the hands of Fraser and Duncan in Edinburgh, now swung back to Glasgow, where throughout the following year the power and leadership of Scottish Chartism was increasingly concentrated.

Most of the universal suffragists appeared to want an end to this interminable squabbling within their own ranks. The General Convention had now become imminent, and preparations had still to be hastily completed, such as the appointment of W. G. Burns as member for Aberdeenshire, and that of Pattrick Matthew for East Fifeshire. In many districts, signatures were still wanted for the National Petition and the National Rent had yet to be collected. Associations were busy canvassing the support of the clergy, the electors and the shopkeepers. The question of their relationship with the corn law repeal movement had also become an urgent matter for discussion. There seemed little time left before 4 February for further strength-sapping internal dissensions.[10]

NOTES

1. *Birmingham Journal*, 8 September 1838.
   True Scotsman, 20 and 27 October 1838; 12 January 1839; 4 May 1839.
2. *True Scotsman*, 27 October 1838; 3, 10 and 17 November 1838; 1 December 1838.
   Northern Star, 27 October 1838; 17 November 1838.
   Add. MSS 27,820, p. 276.
   The Charter, 14 April 1839.
3. *True Scotsman*, 24 November 1838; 1 December 1838.
   Northern Star, 24 November 1838; 15 December 1838.
   Birmingham Journal, 17 and 24 November 1838; 1 December 1838.
4. *Northern Star*, 15, 22 and 29 December 1838.
   Birmingham Journal, 13 October 1838; 8 and 15 December 1838.
   True Scotsman, 1, 8 and 15 December 1838.
   Ayr Observer, 11 December 1838.
   Scottish Pilot, 12 December 1838.
   Add. MSS 27,820, p. 345.
5. *Birmingham Journal*, 1, 8 and 15 December 1838.
   Scotch Reformers' Gazette, 12 December 1838.
   Ayr Observer, 11 December 1838.
   True Scotsman, 15 and 22 December 1838.
   Northern Star, 1, 15 and 22 December 1838.
6. *Northern Star*, 15, 22 and 29 December 1838.
   Add. MSS 27,820, pp. 357–8.
   True Scotsman, 15 December 1838.
7. *Ayr Observer*, 11 December 1838.
   True Scotsman, 22 December 1838; 5, 12 and 19 January 1839.
   Northern Star, 12 and 19 January 1839.
8. *True Scotsman*, 5, 12 and 19 January 1839; 9 February 1839.
   Northern Star, 12 and 19 January 1839.
   Glasgow Argus, 3 January 1839.
9. *True Scotsman*, 12, 19 and 26 January 1839; 9 February 1839.
   Glasgow Argus, 7 January 1839.
10. *True Scotsman*, 12 January 1839.
    Glasgow Argus, 24 January 1839.
    Add. MSS 27,821, pp. 24–5.

CHAPTER FIVE

The Convention

By the beginning of 1839 Chartism had become a well established political force in Scotland. Henry Vincent reported to the *Northern Star* that 'not a large town or village in Scotland was without its Association ... The whole of Scotland [was] united to a man'. This proved to be an over-optimistic assessment, but at this time there were at least 76 Chartist, or Radical Reform, associations and a few Female Radical associations. Lecturers were employed by the Chartists of Perthshire, Forfarshire and the border districts. In Glasgow and a few of the large towns, the associations were based on delegates from the trades, factories and districts. A few associations now held social meetings as a regular feature of their activities, at which concert and propaganda were mixed for the sake of raising funds for the National Rent and for the salary of their member of Convention.

Perhaps most important of all, Chartism now possessed its own press. Besides the importation, in fairly substantial numbers, of the *Northern Star* from Leeds, and of the *Birmingham Journal*, of which Dunfermline alone took seventy copies a week, the Scottish Chartists supported a weekly circulation of about 2,500 copies of the *True Scotsman*. In the north this was supplemented by the *Aberdeen Patriot*, published monthly by the Aberdeen Working Men's Association, and in the west by the *Ayrshire Examiner*, the *Glasgow Saturday Post* and the *Scots Times*.[1]

When it met in London on 4 February 1839, the General Convention of the Industrious Classes enjoyed virtually universal confidence and support from the Chartists of Scotland. Great interest was taken in the proceedings, and growing pride was exhibited over the important roles played by Bailie Craig, the first chairman of the Convention, and several other Scottish delegates. Satisfaction at the sound reason and sober moderation displayed in debates by their representatives was felt by the Scottish constituents. They were delighted at being constantly informed and consulted by Moir, Matthew, Craig and Taylor on these matters of state. The delegates, most of whom were receiving salaries of £25 a month, sometimes supplemented for travelling expenses, were clearly seen to be taking their responsibilities with due seriousness and, whether their delegate blew hot or cold, the electorate were ready with their cheers at the report meetings in the constituencies. If their own delegate found occasion to admire the conduct of a fellow delegate, as was frequently the case, that delegate shared in the rounds of cheering. Dr Taylor, who was the chief recipient of such plaudits, often usurped the place of Feargus O'Connor, and for his 'manly conduct' he also received financial tokens of esteem from his admirers in Alva, Tillicoultry and the Vale of Leven.[2]

It was soon discovered that many well populated localities had not been adequately canvassed for signatures to the National Petition, and during February and March further efforts were made by those Chartist committees on which the self-appointed task fell. The Glasgow and Aberdeen committees, and the county committees of Perthshire, Forfarshire, Ayrshire, Renfrewshire and East Fifeshire, found plenty of work with which to justify their existence. The Edinburgh Chartists distinguished themselves by raising the number of Edinburgh signatures to the National Petition from 5,000 to 16,000. The border districts sent an additional 1,350, and Aberdeen produced 1,600 further signatures. These efforts resulted not merely in shoals of new signatures to the petition, but also more lasting benefits in an increasing crop of local associations. By the end of March the total of Chartist associations in Scotland had risen to more than 130, of which a great many had been mentioned in activity for the first time only since the beginning of the year.[3]

An ominous crack in the unity of the Scottish delegates appeared early in April, when Patrick Matthew returned to Scotland to consult his constituents. He had always made his position clear. His inclination was towards Attwood, Douglas and Salt, though he had felt that the O'Connor party was somewhat justified 'by the tyranny and oppression of the aristocracy'. Recently, however, he had felt obliged to protest against the use of unconstitutional language by members of the Convention at public meetings in London and elsewhere. Now that he had seen the National Petition safely into the hands of Thomas Attwood, he wished to know if his mission was finished. At a delegate meeting of his Perthshire and Fifeshire constituents on 9 April, Matthew's conduct was highly approved, and hopes were expressed for a reconciliation of all parties in the Convention, as the people were certainly unprepared for the use of force, whether that were permissible or not. The Cupar-Angus association demanded, however, that Matthew should return to the Convention or resign. This he had not wished to decide until he had seen whether the Convention would adopt a more temperate course on the 'ulterior measures', but he now felt he should resign.

If you think it fitting to give reason [he wrote in his letter of resignation to William Lovett, on 12 April], state in these words, that it is on account of the intemperate language and ultra character of the major party of the Convention, who have been carrying the minor or more moderate party along with them, and from a conviction that their mode of proceeding is preventing the more intelligent of the Liberal party from joining the Chartist cause and is calculated rather to bring about scenes of destruction and misery, and the discomfiture of the Chartists than the attainment of the rights, and the amelioration of the condition of the people.

Several other Scottish members of Convention were also beginning to feel uncomfortable, and their discomfort was accentuated by the discussions in April on the proposed 'ulterior measures', and on the proposed transfer of the Convention to Birmingham, in May. Alexander Halley, who was noted for his cautious attitude, was strongly opposed to the adjournment to Birmingham and equally strongly to the O'Brien address, 'as it plainly recommended the people to arm'. Its purpose was plainly

to excite the people to acts of violence, and this would compel everyone to oppose us ... He was a working man but he did not come amongst them as a class reformer, seeking the advantage of one at the expense of another ... Every honest reformer who wished to promote the well-being of his country would endeavour to unite all classes and not place them in hostile array against one another.

The only doubt left in his mind was whether or not he should resign. First he did so, then he recanted, and finally went off to Scotland to seek the advice of his constituents.[4]

Halley was supported in his opposition to the proposed Convention address by W. G. Burns and W. S. Villiers Sankey. In the debate on 9 May, Burns declared that if they were really a majority they had only to demonstrate it and there would be no cause for arming; for then their demands must be complied with. If they continued in their violent course, they would lose the support of their constituents and of three-fourths of the Radicals throughout Scotland... They had lost a good deal of time for unless the majority of the people were with them it was useless to tell them to arm. Instead of being a majority we were a minority.

This was corroborated by Villiers Sankey, who had been the most violent of all the Scottish delegates in their public utterances during the early days of the Convention, and whose sudden change of attitude must have been somewhat mystifying to his constituents. On

W. S. Villiers Sankey

6 May he had protested against the language of O'Brien and Vincent. 'The people of Scotland were too calm, too prudent and too humane to peril this cause upon bloodshed.' Even if taken by itself, the Convention address might not be objectionable; when it was taken with other circumstances, such as the exciting language of those who supported it, a case might be made out that it was illegal. Finally, after a strong protest against the adjournment to Birmingham, Sankey resigned, leaving his constituents to decide whether he had lost his nerve or whether, in view of their rather poor efforts to provide him with a reasonable salary, he had merely been seeking an excuse to quit the Convention. They accepted his explanation that with the entrusting of the National Petition to

Attwood his task was finished, and thanked him for his efforts, but appointed John Duncan, the chairman of the Edinburgh and Midlothian Universal Suffrage Association, in his place. Possibly because of the financial weakness of the association, Duncan never took up his appointment.[5]

Questions were now being asked of James Moir, who had returned to Scotland as a Convention missionary in April and had spent a good deal of time agitating in Lanarkshire. At Paisley and elsewhere he was now encouraging the formation of Female Radical Associations, and was finding an interest in education and religion. Unless the 'Voluntaries' marshalled themselves under the banner of the Charter, he would found a new religious sect, with membership based on the principles of universal suffrage. He now appeared loath to leave his shop in the Gallowgate, and explained his lack of haste to rejoin the Convention by his desire to stay in Scotland for the celebration of the anniversary of the Glasgow Green demonstration on 21 May. He was prepared to rejoin the Convention if so required, but he had only promised to attend for six weeks.

Another Convention missionary had been Bailie Hugh Craig, who in April had made a tour of Lanarkshire and south-west Scotland. He had held fifty-four open-air meetings, besides several 'very large' meetings in Glasgow, Paisley and Kilmarnock. On 29 and 30 April he contested the Ayrshire parliamentary election, placing most emphasis in his election address and speeches on total repeal of the corn laws. Although he had been victorious at the hustings on 27 April, he received only 46 votes at the poll, against 1,758 for the Conservative and 1,296 for the Whig. Armed with the plaudits of the Ayrshire Chartists for his 'manly conduct' in the election, he returned to the Convention, where he reported with delight on his Scottish tour. His enthusiasm waned over the proposed adjournment to Birmingham, which he opposed. He did not see how they could leave London until they had presented the National Petition and completed their business. His enthusiasm disappeared altogether when he considered the 'ulterior measures', and before the adjournment of the Convention in Birmingham he left on the train for Scotland, accompanied by Abram Duncan.[6]

Of the Scottish delegates in the Convention, only John Taylor appeared to be unperturbed by recent developments, and once again he emerged as a leader of the 'forcibly, if we must' school. He highly approved of a run down to Birmingham, where they could rally round them the hardy men of Lancashire and York-shire. With an outbreak in Wales, a revolution in Ireland, and England boiling over with revenge, they should not remain in London where they could not distinguish friends from foes. In Birmingham they would be surrounded by a power no Government would attempt to break through. They should make their deaths as useful as their lives had been serviceable to their country.

Outside the Convention, Taylor was to be found advising his audiences to procure arms but to remain quiet at present, for the Whigs and the Tories were trying to goad the people into acts of violence.[7]

At this period Scottish Chartism seemed to be rapidly losing the facade of union which had appeared since the early days of the Convention, and since the eclipse of Brewster. In Edinburgh, there was some division amongst the former constituents of Sankey, and Duncan was not sent to the Convention. In Dunfermline, Stirling and Alloa the views of Halley found strong support, while Patrick Matthew was still very highly esteemed in Perthshire, despite having been denounced by Feargus O'Connor as a 'middle-class traitor'. Neither was replaced in the Convention. Meanwhile the Rev. Patrick Brewster was again appealing to the people of Scotland. He now called for a convention of Scottish delegates, which would reunite the Scottish Radicals and would have power to negotiate a union with the delegates of England, on the principles of the Birmingham Political Union.

This appeal seemed to be well timed. There appeared to be a definite trend of opinion towards the mood in which the Calton Hill resolutions had been adopted. As John Taylor found himself bound to report to the Convention two months later, the people of Scotland considered that nothing short of a physical revolution would be caused by the implementation of the 'sacred month' proposal. Only Forfar, Kirriemuir and Dundee showed any welcome for the 'sacred month'. There was considerable uncertainty how far the constitutional maxims and statutes mentioned in the Convention discussions on the legal rights of the people to possess arms applied to Scotland, and the advice of Dr Taylor on this was anxiously sought by the Dundee Working Men's Association. The Dundee Political Union resolved at the end of April that moral agitation was the only effectual way of obtaining their political rights. A few days later, the Union recommended the possession of arms for 'the protection of life and property'. A week later, the debate ended with a compromise agreement to continue moral agitation, but to warn the government that force would be met by force. There was no apparent relish for civil war, and it seemed clear to most associations that neither they nor their neighbours were at all prepared for armed action.

Confidence in the Convention had been somewhat shaken amongst many of the leaders of the local associations, and to some extent this was reflected in the growing number of votes of confidence in the Convention which were submitted to and by the rank and file. The acclamation which these were invariably accorded indicated that the faith of the masses was quite unshaken. There was little disposition to abandon the Convention in order to return to the empty fold of 'Parson' Brewster, nor to do anything which might weaken the Convention. 'We have confidence in all the members in Convention,' declared the Chartists of Mauchline in a typical message to the General Convention, 'and will be glad to contribute again for their support as soon as we get the word of command.'

Associations which had been deeply divided in the early disputes were reluctant to endanger their harmony with any recurrence of the moral *v.* physical force issue. Even if they distrusted the 'sacred month' proposal, it could surely be kept in the background until they had more fully tried out other possible measures, such as exclusive dealing, abstinence, or even Chartist religious services. For many associations the best answer to the daunting question 'What next?' seemed to lie in a further, but more intensified, programme of agitation, conducted under the auspices of the Convention, with the national figures of the movement appearing frequently to give celebrity lectures. John Adam of Forfar wanted a grant of £20 from the Convention to enable himself and his colleague, Sime, to go as missionaries through the north of Scotland. Dundee thought that W. G. Burns and a deputation from the Convention should be sent to Dundee and the principal towns of the north. The border Chartists complained that their part of the country had been neglected, and that they needed able advocates to open the eyes of the people. Could John Frost and Robert Lowery, therefore, be sent to attend meetings on the border holiday, the 18 May? The Chartists of Stirlingshire, Kincardineshire and Clackmannan wanted the services of O'Connor and Frost for a demonstration in Stirling on 31 May. From the south-west, Mauchline wrote to request the attendance of Frost and O'Brien at a demonstration to be held there on

8 June. Since Ayrshire had stood at the top of the list of contributors to the National Rent, Mauchline suggested that Ayrshire had prior claims in this matter.[8]

When deputations from the adjourned Convention were sent throughout Britain in June, the contingent which toured Scotland was a particularly strong one. A tour lasting three weeks began with a large demonstration on Glasgow Green on Monday 10 June.

Such an exhibition I never saw before [declared John Frost]. I have come 500 miles to witness this demonstration and I am wholly and entirely satisfied with my journey . . . I will let my friends in Wales know how they manage matters of this kind in the north.

The deputation then divided, and while John Collins, Peter Bussey and R. J. Richardson visited the most important towns to the northeast of the Forth, John Frost, Robert Lowery and Bronterre O'Brien toured Lanarkshire, Ayrshire and Renfrewshire. Large demonstrations, usually followed by soirées in the evenings, were held in Stirling, Perth, Dundee, Aberdeen and Alloa in the east, and at Greenock, Paisley and Kilmarnock in the west. The tourists reunited in Edinburgh for a meeting on Calton Hill, and then retreated through the border counties with rallies at Jedburgh and Dumfries. The demonstrations were conducted in fine weather, with an abundance of flags, bands of music, good humour and festive mood. James Moir, Dr Taylor, Abram Duncan and Knox of Durham joined the deputation at various stages of their tour and helped to provide a united front of Convention delegates, with an apparently fixed determination on the main principles of the movement.

Whatever the purpose of the tour, the deputation from the Convention had received a welcome almost as warm as that which had been given thirteen months earlier to the men of Birmingham. John Collins reported to the Convention that, with the exception of Dunfermline, he had 'never seen such spirit manifested in the course of his life'. All the other meetings in Scotland had surpassed 'the most sanguine expectations of the friends of liberty'. In Dunfermline and Alloa there had been coolness to Collins because of an attack he had previously made on Halley, in vindication of whom rival meetings were held. Apart from this, there was no unpleasantness. The demonstrations and the soirées were fully reported in the *True Scotsman*, and Fraser and his local correspondents—normally quick to observe any inflammatory language—could find little fault

with these men. Only Bronterre O'Brien, who gave a series of
lectures in hypercritical Edinburgh, managed to incur any reproach.
The most serious charge against him, however, was his frequent
recourse to oaths and blasphemy. There had been an almost complete
absence of talk of armed revolution, even when they had been
joined by Dr Taylor. The Rev. Patrick Brewster did not raise his
voice to invite the Scottish people to withdraw from the Convention,
and John Fraser felt charitable enough to praise the 'noble' lead
given by Feargus O'Connor in instituting a National Defence Fund
for political martyrs of the future.[9]

NOTES

1. *Northern Star*, 29 December 1838.
   True Scotsman, 17 and 24 November 1838; 8, 15 and 22 December 1838;
      5 and 12 January 1839.
   Parliamentary Papers, 1839; xliii, p. 203.
   Cowan, pp. 160, 189.
2. *Glasgow Argus*, 7 February 1839.
   True Scotsman, 9 and 24 February 1839; 6 and 13 April 1839; 4 and 11
      May 1839; 6 July 1839.
3. Add. MSS 27,822, p. 218.
   Add. MSS 34,245A, pp. 334, 344, 379.
4. Add. MSS 27,821, p. 127.
   Add. MSS 34,245A, p. 280.
   True Scotsman, 23 March 1839; 13 April 1839; 25 May 1839.
5. *True Scotsman*, 18 and 25 May 1839.
   Add. MSS 27, 821, pp. 119, 128–9, 240.
6. *Glasgow Argus*, 25 and 29 April 1839; 2 May 1839.
   True Scotsman, 4, 18 and 25 May; 8 June 1839.
   Add. MSS 27,821, p. 125.
   Add. MSS 27,822, p. 227.
   Add. MSS 34,245B, p. 24.
7. Add. MSS 27,821, pp. 205–6.
8. *True Scotsman*, 4, 18 and 25 May 1839; 15 and 22 June 1839.
   Add. MSS 34,245A, pp. 260, 304, 306, 344, 350, 416, 423, 453.
   Glasgow Argus, 29 April 1839.
   Northern Star, 11 May 1839.
   Scottish Patriot, 13 July 1839.
9. Add. MSS 27,821, pp. 229–241.
   True Scotsman, 15, 22 and 29 June 1839; 6 and 13 July 1839.
   R. G. Gammage, *History of the Chartist Movement*, 1854, p. 130.

CHAPTER SIX

Self-government for Scotland?

Probably the most important change which had taken place in the Scottish movement in the first half of 1839 was the shift of leadership to Glasgow. After May 1838, what leadership had been forthcoming had been chiefly from Edinburgh, and had been concentrated in the efforts of John Fraser and Abram Duncan. The organisation of the east and south had been greatly advanced by them in the summer and autumn of 1838. Fraser and Duncan had become known and trusted leaders in a way that no one in the west could rival. Around Paisley a group of satellite associations had grown up, and for a short period they accepted the patronage of Patrick Brewster. But Brewster had never been accepted outside Paisley as a genuine Chartist, and his genius consisted in playing the role of a solitary rebel leader, concerned with the soul of the movement, not with its strength. The peculiarity of his own position was his greatest asset, and this was rapidly being outweighed by his remarkable capacity for making enemies of his friends and admirers, with his violent reaction to opinions differing only minutely from his own. The other really outstanding personality in the west was Dr John Taylor, who was in many respects well suited to be the counterpart of his friend Feargus O'Connor. The growth of the Chartist agitation came just too late to save Taylor's newspaper; after its collapse he ceased to play any significant role in Glasgow, where he left the building up of the movement to men with many of whom he had little sympathy, and few of whom had the slightest aspirations for power outside their own city.

The Calton Hill episode had not discredited Fraser as much as Brewster, and he still had many followers among the readers of the *True Scotsman*. But he made many enemies. and it was easy to misrepresent his views in Glasgow and the west of Scotland, where his paper never achieved a satisfactory circulation—about 600–700 copies at its peak. With the constant growth of organised Chartism, Fraser's influence was declining relatively. However, Fraser evinced little desire for power in the movement. All he demanded of his colleagues was respect—and judicious conduct.

With the election of Convention delegates, each with a fairly well defined region, the local associations looked to these delegates for leadership. This allegiance was quickly transferred to the Convention, but the local committees carefully scrutinised all advice and recommendations from the General Convention before giving their own support. Generally, they expected the Convention to canvass support for the National Petition. Once that was accomplished, there would be fresh plans on which they would be asked to act. They had confidence in the Convention, and expected it to lead. But the months passed and the Convention was still not leading in any definite direction. The local associations wanted to know what were the best ways in which they could help. Recently formed associations were always busy enough building up their organisation, and allowing their members to go through the process of declaiming the principles of the Charter to each other. The older associations, however, were beginning to be bored with the same old stories reiterated by the same old voices. Their committees had often been meeting twice a week, and they wanted to discuss fresh, concrete tasks.

There was certainly no intention of looking to Glasgow rather than to the Convention for leadership, but there was a growing tendency to consider that Glasgow should be the prime mover in all Chartist plans for Scotland. While the Scottish movement had been gaining strength in 1839, the prestige of Glasgow had been slowly rising and the influence of Edinburgh steadily declining. This trend had been accentuated by the relatively poor performance of the Edinburgh Chartists in their contributions of signatures to the National Petition, and of money to the National Rent. Glasgow was increasingly attending to missionary work in its region. Its Chartist committees were becoming more self-confident, and ready to accept further responsibilities. Their members were largely drawn from the trades organisations, and several men were emerging from the non-commissioned officers of the trade union world who had qualities of leadership and imagination. Of these the most important were William C. Pattison and William Thomson. The former was the secretary of the steam-engine machine makers' union, an active corn law repealer, and secretary of the standing committee of the Glasgow trades. The latter was an exponent of retail co-operation, formerly secretary of the Scottish National Association for the Protection of Hand-loom Weavers and editor of the *Weavers' Journal*.

Impetus was added to this swing of power to Glasgow with the publication on 6 July 1839 of the *Scottish Patriot*, which was to be the press organ of the Glasgow Chartists. It was owned, printed and edited by Robert Malcolm, of the half-Chartist *Scots Times*, who was to be guaranteed against financial loss in the first year by its sponsors, the delegates of the trades and the directors of the Universal Suffrage Association. It was designed to appeal not merely to Chartists but to a wide range of reformers, and its first declaration of policy comprehended a vast field of political, social and economic reform, including free trade, direct taxation, reduction of defence expenditure, reform of the Post Office, the abolition of capital punishment and a national system of education. In Chartist affairs, its editorial policy would be to ignore as far as possible internal squabbles and all those who fomented them. Its appearance coincided with the Chartist riots in Birmingham and the arrests of Lovett, Collins and Taylor, to which it paid considerable attention, and also with a fresh appeal from Patrick Brewster, which it ignored.

Brewster saw impending disaster for the movement unless it were immediately purged of the 'physical force men'. This troublesome question was aired once again in the *True Scotsman*, and on this occasion there was rather more response to Brewster's call. Aberdeen and Perth held soirées in his honour, and the excitement over the current events in Birmingham added considerable emphasis to his warning. Moreover, the discussions in the Convention on the 'national holiday' were creating nervousness in some towns, and several local associations felt the need to assert their 'fundamentally peaceful' character.[1]

This disquiet was reflected at the Convention by the Scottish delegates. James Moir departed without permission from the Convention, immediately after the presentation of the National Petition on 12 July, ostensibly to consult his constituents, though he had received their instructions at the Glasgow Green demonstration only a few weeks previously. He had, however, no intention of returning to the Convention, as he regarded the 'sacred month' as tantamount to the commencement of a disastrous revolution. Bailie Craig was less equivocal in his attitude. The cause of the people was not going to be achieved by fines and martyrdoms. Any unsuccessful attempt at unconstitutional means would only throw more power into the hands of the government. He therefore left the Convention and met his constituents with the incontestible plea that Ayrshire was unprepared for ulterior measures. This was not acceptable to half the Ayrshire Chartists, who regarded Craig as a traitor to the cause, obtained his resignation, sued him for repayment of unearned salary which had been paid in advance, and replaced him with John McCrae, the convenor of the county committee. When the vote was eventually taken in the Convention on the 'national holiday' proposed for 12 August, only Abram Duncan and W. G. Burns were present to represent Scotland. Both voted against the proposal.[2]

Within a few days of the news of the Birmingham troubles, special meetings were being held in most localities to protest at the 'unlawful conduct' of the government in sending Metropolitan policemen to Birmingham and incarcerating the leaders of the movement. These events sent a thrill throughout the movement; they excited a feeling of self-importance and a sense of purpose which had been absent since the early days of the Convention. Instead of some clear division emerging between 'morals' and 'physicals', most associations became more united than ever. Several associations decided to respond to the government by refraining from exciseable goods, or by exclusive dealing. Campsie, Alloa, Barrhead and the Vale of Leven were especially concerned over Dr Taylor's treatment in gaol, when his glorious locks were shorn. In the House of Lords, Lord Melbourne expressed his concern to Lord Brougham, and promised to call the attention of Lord John Russell to these 'well-grounded complaints'.[3]

On the question of the 'national holiday' due to commence on 12 August, there was great uncertainty. Several associations asked Glasgow whether or not they should follow the recommendation of the Convention on this—and Glasgow advised against any such action. The demand for a Scottish delegate conference, which had first been voiced by Brewster in May, was now being reiterated by many parties. Stonehouse wanted Glasgow to convene a meeting of delegates from all Chartist associations in Scotland to discuss the 'existing emergency'. The Renfrewshire Political Union wanted a delegate conference to improve the organisation of the movement, especially in Lanarkshire and Renfrewshire. In Glasgow, on 11 July, a public meeting deplored the 'late, rash, ill-advised and wanton attack upon the people of Birmingham by the London Police', and memorialised the Queen to institute an inquiry into the 'disgraceful and bloody riots in Birmingham'. It declared its confidence in the Convention, which would be supported 'in all constitutional measures', and then resolved that it was 'advisable to hold a delegate meeting, to take into consideration the best method of organising Scotland, and ... that all advice may be given to the Convention'.

Thomas Gillespie, the secretary of the Glasgow Universal Suffrage Association, sent out circulars to the principal Scottish associations. Did they favour the holding of a delegate conference to consider the best means of organising Scotland? If so, where should it be held? By the end of July, Gillespie had received fifty replies. Of these, forty-nine approved of the proposal, and forty thought the conference should take place in Glasgow. Even the Edinburgh association opted for Glasgow, with only Alloa and Clackmannan expressing a preference for Edinburgh.[4]

A delegate meeting was therefore summoned to meet in Glasgow on 14 August, and the preparations for it were completed almost unobtrusively. August 12 passed over quietly, with the occasion apparently regarded more as a festival than as a political crisis. The greatest excitement was probably at Newmilns, where the Chartist magistrates swore in all the Chartists as special constables lest the Whigs or Tories might 'meditate some disturbance', and headed the procession to the town green, where John McCrae, member of Convention, addressed the local Chartists, augmented by deputations from Mauchline, Darvel, Cumnock, Galston, Kilmaurs and Kilmarnock.

Feargus O'Connor had himself appointed the representative of the General Convention, and travelled north to ensure that he, not the Rev. Patrick Brewster, would act as the presiding genius this time. On the eve of the conference, several delegates spoke at a public meeting in Glasgow. The 'delegate' from Newcastle dwelt on the value of organisation. If Lanarkshire and Renfrewshire were as well prepared as Durham, Cumberland and Northumberland, universal suffrage might soon be the law of the land. The delegates of Penicuick and Juniper Green expressed strong opposition to physical force—especially while most physical force was in the hands of the aristocracy. James Moir, whose solicitude for his safety and his

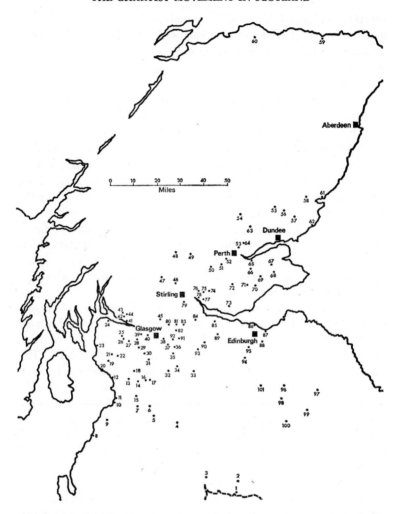

Chartist Associations in Scotland

(1) Annan. (2) Ecclefechan. (3) Dumfries. (4) Sanquhar. (5) New Cumnock.
(6) Cumnock. (7) Ochiltree and Sorn. (8) Girvan. (9) Maybole. (10) Ayr.
(11) Prestwick. (12) Irvine. (13) Kilmarnock. (14) Galston. (15) Mauchline.
(16) Newmilns. (17) Darvel. (18) Fenwick. (19) Dalry. (20) Saltcoats. (21) Kilbirnie. (22) Beith. (23) Largs. (24) Greenock. (25) Bridge of Weir. (26) Kilbarchan. (27) Johnstone. (28) Paisley. (29) Barrhead. (30) Newtonmearns.
(31) Eaglesham. (32) Strathaven. (33) Lanark. (34) Stonehouse. (35) Hamilton.
(36) Bellshill. (37) Uddingston. (38) Shettleston. (39) Govan. (40) Renfrew.
(41) Dumbarton. (42) Vale of Leven. (43) Alexandria. (44) Bonhill. (45) Balfron. (46) Doune. (47) Callander. (48) Comrie. (49) Crieff. (50) Auchterarder.

business had recently been vindicated by his constituents, declared that he would be found in his place in the General Convention when it resumed on 26 August, if his constituents so wished. He could not, however, pledge himself to remain at the Convention throughout the winter, but they should not decide upon the matter until the deliberations of the Scottish delegate conference were known.[5]

On Wednesday 14 August 1839 the Scottish delegate conference assembled in the Universalist Church, Dovehill, Glasgow, and fifty-two delegates presented their credentials. They were joined by late arrivals, and eventually at least eighty-four towns and villages were represented by sixty-four delegates. Of the associations which had notified agreement with the proposed conference, forty sent representatives. Glasgow and Paisley were each allowed two representatives, and four delegates represented two towns each. One delegate represented at least twenty-two local associations, and with the exception of Dumfries, Kirkcaldy, Arbroath and Inverness, all the important towns in Scotland were represented.

John Duncan, a small shopkeeper and newsagent, who had emerged as the leading figure in the Edinburgh and Midlothian Universal Suffrage Association, and who had been the mainstay of support for the Convention in Edinburgh, was appointed chairman. He was a mild man, who strongly disbelieved in the value of violence, but who was nevertheless a firm believer in the justification of threats of force. The proceedings were opened with a 'short and impressive prayer' by Arthur O'Neill of Maryhill, a young man of twenty-one, half Irish, who had been a student of theology, electricity and physiology, and who derived a living from lecturing engagements in working men's associations and scientific institutions. Reports on local progress and policy from each delegate then

---

(51) Dunning. (52) Crossgates. (53) Bridgend. (54) Blairgowrie. (55) Kirriemuir. (56) Forfar. (57) Letham. (58) Brechin. (59) Banff. (60) Elgin. (61) Montrose. (62) Arbroath. (63) Cupar-Angus. (64) New Scone. (65) Newburgh. (66) Auchtermuchty. (67) Cupar. (68) Ceres. (69) Kettle. (70) Markinch. (71) Leslie. (72) Kinross. (73) Dunfermline. (74) Dollar. (75) Tillicoultry. (76) Alva. (77) Clackmannan. (78) Alloa. (79) Bannockburn. (80) Lennoxtown. (81) Milton. (82) Kirkintilloch. (83) Kilsyth. (84) Falkirk. (85) Linlithgow. (86) Leith. (87) Musselburgh. (88) Dalkeith. (89) Bathgate. (90) Whitburn. (91) Airdrie. (92) Coatbridge. (933) Shotts. (94) West Linton. (95) Penicuik. (96) Galashiels. (97) Kelso. (98) Selkirk. (99) Jedburgh. (100) Hawick. (101) Innerleithen. *Note:* within the major towns—Glasgow, Edinburgh, Dundee and Aberdeen—there were numerous local associations (see p. 273).

took up most of the time of the conference. The main topics in these reports, the 'ulterior measures', attitudes to the Convention, and the need for more effective and widespread measures of organisation, were raised by almost every delegate.

Many delegates testified to the beneficial results of the Birmingham 'outrages'. Aberdeen could report a fivefold increase in membership since then. Dundee, Lanark and other localities reported a merging of their moral and physical force associations as a result of the healing of divisions by the Birmingham affair. Johnstone and Kilbarchan appeared to think that the issue of peace or war was being decided and pledged themselves to abide by the decisions of the majority. Renfrew had fifty men 'ready for anything', and Elderslie and Rutherglen also declared themselves ready for any measures. Old Cumnock, Aberdeen, Barrhead, Forfar, Edinburgh, Paisley and Dunfermline all reported some men under arms. Many associations declared their willingness to use only legal and peaceful means of agitation. These included Ayr, Anderston, Hamilton, Lanark, Kirkintilloch, Stonehouse, Stirling and Strathaven. Penicuick considered all who spoke violently as enemies to the cause, while Juniper Green expelled such people from its association. Springburn and Tillicoultry were representative of those associations which consisted of a 'happy mixture' of moral force and physical force men, but which considered that the Chartists were entirely unprepared for physical force. Several delegates considered that no useful purpose could be served by further discussion of the issue of moral *v.* physical force.

There was universal agreement that whatever the merits of the 'sacred month' proposal, the country was quite unprepared to put it into practice, and exclusive dealing appeared to be the most popular of the ulterior measures. Several delegates reported the application of sanctions against non-Radical shopkeepers, but, as the Paisley delegate explained, its success depended on the co-operation of the wives. At Musselburgh a co-operative store had been founded by an exclusive-dealing association and fifty members, who had each paid 10s. Bridgeton, Bathgate and Galston advocated the adoption of total abstinence from spirits and other dutiable articles, while Paisley prided itself on having been instrumental in causing friendly societies to lift £950 from the savings banks.

The Glasgow representatives were insistent that the agitation must be kept alive until 'some favourable accident' brought about universal suffrage. Efficient organisations at local, county and national levels, for the creation, mobilisation and direction of public opinion, was regarded as the vital key to the Charter. Two methods were advanced as the most promising means towards achieving this aim. One was the employment of as many political missionaries as possible—'not firebrands and ignorant declaimers . . . but men of calm, correct judgement, extensive knowledge, good rhetorical powers, and . . . of unblemished moral character'. The other method was the dissemination of knowledge of the 'details of legislative misrule' and the rights owed to the people by Society, together with an explanation of the power of an unorganised nation in redressing its own grievances, through the medium of small tracts. Most associations felt that, while it might be folly to expect any redress of their grievances by petitioning the House of Commons, petitioning was the only plan which offered a safe, legal and popular basis to the movement. Aberdeen wanted to have no more petitions, but Stonehouse wanted to keep the table of the House of Commons groaning under the weight of thousands of them.

Feargus O'Connor joined the ranks of the organisers. The error of the General Convention, he confided, had been to try to direct public opinion before it was properly organised. Had the Convention known the feeling of Scotland regarding the 'sacred month', it would not have voted as it did. He had always opposed the 'sacred month', and he hoped that the premature steps taken in England would be a 'light to warn them from the rocks'. Moral force would be all that was requisite, and physical force, if required, would come like 'an electric shock to its aid'. But the man who talked about it was a knave, and the man who recommended it was a fool.

Amongst the resolutions adopted by the conference was one eulogising the service rendered to the people's cause by the 'National Convention' during its first session. They would look with suspicion 'upon any person who, from motives of pique, jealousy, or personal ambition, shall, by menace, threat, or slander, endeavour to throw discredit upon the General Convention'. A further resolution pledged renewed efforts 'to raise, for National Rent, those funds which are indispensable for the prosecution of the cause of the people'.

The most important decision to be taken, however, was that to establish a Central Committee for Scotland. This body would be supplied with funds from the district associations, in proportion to membership. These funds were to be 'appropriated to the purposes of engaging lecturers, printing and circulating political tracts, and doing all in their power to disseminate knowledge among the people with a view to organising Scotland'. Of the fifteen members appointed to this committee, only John Duncan of Edinburgh lived more than five or six miles from the centre of Glasgow, while six were directors of the Glasgow Universal Suffrage Association. Only one member of Convention, James Moir, was elected.[6]

The delegate conference ended on 16 August amidst general satisfaction that decisions which would have far-reaching consequences had been taken. Even John Fraser, though he complained that the Glasgow papers had not reported the opposition which some resolutions had encountered, could scarcely forbear from a mild cheer for much that was excellent in them. He was uncertain, however, whether there was any guarantee that the Central Committee for Scotland—to which he justifiably referred as 'the Glasgow Committee'—would remain 'firm to moral principle'.

O'Connor wrote to the Secretary of the Convention on 18 August, expressing his complete satisfaction with the Scottish conference. He then spent a week touring Scottish associations, and holding 'large meetings' at Glasgow, Elderslie, Perth, Auchterarder, Dundee, Edinburgh, Kilmarnock and Hawick. At Kilmarnock he was suitably impressed by the 'whole population' singing *Scots wha hae* in perfect harmony. When he reported back to the General Convention, he waxed enthusiastic about the progress of the movement in Scotland:

Scotland is being thoroughly organised ... Where there was one milk and water Radical eight months ago, in Scotland, there are now fifty staunch ones ... In Scotland the trades are with the people to a man ... In Scotland the middle class are better men, and always attend the meetings to judge for themselves, and they decide accordingly to the arguments they hear, while in England they decide by physical force and perjury.[7]

NOTES

1. *True Scotsman*, 6 and 13 July 1839.
   Scottish Patriot, 6 and 13 July 1839; 14 October 1839.
2. *True Scotsman*, 20 and 27 July 1839.
   Scottish Patriot, 20 and 27 July 1839; 3 August 1839.
   Northern Star, 27 July 1839.
   Glasgow Argus, 23 July 1839.
   Add. MSS 34,245B, pp. 58, 65.

3. *True Scotsman*, 17 August 1839.
   Scottish Patriot, 13, 20 and 27 July 1839; 17 August 1839.
4. *True Scotsman*, 18 May 1839; 6, 20 and 27 July 1839.
   Scottish Patriot, 13 July 1839; 3 August 1839.
5. *Scottish Patriot*, 3, 10, 17 and 24 August 1839.
   Northern Star, 31 August 1839.
   Glasgow Argus, 14 August 1839.
6. *Scottish Patriot*, 17 and 24 August 1839.
   True Scotsman, 24 August 1839.
   Northern Star, 24 and 31 August 1839.
7. *Scottish Patriot*, 7 September 1839.
   Add. MSS 34,245B, p. 194.

CHAPTER SEVEN

The petitioning issue

The impetus given to the Scottish movement by the Birmingham incidents and the efforts to enforce the ulterior measures was not completely spent by the Glasgow delegate conference and the establishment of the Universal Suffrage Central Committee for Scotland. In many districts there was determination to apply sanctions against their opponents, and to extend the scope of their organisation. In Glasgow, W. C. Pattison was insisting that organisation should take precedence over all other matters, and that fresh efforts should be made to increase the support of the Glasgow trades. Attention was given to the work of arousing the little townships around Glasgow, such as Govan, which had been active on the Church question and on the corn laws but which had remained apathetic about universal suffrage. A Glasgow Universal Suffrage Electors' Association, with Bailie Hedderwick as President, was formed, which resembled the now defunct Glasgow Political Union, and social meetings were organised on a regular basis to increase the funds available for organisation.[1]

Ever since the beginning of the agitation for the Charter, there had been a few counties in which local associations were grouped into county or regional organisations for common purposes, such as the election and maintenance of members of the Convention. During the autumn of 1839, this habit spread, with permanent secretaries being appointed in Stirlingshire, Fifeshire, Forfarshire, Midlothian and in the Border districts, to correspond on behalf of their county committees with the Central Committee for Scotland. Their chief tasks were to perfect their organisation and to raise funds for the Glasgow centre. At first it was understood, in Forfarshire at least, that all funds for the maintenance of lecturers were to be paid to the Central Committee in Glasgow, but after a few weeks it recognised as more practicable to employ lecturers on a county basis.[2]

Meanwhile the Universal Suffrage Central Committee for Scotland had been finding that its title was rather more imposing than its power. While it had received a mandate to promote organisation by the provision of a plentiful supply of agitators and cheap tracts, the Central Committee found itself lacking the funds whereby it could finance the activities expected of it. Although it had been agreed that the central body should be financially supported by the local associations in proportion to their membership, few associations made haste to pay either their share of the expenses of the delegate conference or their first instalment of monthly dues on the basis of ½d per member which the Central Committee demanded. It soon found itself, therefore, in grave danger of lacking the means to prove its utility to the movement, and of forfeiting what semblance of authority it had received from the conference. Yet the annual cost of maintaining three or four lecturers in the field plus the printing and circulation of tracts in sufficient quantities would require as much money as had been contributed by Scotland to the National Rent.

This fear that the Central Committee might be doomed to ineffectiveness was, however, soon relieved by the adoption of a plan, produced by W. C. Pattison, for the production of a four-page folio or eight-page octavo publication, designed after the style of the *Anti-Corn Law Circular*. It would have no pretensions to be a newspaper and since it would escape stamp duty it could be sold for a halfpenny, provided it could maintain a circulation of 8,000. The immediate obstacle of the empty exchequer was surmounted by persuading the treasurer, George Ross, a prospering shoemaker, to provide financial backing for the first number. Ross then procured 'an abundant supply of paper', and with the services of a good printer, the *Scottish Chartist Circular* was published on 28 September 1839.

The first number of the *Circular* had a circulation of over 20,000, and throughout its first year it maintained its weekly sales at an average of 22,500. Edited by William Thomson, the secretary of the Central Committee, and formerly editor of the *Weavers' Journal*, the *Circular* provided little news of the progress of the movement, eschewed controversial issues and confined itself to the propagation of the principles of the Charter, the exposure of abuses in the existing social and political structure of Great Britain, and the extolling of the heroes of past struggles for national freedom. Its main object was the provision of a self-financing substitute for the tracts and lecturers which the Central Committee could ill afford. Its editor's policy was to ignore the divisions which existed within the Chartist ranks, while providing readers with an awareness of social and political evils, and an encyclopedia on the history of democracy and popular freedom.[3]

The successful launching of the *Chartist Circular* was widely regarded as an outstanding achievement. While it could hardly provide the basis for a fresh agitation, or the rallying point around which the Committee could maintain the existing strength of Scottish Chartism, the *Circular* provided its promoters with reassuring confidence in their own abilities and enhanced the prestige of the Central Committee. The importance placed upon the *Circular* was indicative of the current attitude of most of the Scottish Chartists. No bloody insurrection was necessary for their purpose. All that was required was the vigorous dissemination of Chartist principles. Truth and justice would eventually prevail, and public opinion was the main weapon to be used to win their cause. A great portion of the people still remained ignorant of Chartist principles, and their instruction in the principles of freedom, democracy and justice was an essential preliminary to the granting of the Charter. This would best be done by putting 'that mighty engine, the press' into full operation on the side of the people, and by frequent orderly meetings.

In this work the practice of petitioning could also play a valuable dual role. Not merely could petitions keep Chartist claims constantly before the public, but it was the best way in which the agitation could be kept alive without fear of interference from the law. Petitioning had been robbed of most of its glamour by the failure of the National Petition to achieve any reform of Parliament or induce the slightest change of heart on the part of the ruling classes. But it was not considered more futile to petition again for universal suffrage than to petition constantly for the repeal of the corn laws. While it might be folly to expect any redress of grievances by petitioning, Moir, Pattison and other influential Chartists regarded it as the only plan which could provide a safe and legal impetus to the movement. In order to arouse the dormant feelings of their fellow countrymen, and the sympathy and sense of justice of the middle classes, 'petitions should be poured into Parliament from every town, village and hamlet in the kingdom'. Moir wanted the Convention to petition again, 'with thousands of little petitions'. Pattison, who had become the dominant personality on the Central Committee, believed that the success of the Chartist cause depended largely on the amount of aid which could be obtained from the middle classes, and that this required a long-term policy of education and propaganda, abjuring all violent methods of agitation.[4]

At the Scottish delegate conference in August such views had been strongly voiced, but there had been dissension on the point, and the issue had been left in abeyance for deliberation by the Central Committee, once the feelings of the country had been ascertained. On 12 September, two days before the dissolution of the General Convention, there was further discussion on the question by the Central Committee, which decided that the means to be employed in the agitation should be 'strictly peaceful, legal and constitutional'. Registers should be prepared listing the names, ages, trades and residence of all male inhabitants of Scottish towns, villages and hamlets who were favourable to the principles of the Charter. In each of these localities, petitions should be prepared for separate submission to the House of Commons.

Little attention appears to have been paid to this pronouncement by 7 November, when, shortly before the news of the Newport rising reached Glasgow, Pattison again submitted to the Central Committee that only by assuming the character of a petitioning body could they legally keep alive their agitation. His demand that the Committee should declare their intention to petition again was supported by almost the entire committee, but was hotly denounced by Thomas Gillespie, the former secretary of the Glasgow Universal Suffrage Association and leader of the Glasgow Republicans and Ultra-Radicals.

The Central Committee was falling into the same error as the General Convention, complained Gillespie. They were taking too much upon themselves, and recommending measures before consulting the country on whether it was likely to carry them into effect. Many leading Chartists had declared their opposition to further petitioning, and the Committee ought to consider the danger of creating fresh scisms. He refused to be convinced by Secretary Thomson that, since the delegate conference, the voice of the country had been heard in favour of re-petitioning. Nor would he be persuaded by Pattison that the Central Committee had the right to decide on the question without being required to paralyse itself by continuing to test the opinion of the country time after time.

Gillespie, who had been employed on the staff of Dr Taylor's *New Liberator*, had acted as secretary of the defence committee for the Glasgow cotton spinners and had been chiefly responsible for the organisation of the Dovehill delegate conference in August 1839. He was a young man of about 28, whose vanity inclined him to be pompous and open to ridicule, which he bitterly resented. In the Central Committee he regarded the cautious Pattison as his chief rival, and resented Pattison's growing dominance at a time when his own employment made attendance at committee meetings difficult. When the Glasgow Universal Suffrage Association adopted the petitioning recommendation of the Central Committee, and rejected Gillespie's contention that the Central Committee were acting unconstitutionally, he and his chief associate, Allan Pinkerton,* a young policeman, retired in high dudgeon.

With the support of the recently established *Scottish Vindicator*, which declared itself 'thoroughly disgusted with the abominable humbug of petitioning men—deaf as adders to the appeals of suffering humanity, the voice of reason, of nature, and naked unerring justice', Gillespie and Pinkerton now formed the Glasgow Democratic Association. Their motto would be 'We are determined to carry the People's Charter, peaceably if we may, forcibly if we must'. Their main contention was that no further petitioning should take place before consulting England, and without obtaining a favourable majority in both countries.[5]

From the Renfrewshire Political Union, and from Aberdeen, the same argument was heard. On 2 December, Thomson reported on correspondence with Edward Polin, secretary of the Renfrewshire Political Union. The Renfrewshire Chartists were opposed to petitioning and would accede to the plan only if it could be shown that a majority of the Chartists of Scotland and England favoured it. Otherwise, petitioning would be the cause of more disunion, and in the present state of England and Wales it was improper and inconsiderate to risk this. The opposition from Aberdeen was in less measured terms, and in the *Northern Star* of 7 December,

---

* Allan Pinkerton (1819–84) emigrated in 1842. He survived being shipwrecked on his way to the United States, where he established the famous detective agency.

George Ross, the chief secretary of the Aberdeen Working Men's Association, was given space to attack 'that immaculate body, calling itself the Central Committee for Scotland'. The Radicals of Scotland should not permit 'a few individuals, in whom they have no confidence, to misdirect the movement in their name'.

In reply to these attacks, the Central Committee appealed to its countrymen 'not to allow any man, or any set of men . . . to peril the movement by schemes of violence, which will be as futile in their effect, as they will be dangerous in their operation'. It should not have astonished Chartists in Renfrewshire or elsewhere that the Central Committee were favourable to petitioning. More than ten weeks previously they had published a series of resolutions on the subject, and had in particular invited the attention of the Renfrewshire Political Union. They were endeavouring, by all means at their disposal, to test the feelings of the Scottish Chartists, but they must confess they did not know how to test England—even if they were authorised to interfere there. There was no Convention, no Central Committee, nor indeed any 'large properly organised district' with which they could communicate. Moreover, the minds of their English brethren had been 'too much irritated of late by doctrines of physical resistance—by disappointed hopes and furious and vindictive persecution—for them to enter dispassionately into the bearings of such a question!' A physical force agitation would not now do in England—it was too full of spies and informers. The insurrection in Wales was a

melancholy proof of this; consequently the spirit of agitation will die here in a short time if there is not a new tone given to it. It belongs to Scotland . . . to give it a fresh impetus, and this can easily be done, were our Scottish Chartists unanimously to adopt our plan of petitioning, and then . . . our example would renovate the movement.

Considerable support, however, had been forthcoming for the recommendation to petition. When the Glasgow association discussed the question, Pattison was able to claim that twenty-four associations in Forfarshire, and twenty-two in Fifeshire, besides 'a great meeting in Edinburgh', had responded to the recommendation to prepare for petitioning. Widespread approval of the decision of the Central Committee was reported by Abram Duncan. Accompanied by Robert Lowery, who had recently been appointed county lecturer for the Forfarshire Chartists, Duncan had addressed more than twenty meetings in the south of Scotland and in Forfarshire between mid-October and mid-November, and he expressed his confidence that government spies could not succeed in Scotland as in Wales. The decision of the Central Committee for petitioning had 'given great satisfaction' everywhere, and there was a desire for a new Convention to look after the presentation of petitions.[6]

Robert Lowery

Amongst those who welcomed the decision of the Central Committee was John Fraser, who had recently been conducting a newspaper feud with the *Scottish Patriot* over its policy of studiously ignoring the *True Scotsman* and its editor, which Fraser found intolerable at a time when his paper was seriously losing circulation. Fraser had initially regarded the Central Committee with complete indifference, but he now found its emphasis on a constitutional basis for Scottish Chartism wise. He wished to see 'separate petitions from every city, town, village, hamlet, trade and section of the people'. Another Convention should be elected to superintend the petitions and 'for nothing else whatever'.

Praise was also forthcoming from England, particularly from the *Champion*, which had previously noted with approval the intention of the Scottish Chartists to petition.

The Scottish Radicals [J. P. Cobbett declared] were among the most energetic in the island in getting up the 'General Convention of the Working Classes'. To their very great honour, when that Convention had proved a failure, instead of being cast down, they were the first on their legs again—they were the first actively engaged in taking new steps to promote the object for which they originally combined.[7]

The wrangling over petitioning continued, however, throughout December and January, and it was not until 13 February that the Central Committee designated 2 March 1840 as the 'appointed day' for the commencement of the petition movement. At the same meeting, Thomas Gillespie, who had been fighting a delaying action with some success, was replaced on the executive council of the Central Committee by James Proudfoot. The procrastination in taking the final decision, however, had not been entirely due to dissension over this issue, as several other issues had assumed considerable importance and urgency since November.

Foremost amongst these was the question of support for John Frost and the imprisoned Welsh insurrectionaries, but almost equally absorbing was the question of Chartist tactics towards the intensification of the corn law repeal campaign, in which large demonstrations were planned as the preliminaries to a 'repeal festival' in Manchester, at a time when trade had slumped seriously in Paisley, Dundee, Aberdeen and elsewhere.

Zest for organisation was being exhibited in many parts of the country, and considerable energy was now being expended on the organisation of Chartist Sabbath worship services, and on the establishment of Chartist co-operative stores. In Glasgow and Lanarkshire there were renewed efforts to implement the plan which W. C. Pattison had produced for connecting the committees of the trades in Glasgow with the committees of the Chartist district associations throughout the county, forming one general association for Lanarkshire.

During such a period of Chartist excitement there was in fact little need of a petition movement in order to keep the agitation and the local associations alive. Nor was there any likelihood of repressive interference from those responsible for law and order. The patently peaceful nature of their activities could well be relied on to safeguard the participants from that. Nevertheless the Central Committee were determined to persevere with their petitioning project. It would confirm the peaceful nature of their agitation, while giving the movement a sense of direction and satisfaction from positive action. Its effects on the 'apathetic repressed Chartism of England' must be highly beneficial; the English Chartists would be

97

shown the paths of prudent, peaceful and safe agitation, and encouraged to revive their faith in the Charter. Thereby the House of Commons would learn that Chartism was still alive and vociferous.

Petition! Petition! Petition! [called the *Scottish Patriot*]. Remember the 2nd Day of March. Let nothing divert you from this important duty. The eyes of all England are upon you . . . So soon as [the plan of petitioning] is generally known and understood, we are convinced that every true Chartist in the kingdom will adopt it.

Specimen petitions were to be copied from the Chartist newspapers, and the House of Commons was to be inundated by petitions from individual Chartists and groups of Chartists.[8]

Under the impetus of the petition movement, many meetings were held and hundreds of petitions were forwarded to members of Parliament—from individuals, from universal suffrage associations and from factories. In Fifeshire and in the borders there was considerable activity, but it was chiefly in the area near Glasgow that enthusiasm was displayed. There were petitions from Anderston, Burnside, Bridgeton, Calton, Cambuslang, Gorbals, Govan, Hutchesontown, Laurieston, Tradeston, Woodside and all the districts of Glasgow, and from Lanarkshire there was good response from Airdrie, Biggar, Denny and Strathaven. Denny sent a petition praying for both the People's Charter and abolition of the corn laws, which was signed by 450 people, while Strathaven alone sent off more than 300 petitions in one week. Even in Glasgow town council there was a move to support the universal suffrage movement.

Most of the petitions were directed to John Dennistoun, the member for the city, who acknowledged most of them with courtesy, promptness and apparently 'warm approval', for which he received the plaudits of the Chartist newspapers. Another recipient of numerous petitions was General W. A. Johnston, who, along with Dr Thomas Wakley and Mr Leader, assured the petitioners of his warm support. G. F. Muntz presented all the petitions forwarded to him, but saw no need to inform the petitioners of having done so. Joseph Hume found 'pleasure' in presenting the many petitions entrusted to him, and to the Gorbals Female Universal Suffrage Association he expressed his desire to 'see taxation and representation co-extensive'. Union between the working and middle classes, he explained to the petitioners, could be best promoted by the former joining in the demand for a repeal of the corn laws and for suffrage reform.

Petitions, however, should be numerously signed in future, and not sent merely from individuals. The corn laws, moreover, should be strongly denounced 'as the immediate evil from which the working classes are suffering'.

It [was] only because the people [were] denied a fair share of power in their House of Commons that the odious Corn Laws, and other bad laws bearing heavily upon the working classes, are allowed to remain on the statute book ... Every man who earns his bread by his labour, should raise his voice against the Corn Laws, as pressing immediately on them, and producing a stagnation of trade, a want of work, and starvation.

Less sympathetic were Lord James Stuart, who would present Ayrshire petitions, but who regretted his ability to agree only with the demand for the ballot, and Captain Wemyss of Fifeshire, who, being afraid of being tricked into presenting many fictitious petitions, returned them all to local ministers to ascertain the authenticity of the signatures. Wemyss demanded that those who signed petitions must also send certificates from their ministers. One petition, from the North West Quarter branch of the Lanarkshire Universal Suffrage Association, was sent to a Tory, Sir Robert Peel, who returned it with the suggestion that it should be placed 'in the hands of some member more favourable to a compliance with the prayer' than himself.

By the middle of March this paper war against the House of Commons was adjudged to be a great success.

Showers of petitions of all shapes and sizes now wing their way daily to the House of Commons [exulted the *Scottish Patriot*]. The Universal Suffrage Central Committee have not appealed in vain ... The people are neither wearied out by waiting, nor less energetic than before. The movement here wears a youthful, healthy and hopeful appearance ... We have assurances too, that our English brethren are not blind to good example. We observe from the columns of our able contemporary the *Northern Star* that meetings have been held in various towns of England where petitioning was agreed to.

In claiming for the Scottish Central Committee the credit for this development, the *Scottish Patriot* had the support of James Mills, late member of the General Convention, who on 9 March proposed that the Cobbett Club at Oldham should tender their heartfelt and most cordial thanks to the Universal Suffrage Central Committee of Scotland, and especially their unremittingly persevering Chairman, Mr James Moir, for his strict adherence to the only proper way of making known their grievances, namely by petitioning.

Rather less predictable, and certainly more ambiguous, support was forthcoming from George Julian Harney in an address to the Democrats of Great Britain in March 1840:

The men of Scotland have recommended petitioning. Shall we join them in that? My answer is—Yes! Not because I imagine petitioning will get the Charter ... Neither do the men of Scotland; but they adopt it as a means of furthering their organisation, and of annoyance to their oppressors ... I still believe that it is physical force, or the fear of it, to which in the end we shall be compelled to resort ... It was not praying and petitioning, but his gore-dyed sword that enabled Wallace to resist successfully the invaders of his own lov'd land ... It was not the moral-force psalm singing section of the Covenanters that gained religious freedom for Scotland. No! It was the men who took to the hills for their homes, and had the heather for their bed. They prayed, I grant you, but it was with the Bible in one hand, and the claymore in the other.[9]

NOTES

1. *Scottish Patriot*, 24 August; 14 and 21 September; 5 and 19 October 1839.
2. *Scottish Patriot*, 7, 14 and 21 September 1839.
   True Scotsman, 14 September; 2 November 1839.
   Northern Star, 9 November 1839.
3. *Scottish Patriot*, 7 September 1839.
   Chartist Circular, 12 October 1839; preface, 23 October 1841.
4. *Scottish Patriot*, 3 August; 7 September 1839.
5. *Scottish Patriot*, 14 September; 9 and 23 November; 7 and 21 December 1839.
   Scottish Vindicator, 2 November 1839.
6. *Scottish Patriot*, 23 November; 7, 14 and 21 December 1839; 4 January 1840.
   Northern Star, 23 November; 7 December 1839.
   True Scotsman, 23 November 1839.
7. *True Scotsman*, 21 and 28 September; 5 and 19 October; 23 November; 28 December 1839.
8. *Scottish Patriot*, 11 and 25 January; 15, 22 and 29 February 1840.
   Glasgow Argus, December 1839.
   True Scotsman, 22 February 1840.
9. *Scottish Patriot*, 7 March–20 June 1840.

CHAPTER EIGHT

Physical force, Welsh victims and English 'spies'

If the term 'physical force Chartism' were to be applied only to
those who believed that violent measures would be required if they
were ever to gain the demands of the Charter, then it would be
difficult to find more than a handful of 'physical force Chartists' in
Scotland. There was no school of thought which preached violent
revolution; nor was there any body of Chartists which preached
unconditional submission to tyranny. Nevertheless, the unity of
Scottish Chartism was frequently disturbed by the issue of 'physical
force'.

This division arose mainly as a consequence of a conflict of
personalities, and their varying attitudes towards obedience to
constituted authority. The Rev. Patrick Brewster of Paisley, who
more than any other inspired this disunity, actually believed that
tame submission to tyranny was 'sinful and unchristian'. Such an
attitude was at best 'a beautiful chimera of overstrained and self-
immolating charity'. The existence, however, of adequate constitutional freedom to advance political claims made all violence treasonable, and in Britain, where a free constitution supplied the means of
correcting every abuse, advocates of violence were either reckless
men and virtual enemies to the cause they espoused, or they were
government agents paid to foment premature insurrection. The first
essentials for any political agitation in Britain, therefore, were
complete renunciation of any intention to use physical force under
any circumstances whatsoever, and complete readiness to obey
constituted authority. Even the use of unconstitutional force by the
government against the people did not warrant resistance. By non-
resistance, the people would enlist the sympathies of the influential
sections of society.[1]

This view was very strongly held by its supporters, but it was never very widely held, and repeated efforts by Brewster to have it accepted as the essential basis of Chartist organisation never resulted in its adoption by more than a handful of associations. 'New Moral Force Associations' were established in Edinburgh, Perth, Paisley, Hamilton, Leven, Douglas, Elie and Saltcoats, which refused to have dealings with any organisation which had not adopted this basis. Several other associations could be induced to disavow violence for Brewster's reasons, but could not be persuaded to break off relations with those who refused to follow suit. Amongst these were Stirling, Juniper Green, Penicuik and Kirkwall. The associations in Edinburgh, Paisley and Kilmarnock constantly fluctuated in their adherence to this policy, and after the autumn of 1839 the Dunfermline association remained hopelessly divided.

Refusing to subscribe to Brewster's 'unconditional obedience' policy was a broad coalition whose members differed widely in their attitudes to 'physical force', and whose only common distinguishing feature was their insistence that obedience to authority was conditional on the enjoyment of constitutional rights. Within this broad category fell the great majority of the Scottish associations, with most of them comprising an amalgam of individuals subscribing to three main trends of thought.

There was often a small extremist section which declared the necessity of possessing arms, and their willingness to adopt any measures. The extremists were influential in Forfar, Renfrew, Elderslie and the Vale of Leven, but their spokesmen at conferences, who blustered in the excitement of the moment, were seldom able to match their local actions to declarations of 'readiness to adopt any measures'. The principal exponents of this attitude were Dr John Taylor, John McCrae and Thomas Gillespie. Most of the extremists were determined to maintain the most aggressive bluff to alarm their enemies, without pushing their friends into military preparations. Among the Scottish Chartist leaders, only Dr Taylor could be fitted without unfairness into the 'physical force' category. Taylor was convinced that measures short of the threat of imminent revolution would never succeed; yet he tried hard to convince himself that the 'stopping of supplies' by his D'hurna societies might be sufficient, and he did not believe that physical violence was justified until all peaceful means had been tried in vain. In none of his half-developed plans for large-scale rebellion does Scotland appear to have figured in his calculations. Even in the desperate schemes which he was hatching in the Carlisle area in November and December of 1839, Taylor seems to have discounted the possibility of obtaining armed support from Scotland.[2]

The most numerous section of the 'conditional obedience' school consisted of those who agreed with Taylor and O'Connor that the threat of force was necessary, but who were unwilling to subscribe to any declaration that moral means were unlikely to prove adequate. Most of this group had as great a fear of civil war as had the associates of Brewster, but they accepted the dictum that moral force had never been productive of any good unless it were strengthened by the underlying threat of force. Their oppressors would not heed moral force unless they were convinced that potential physical force lay behind it. For the first eighteen months of the agitation this attitude was characteristic of the Glasgow Universal Suffrage Association, and several Ayrshire associations—particularly Ayr, Cumnock and Irvine—insisted on it. This point of view was strongly held in those associations where Feargus O'Connor or John Taylor had many admirers, such as Alva, Clackmannan and Tillicoultry. But most of the leading Scottish Chartists could be found, at some time, to be expounding this line of thought. Apart from Halley and Brewster, most of the leading participants at the Edinburgh conference of December 1838 had adopted this standpoint. Even John Fraser, who later denounced the least suggestion of threats at physical force as violently as 'Parson' Brewster, had been not less insistent on the value of such threats during the early months of agitation.

Most of the Scottish leaders who refused to disavow all intention of ever using physical force limited any threats to which they gave vent to maintaining the right of the people to repel the unconstitutional use of force. Several of these, such as W. S. Villiers Sankey and James Moir—who had threatened to unsheath his sword and not return it to the scabbard if the people were attacked—could soon be seen slipping into the third section of the 'conditional obedience' coalition. This consisted of the advocates of a purely peaceful agitation, simply because they considered it inexpedient and foolish to talk of physical force before they had adequate physical strength to implement any threats they made. W. G. Burns, of Dundee, was a good exponent of this attitude. The General Convention had failed, not from its measures being bad but from the 'want of power in the assembly to carry their deliberations into effect'. They ought never to make a threat until they were prepared to act upon it.[3]

In addition to these two main schools of thought, a third emerged, whose main desire was to prevent further discussion of the physical force issue. Within this group could be found many of the enthusiasts for organisation, self-reform and education, including W. C. Pattison, Arthur O'Neill, John Duncan, Partick Matthew and Alexander Halley. To them the most important issue was the unification of the movement, and they tended to have a strong influence in moderating the conflicts between the more extreme Chartists. After the Calton Hill fiasco had threatened to split the movement, they succeeded in reconciling all but the small faction which supported Brewster in support for the General Convention. While this group might be willing to admit the right of Chartists to possess arms, they deprecated any allusion to, or encouragement of, the possession of arms, and denounced any intention of using arms in terms almost as violent as those of the Rev. Patrick Brewster. All of them believed that talk of violence inevitably alienated many friends of Chartism.

There was indeed a good deal of sense in the attitude of each of the different schools of thought. There was much justification for the belief of those in the extreme revolutionary position that the government might never again be so vulnerable to the vengeance of a fiercely discontented people. There was sense in the moderate position, that the people were neither organised for rebellion nor even contained a clear majority in favour of the Charter. There was even sense in the extreme pacifist position in its warning to the moderates that they might make a doomed rebellion possible by the very success of their organisational efforts if they did not divorce themselves from revolutionaries and government agents.

Few, therefore, of the Scottish Chartists had ever any desire to attack the authorities with weapons other than reason, remonstrance and demonstration. Some of their leaders might occasionally say rather violent things, but they were known to be free of any really seditious intent, and the suggestion that demonstrations, on Glasgow Green or Calton Hill or elsewhere, of physical—or even armed— strength were intended as rebellion was to most Scottish Chartists as ridiculous as any suggestion that the Whig–Radical reform demonstrations in 1831–32 were acts of sedition.

This moral *v.* physical force conflict was, as far as Scotland was concerned, rather a sham fight. The real issue was the question of leadership, with the exhuberant Feargus O'Connor playing the key role. After the 'defection' of the Birmingham leaders, O'Connor became and remained, almost universally in Scotland, the object of admiration. Those Scottish leaders who distrusted O'Connor found it impossible to dissociate themselves from him without divorcing themselves from the rank and file of the movement. Those inclined to this attitude preferred to look to William Lovett rather than to Patrick Brewster, who had such a wonderful capacity for alienating his allies. Several would have welcomed leadership from the parliamentary Radicals, such as Joseph Hume, Sharman Crawford or J. A. Roebuck, but support for this would have been confined to the more intellectual Chartists, and any such move would inevitably have been killed by association with the name of Daniel O'Connell.

The most important effect of the Welsh insurrection in November 1839, as far as Scotland was concerned, was to confirm the leadership of the movement in the hands of the 'moderates', who could sympathise with their 'physical force' colleagues but who were incapable of departing from a 'moral force' agitation. There had never been any danger of widespread Chartist insurrection in Scotland, but after the Newport rising there could no longer be any question of it.

The immediate effect, however, of the news from Wales, was a spontaneous wave of sympathy for John Frost, who had won golden opinions on his Scottish tour in June. It was difficult for soberminded Scotsmen to see in Frost a revolutionary firebrand. Fraser found an explanation for the rising in the history of the Welsh nation. They had been driven to insurrection not so much by want and distress as by centuries of harsh treatment, by love of country and by hatred of oppression. Even those who regarded such outbreaks of violence as grave hindrances to the winning over of public opinion to Chartism, as did the Central Committee for Scotland, suspected this one to have been a government plot into which some of their less intelligent and more reckless friends had been trapped—as in Scotland in 1817 and 1820—by the machinations of spies and *agents provocateurs*.[4]

Like the Birmingham incidents in July, the Newport rising infused a fresh vitality into the agitation and, perhaps surprisingly, tended to reunite all factions. The serious predicament of Frost, Williams and Jones called for positive measures, and despite an undercurrent of disapproval of their reckless behaviour, a Frost Defence Fund Committee was appointed by the Central Committee for Scotland to launch an 'Appeal to the Unprejudiced Public'. The fund committee organised the issue of a large number of subscription sheets, and sent deputations to speak in many factories and mills where there was known to be Chartist sympathy. Its efforts to place the fund on a well organised basis were rewarded with a large number of small collections which brought the total to an impressive sum. Although its activities were confined to the area within a radius of about five miles around Glasgow, within a few weeks the proceeds of 'social entertainments', raffles, religious services and contributions from individuals, shopkeepers and trade unions provided over £200 for the legal expenses of defending Frost and his colleagues.

Reports of the trial of John Frost were closely followed throughout Scotland. Few Chartists continued to believe that Frost was blameless, and opinions varied considerably from those who insisted, as in Lochee and Lennoxtown, on his innocence, to those in Dunfermline who held that armed attacks were to be deeply detested and merited heavy punishment. A fairly common explanation of Frost's conduct at Newport was that he had been trying to preserve order —as he had already done successfully at the time of Vincent's trial. The *Scottish Patriot* declared its conviction that

Sir Frederick Pollock clearly proved that when Mr Frost, at the head of the Welsh Chartists, marched into Newport, he did not more unequivocally appeal to physical force, or commit high treason, than did the Reforming Ministry of the year 1831–2. If it were treason to assemble in large masses, and threaten by even a show of physical force, then had Lord Melbourne and his colleagues themselves been guilty of that crime . . .

The reaction to the death sentence on Frost, Williams and Jones was, however, both immediate and fierce, and in many parts of Scotland throughout the second half of January numerous meetings were held to protest against the severity of the sentences. Even from Dunfermline, where the Chartists felt unable to demand a 'full and free' pardon, a petition for the mitigation of Frost's sentence was supported by the provost and magistrates. In Aberdeen, the Female Radicals organised a public meeting to contest the death sentence, while the male Chartists held meetings which opened with prayer and closed with the singing of the fourth Paraphrase.

From Edinburgh, where only 5,000 had initially signed the National Petition, a petition was sent to Lord Brougham containing more than 22,000 signatures. In Paisley the town council, with all the dignity the provost, town treasurer and magistrates could command, decided to petition for Frost. Within fourteen hours the Paisley petition received 14,784 signatures and measured 56 yards.

In many localities, as at Paisley and Dundee, where 20,523 people signed, the Chartists were able to pride themselves on managing to persuade 'persons of all classes and all grades in politics to unite in this act of humanity and Christian philanthropy'. Ill-feeling against those sufficiently lacking in Christian charity as to refuse to sign was directed mostly against clergymen. At East Kilbride, four doctors, two ministers and several kirk elders refused to sign. At Stonehouse the Chartists were delighted at obtaining 639 signatures from 1,700 inhabitants, which was equivalent to 90 per cent of those over fourteen years of age, but were annoyed with the refusals of the Dissenting ministers and several elders from both congregations.[5]

To many associations the Welsh outbreak, in offering them a specific task in what they found to be an inspiring cause—the defence of the persecuted against governmental tyranny—provided a new lease of life. The outburst of excitement and indignation which it generated provided Chartists of all descriptions with a safe outlet for any violent emotions which the moral agitation might have repressed, and, despite the tendency of the middle class press to couple Chartism with bloody violence and attacks on property, the fears of some of the members of the Central Committee that the Welsh insurrection would have a damaging effect on the relations between middle and working classes did not seem to be borne out.

It was into an unduly spy-conscious Scotland that several suspicious strangers ventured in the winter of 1839–40. They were John Sibon, 'a gentleman of Kent', who claimed to be a missionary of the Northern Political Union, and two former members of the General Convention; William Cardo, who was being denounced as a 'paid agent' by George Edmonds of Birmingham, and the more notorious George Julian Harney.

By 20 January each of these gentlemen was reported to be busily engaged in converting the Scottish Chartists to a hatred of Whiggery. From Perth, on that date, Sibon was reported as 'scarcely equalled among the Chartist orators we have heard from England; his language is modest yet energetic and convincing'. In Kilmarnock, on the same evening, Julian Harney was reported to have delivered 'one of the most savage harangues ever uttered in old Killie', in the course of which he asked for one hundred good men and true who would cross the border with him, in order that the Charter would be the law of the land within a week. At a meeting in Whitefield Chapel, Edinburgh, on the same evening, William Cardo was meeting with even less success, and was refused permission to speak. This was at the instigation of John Fraser, who insisted that strangers should make known their 'public and private character' before being permitted to address public meetings. Cardo refused to fulfil these conditions, and also declined to 'give any information as to the gentlemen who were financing him'.

The appearance of Julian Harney, in particular, was hardly calculated to ease the minds of the Central Committee members. This fiery young man had been denounced by no less an authority than Dr John Taylor for his injudicious and irresponsible conduct in the early stages of the Convention, and it was widely suggested that such an avowed revolutionary could only owe his liberty, at such a time, to employment as a government agent. The men of Scotland, counselled the *True Scotsman,* should disdain from giving Harney any countenance:

They should send him back again to his friends in England; whom he has done his best, in his great ignorance and blinded zeal, to commit to the dungeon and lead to the scaffold ... He may be an honest man but he is a fool ... He was one of the most furious agitators in England and did his best to produce a revolution ... and after having been instrumental in producing the deplorable state of Radicalism in England, he, coward-like, deserts the scene of desolation and ruin to travel to Scotland, leaving England without the benefit of his patriotism, his advice and his wisdom.

Harney received a somewhat inhospitable reception in Glasgow, where his arrival had been preceded by reports of inflammatory speeches alleged to have been made by him at Kilmarnock and Ayr. The directors of the Glasgow Universal Suffrage Association hastened to advertise in the liberal *Glasgow Chronicle* that they disclaimed all connection with Harney. They then informed him of the nature of the reports, rumours and suspicions which existed in Glasgow concerning his character, and drew from Harney a confession about his past foolishness. He protested, however, that he had now been reconciled with William Lovett and was convinced of the need for all parties to direct their energies to the attainment of their rights by moral means. The *Scottish Patriot* noted 'the absence of direct evidence' against Harney, and in a cautious but almost friendly editorial found that the manner of his address in Glasgow on 27 January had been very different in tone from that ascribed to him by report.

The Glasgow leaders instituted enquiries into Harney's recent conduct and speeches, especially the speech at Ayr, from which it appeared that he had come to Scotland neither as a government spy nor as a needy adventurer, but at the invitation, or suggestion, of the newly formed Glasgow Democratic Association. They concluded that Harney had been badly treated by both the press and his Glasgow sponsors, who had failed to make public their connection with him. Despite this, they remained reserved and suspicious towards Harney, but he suffered no further abuse, and for over a month he toured the west of Scotland, praising the work of the Central Committee for Scotland.

Outside Glasgow, Harney enjoyed the confidence of the rank and file of the movement and found no difficulty in obtaining invitations to address meetings. In January and February he spoke at thirty-five meetings, obtaining votes of confidence wherever he went, from Campsie to Dumfries. At Paisley he was challenged as a spy but obtained a resolution of sympathy for the prejudiced reports in the press, and at nearby Barrhead it was hoped that England would send more 'spies' like Harney—'this straight-forward, honest Reformer'. When he left Dumfries on the way to stand trial at the Warwick assizes, his Scottish friends had made sure that he would not have to walk.

In a valedictory address to the 'Democrats of Great Britain', on the eve of his trial, Harney thanked God that the humiliating disorganisation, apathy, distrust and despair which pervaded the English movement were absent in Scotland, 'where the banner of the Charter floats gloriously on the breeze'. The men of England should follow the example of the men of Scotland. In particular they should recommence petitioning, not because it would gain the Charter but because it afforded them a legal excuse for assembling together, and as a means of annoyance to their oppressors. Parliament should be bombarded with halfpenny individual petitions. Organisation was the next most important thing. In this 'the people of Scotland are acting wisely—slowly and cautiously, it is true—but with the moral certainty of ultimate success.'[6]

John Sibon had appeared in the west of Scotland in December 1839, lecturing in Mauchline and Newmilns on the 12th and preaching in Newmilns on the 15th. On 25 December he sent a note to a surprised Thomas More, secretary of the Hamilton Chartists, announcing that he would address the Radicals of Hamilton on the 28th, and that a subscription should be made to defray his expenses. When Sibon arrived in Hamilton he was offended to find that no public meeting had been arranged for 'Sibon, Missionary of the Northern Union'. He was incredulous that the Hamilton Chartists had not noticed his name in the *Northern Star*, and considered it ridiculous that he should be expected to advertise in the *Scottish Patriot* and the *True Scotsman*. He boasted of great meetings wherever he went, and promised to put life into their dead souls if they would get up a meeting for him. He condemned the Convention as a 'batch of cowards and traitors', and the Cobbetts as 'damned scoundrels' who had driven their father to his grave. Sibon talked of places which were armed and ready, and of meetings where he had spoken with drawn swords placed above his head, but avowed himself a complete moral force man when More observed that too many blows had already been struck.

Since Sibon talked of remaining in Scotland for some time, and as he could produce no credentials, the Hamilton Chartists directed him to Glasgow and the Central Committee, from whom he might obtain recognition. Little attention was paid to him until More realised that, despite his failure to obtain recognition from the Central Committee, Sibon was still active in Scotland at the end of January 1840. More therefore warned his fellow countrymen against such men, who must be either spies or needy adventurers. Dr Taylor, with whom he claimed to be intimate, had disclaimed any knowledge of the man. Nor would the secretary of the Northern Political Union substantiate Sibon's claim to be a missionary of that organisation.

This warning antagonised John Adam, secretary of the Forfar Political Union, who replied that the Dundee Democratic Council had examined the charges made against Sibon and had concluded that they were groundless. Adam had also been authorised to recommend Sibon to the other towns in Forfarshire by the Forfar council, which accepted his credentials. No lecturer had ever given more satisfaction than Sibon, and so long as he pointed out peaceable and legal measures as the only mode of carrying the Charter, even guillible Forfarians would never take him for a spy.

Support was also forthcoming from Perthshire, where Sibon had lectured in many villages. T. McPherson, the county lecturer, thought that the Hamilton Chartists had been over-hasty in imputing bad motives. Whatever this mild and dignified-mannered man might have possessed at Hamilton, he now held 'undoubted credentials from known and tried friends of the cause'. More refused to be impressed with this testimony. He granted that Sibon was good-looking, agreeable and undoubtedly very clever, but he had made boastful lies, had spoken in an absurd and dangerous manner, and had acted dishonestly towards William Hamilton of Stonehouse, who had befriended him. He could be relied upon to spout any doctrine which he thought would please his hearers and bring him funds to scour the country.

Let us employ men, [concluded More] in whom we can place full confidence, and not unknown adventurers—fellows who foist themselves on the public, and are ready to do anything rather than settle at home, and work their work . . . Let them stay at home in their own country where they are known, and further the cause; there is more need for them than here.[7]

The visit of William Cardo was also marked by rather inhospitable behaviour on the part of his erstwhile Scottish friends:

This gentleman, member of the late Convention [reported the *True Scotsman* on 18 January] gave a lecture in Whitefield Chapel, last Wednesday night, on the foreign policy of Great Britain, to a crowded audience, who were little satisfied with the speaker . . . We think our friends should beware of all such individuals and give no encouragement to men of whose character they know nothing and as little of the gentlemen, who Mr Cardo says, sent him out, and pay his expenses.

Fraser's advice was followed and Cardo was refused a hearing at his next Edinburgh meeting. Nor was he welcome in Glasgow, where James Moir had recently received a letter from R. J. Richardson of Manchester explaining his suspicions of Cardo, who appeared to be excessively well informed about the spy system in operation. His plans for introducing David Urquhart's foreign policy campaign were postponed, and although Urquhart visited Glasgow in January to discuss his ideas with the Chartist leaders, it was not until March that Cardo introduced the campaign in a series of lectures on 'The effects on industry of the foreign policy of the government'.

The distress of British merchants and manufacturers, he said, was due to mismanagement of colonial affairs. The alienation of America had made possible the first partition of Poland, which had been the first step in the Russian plan to possess half of India and destroy the trade and commerce of Britain. Lord Palmerston, who was pretending to counteract Russian schemes, was treacherously aiding them. Russia had in fact concocted the war with China and was endeavouring to get up a war between Britain and America. This could be stopped, and Russian power destroyed, by ending trade with Russia. Now that Russia had twenty-seven sail of the line in the Baltic the British Home Fleet could no longer protect the country, and strong measures were required from the Foreign Office. But if the country were to be redeemed, it must be by 'the simple-minded working man'. He regretted the degradation of the country by the influence of party spirit, which made it impossible to discuss a question involving the interests of all parties without exciting suspicion and obloquy.

David Urquhart's own approach was much less to the simple working man. His semi-private approaches to Pattison and other Glasgow leaders alarmed the editor of the *Scottish Patriot*:

If Mr David Urquhart wishes to convert the operatives of Glasgow to his views, why not at once call a public meeting in one of our large halls, and lay these before the inhabitants, instead of throwing away a vast amount of useful knowledge concerning Russian policy, Turkish Treaties, Palmerston's Treason etc. upon a mere handful of Chartists, in the large room of the Star Hotel? . . . Are his Tory friends afraid that the Rads will perhaps muster even there in considerable force, and after listening to one of Mr Urquhart's splendid lectures, carry the usual amendments?

Robert Malcolm found it somewhat surprising that his Chartist friends, 'usually so sharp-sighted on matters of a public nature', could not perceive that the whole purpose was to invite working class co-operation to assist the commercial interests of a certain party vitally interested in diplomatic relations with the East. He was disquieted to find W. C. Pattison accepting Urquhart's information as 'the most important' he had ever received, and was not completely satisfied with Pattison's contention that what he said was 'the most important on the subject of foreign policy'. If ever there was a man 'infatuated with his subject and who has conceived an exaggerated opinion of his own powers and knowledge with respect to that subject, it is David Urquhart with respect to Russian policy'. As for Urquhart's paid lecturer, Cardo, this man was playing an equivocal game 'by striving to ingratiate himself into the good graces of the Chartists by pandering to their prejudices. Even when he was in the Convention, there were suspicions of this man . . .'

Despite Malcolm's misgivings the response of the Glasgow Chartists to the foreign policy campaign remained cool. There was much in this propaganda which appealed to Radical feelings, but, with some judicious prompting from James Moir, the purity of Glasgow Chartism was preserved. It was agreed that all the information which Cardo had to offer only afforded additional reason for urging 'the whole Charter and nothing but the Charter', and Cardo's conclusions were always countered by resolutions that these evils could be rectified only by universal suffrage.

Apparently undaunted, William Cardo then moved on to Ayrshire and other more congenial parts of the West of Scotland, occasionally appearing on platforms with John McCrae and Julian Harney, who now also had strong opinions on foreign affairs, as well as an Ayrshire wife. At Greenock and several other towns Cardo was well received, although his lectures there dealt more with Chartism than with foreign policy.[8]

NOTES

1. P. Brewster, *Seven Chartist and Military Discourses*, 1843, pp. 279–99.
2. *The Chartist Correspondence*, Sheffield Free Press Serials No. 13, 1856 (letters Nos. 4, 8, 10, 15, 17–19, 26).
   W. Lovett, *Life and Struggles of William Lovett*, 1876, vol. ii, pp. 208–11.
3. Add. MSS 27,821, pp. 128, 209.
   True Scotsman, 13 April; 18 and 25 May; 15 June 1839.
4. *True Scotsman*, 16 and 23 November 1839.
5. *Scottish Patriot*, 11, 18 and 25 January; 1, 8 and 15 February 1840.
   True Scotsman, 18 and 25 January; 1 and 8 February 1840.
6. *True Scotsman*, 18 and 25 January; 1 February 1840.
   Scottish Patriot, 1 and 8 February; 14 and 21 March; 25 April 1840.
   Glasgow Herald, 25 January 1840.
   Northern Star, 25 April 1840.
7. *Northern Star*, 21 December 1839.
   True Scotsman, 25 January; 8, 15 and 22 February 1840.
8. *True Scotsman*, 18 and 25 January 1840.
   Scottish Patriot, vol. ii, pp. 147–8, 165, 200, 233, 249, 281, 384.
   The Chartist Correspondence, No. 23.

CHAPTER NINE

1840: the year of organisation

Faith in the efficacy of organising popular opinion remained the keynote of Scottish Chartism throughout 1840. Strongly held by the members of the Central Committee for Scotland, it was voiced in the Chartist press and echoed at all levels of the movement. Both to those who believed that the key to power was knowledge and the conquest of public opinion by rational means, and to those who believed that continuous demonstration of organised strength was necessary to overawe opponents of Chartism, the pursuit of more efficient organisation was a compelling goal of Chartist policy.

This zest for organisation found expression in the social reformist offshoots of the agitation, in the Chartist co-operative movement, the Chartist temperance movement and the Christian Chartist church movement, as well as in more orthodox activities such as the petitioning movement, the employment of lecturers and the development of county associations. The principal objectives remained constant—the unification of the working classes, some degree of reconciliation with the middle classes, and the spreading of the Chartist gospel to all corners of the country by the establishment of an efficient system of propaganda, serviced by Chartist press and political lecturers. Few of the leaders, at least, held out much hope of rapid achievement of the Six Points. These principles, declared Matthew Cullen, the president of the Central Committee, had taken deep root, but they could not be carried in 'less than some years'.

Especially in an old country like ours [warned the *True Scotsman* on the eve of the new year, 1840], the errors of a nation are not to be changed in a day or a year ... The past year has given birth to the movement, the existence and nature of which will now constitute a very important part of the political history of Great Britain ... We trust that the year to come will be signalised by the abundant use of those exalted and intellectual means now only partially begun ... The tract system, now issuing from Glasgow, is admirably calculated to maintain unity of action, diffuse knowledge and give wise direction to the popular will. The missionary system, yet but very partially carried out, must be adopted as the great means of convincing and converting foes, multiplying friends.

Lack of funds, however, remained a crippling problem for the Central Committee, and responsibility for this was seldom shouldered by those who made the most incessant demands for the provision of more lectures and tracts. James Robertson of Perth found it painful

to see men of talent, respectability, and stern integrity, under the necessity of pleading for the means necessary to carry on their operations ... I know how many of my friends have great reliance on the circulation of the *Chartist Circular*—they speak as if 25,000 numbers of that valuable periodical scattered over the face of the country were sufficient ...

From Kirkintilloch, Thomas Baird complained of the seeming indifference amongst universal suffrage associations to supplying the Central Committee with the necessary money, and proposed a system of national missionaries. These would be appointed by the Central Committee and furnished with credentials, on the basis of the number of local associations pledging themselves to accept a minimum number of visits, costing 10s.–12s. per visit, within a given period.

During the period August 1839 to March 1840, in the course of which over £400 was raised in Scotland for various defence funds, George Ross received for the work of the Universal Suffrage Central Committee less than £80, of which £44 were earmarked for liquidating the expenses incurred at the inaugural conference in August 1839. The most zealous of the financial supporters were the associations in the Vale of Leven, Campsie, Alloa, Markinch and both the male and female associations of Tillicoultry. Tillicoultry, which had contributed seven guineas, appealed to all other districts to follow its example, and on a more modest scale Linlithgow also set a good example by sending in regular contributions of fifty halfpennies each month. Rutherglen paid for a membership which appears to have declined gradually from 100 to 70 over a period of nine months. Apart from W. C. Pattison, the architect of organisation, who contributed £2 10s., no individual made a substantial contribution.

Among the trade unions, the most zealous in this respect were the Operative Stone Masons and the Chartist Boot and Shoemakers' Association.[1]

Despite this financial limitation, a considerable amount of missionary activity took place in the first half of 1840, and many villages which had never heard of Chartism were visited by Chartist lecturers, most of whom also took the opportunity to preach Chartist sermons. Where the intimidation of mill owners, brewers and clergymen could be overcome, committees were formed and branches established. Some of this work was done by freelance agitators, but mostly it was carried out by Chartists with local reputations who were employed on lecture tours by county committees.

In January and February the newly formed Lanarkshire association engaged Arthur O'Neill for a five-week tour of the county, mostly in the mining districts. In Stirlingshire and Clackmannan during February, William Tait of Auchinearn was reported to have done wonders at about twenty places. More than a dozen Fifeshire towns were visited in February by William Bowie and James Lowe of Dundee, whose work was continued throughout March and April by Abram Duncan. In April and May, John Adam of Forfar gave many lectures, especially in the Kirriemuir district, while George Julian Harney, on his return from Warwick assizes, resumed his activities in the west of Scotland. Harney was the moving spirit behind an attempt to revive the Ayrshire association, but he found that plans which had been formulated many weeks earlier at a delegate conference in Kilmarnock had remained a dead letter, and his efforts met with little success. 'Your chiefs in Glasgow are labouring day and night for you,' he scolded the Ayrshire Chartists. 'Have you supported the Central Committee as you should have done? That Committee has proposed to the country the most wise and beneficient measures.'[2]

The Lanarkshire Universal Suffrage Association was considered a great success, and in March the Renfrewshire Political Union was reformed on the basis of the Lanarkshire association rules. Elsewhere the county associations which had been established in 1838 and 1839 continued to function in the border district, Fife and Kinross, Forfarshire, Perthshire, Stirlingshire and Midlothian. Forfarshire and Fifeshire, in addition to Lanarkshire, had particularly energetic office-bearers and executive councils. These efforts were constantly applauded by J. P. Cobbett's *Champion*. 'Now, while

England is doing nothing,' it declared, 'Scotland is as busy as if her exertions were just commencing, and as if she knew that England was ready to back her.'

To a considerable extent the maintenance of a successful organisation amongst the Scottish Chartists was becoming dependent on the existence of rival agitations, though it was widely recognised that any Chartist associations which decided to wage unremitting warfare on all other agitations might antagonise and lose members and sympathisers with divided loyalties. This became a serious issue in the latter part of 1840, but earlier in the year the agitation was adequately fed with fresh grievances, and the impetus given to the Scottish movement by the actions of the authorities in England was probably as great as any measures adopted by the Chartist organisations themselves. Each month seemed to bring a fresh focal point for the agitation. In January and February there were numerous excited meetings on behalf of John Frost and his colleagues. In March and April the surplus energy was devoted to petitions for universal suffrage, and to prayers for the dismissal of those Ministers who had hastily transported Frost before honouring their pledge not to do so until the case had been fully investigated by the House of Commons. These were followed in May and June by protests against the treatment of Feargus O'Connor and other political prisoners as common felons. Such treatment had not been meted out to Cobbett, Hunt, Burdett or Hobhouse, and petitions for O'Connor's release from York Castle were often coupled with denunciations of his compatriot, Daniel O'Connell.

No Scottish representatives were sent to the conference at Manchester in July, which projected a National Charter Association, but the release of Lovett, Collins and McDouall aroused much rejoicing, and Arthur O'Neill and W. S. Villiers Sankey were present at the Lovett–Collins liberation demonstration in Birmingham. O'Neill, who was appointed secretary of the delegate conference held there, became enthusiastic about the plan for a national association and seconded the resolution which proposed its establishment. After his return to Scotland, however, objections were raised regarding the legality of the proposed organisation, and although Edinburgh, Dumfries and Renfrewshire had previously aired proposals for such an association, no Scottish associations joined the National Charter Association in 1840 or 1841.[3]

In August and September there was a re-emergence of the physical force issue, when Patrick Brewster produced a fresh project for a Grand National Association of Moral Force Chartists. This was to be formed after delegate conferences, at Dunfermline on 11 September for the north and east of Scotland, and at Paisley on 16 September for Lanarkshire, south and western Scotland. Earlier in the year, Brewster had been outraged by the attitude of the Central Committee towards corn law repeal. In an address 'To the Moral Force Chartists of Scotland', he had explained the necessity for throwing off the incubus of physicalism and the rank, hardly disguised Toryism of the Central Committee. The 'Physicals, who are the creatures of Toryism, are uniformly opposed to repeal', and were preventing the subject of the corn laws from being made an open question.

The projected conference in Dunfermline failed to materialise, but the issue was speedily resolved at delegate conferences in Paisley and Glasgow. At the Paisley meeting on 17 September, delegates from Glasgow, Barrhead, Tradeston, Gorbals, Parkhead, Stewarton, West Kilbride, Saltcoats and Cumnock presented their credentials. Brewster then insisted that the meeting was only for those who disapproved of the Universal Suffrage Central Committee. Although the meeting had been advertised as a delegate conference, it was not really a delegate meeting, and was meant to be attended only by moral force persons. Despite his membership of the Central Committee, Arthur O'Neill would be permitted to represent Cumnock.

Brewster did not wish to impugn the Central Committee with having acted 'in anything but a moral manner', but it had been established by delegates from associations which had approved of the Convention dictum 'forcibly if we must'. Under certain circumstances, physical force might be necessary, but he refused to act with those who refused to repudiate it. They should rescue such men as John Collins and Dr McDouall 'from the guidance of men pledged to physicalism', and form a new National Association based on moral force principles.

All the others present thereupon insisted that they had been sent by persons and associations approving of moral force principles, and James Moir denied that there was a physical force association or committee in Scotland. He saw no reason, therefore, against union with those calling themselves 'moral force Chartists'. Arthur O'Neill carried a resolution that it was their intention 'to obtain the Charter by no other means than those that are legal, peaceful and constitutional', and the conference then resolved that it was unnecessary to form any separate body in Scotland.

At the delegate conference convened by the Central Committee for Scotland, in Glasgow, on 22 and 23 September, Brewster was present, supported by Cochran and Coats of Paisley, and Morrison of Dunfermline. Their attendance was very brief, as they resigned after the refusal of the conference to repudiate physical force in what they considered a sufficiently explicit fashion. Brewster, however, remained to resume the discussion on physical force. Eventually a resolution from William Thomson was adopted as one of the principles of the Central Committee:

That the Universal Suffrage Central Committee shall use to the utmost of their power all legal, peaceful, and constitutional means, to establish by law the principles embraced in the People's Charter; and that they shall neither sanction nor support any party who may adopt or advocate any other means than these, viz. peaceful, legal and constitutional.

The conference decided to appoint another Central Committee for the next year, and eleven out of the fifteen who had served on the original committee were re-appointed, along with some new blood. At the instigation of John Collins, it was agreed to send a delegation to Birmingham to act as missionaries in England, once funds were supplied. Collins subscribed £1 'anonymously' in the hope that Arthur O'Neill would be sent. It was also decided to send a delegation to convert Ireland to Chartism, once funds became available. In the meantime only addresses would be sent to each country.[4]

Much rekindling of Chartist fervour resulted from the lengthy tour of John Collins and Dr Peter Murray McDouall during September and October, with demonstrations and soirées organised in their honour at Airdrie, Alva, Coatbridge, Dalkeith, Dumfries, Dumbarton, Dunfermline, Edinburgh, Forfar, Kilmarnock, Linlithgow, Markinch, Montrose, Stirling, St Ninians, the Vale of Leven and a few other places. In Glasgow, antagonism was met from the employers and master manufacturers, among whom there was alleged to be an 'illiberal and scandalous' agreement to refuse permission to attend, on threat of dismissal. Nevertheless, at the demonstration on Glasgow Green, on 21 September, eighteen trades unions marched in procession with the upper ward of Renfrewshire and twenty-two districts of Glasgow. The 'old Radical spirit' had revived, claimed the *Scots Times*. 'The demonstration on Monday exceeded that held when the Earl of Durham visited Glasgow, and was scarcely equalled by that of O'Connell. Chartism is supreme in Glasgow—Monday has settled that.'

Most of these events were highly successful, but there was considerable controversy over the demonstrations in Paisley and Dunfermline. The *True Scotsman* accused the *Scottish Patriot* of 'false reporting' in magnifying the success of these meetings and demonstrations. The *Scottish Patriot* retorted that wherever Fraser, 'or his equally anomalous coadjutor, Mr Brewster of Paisley, are found agitating in its favour, there the cause is sure to recede or stand still.' The contentions of both parties seemed to be borne out by most reports from Dunfermline, Paisley and Kilmarnock, where Chartist apathy throughout most of 1840 was in striking contrast to the leading part these towns had played in the agitation of 1838 and 1839.[5]

Another tourist in Scotland in the autumn of 1840 was Julian Harney, who returned once again as a self-appointed missionary in August. On this occasion he confined most of his attention to the east coast, where he lectured at Ceres, St Andrews, Arbroath and Kettle on the profligacy of the rulers of the country, the swindling system of the Jews, the corruption of the priesthood, and the need for the wider diffusion of political information. In Dundee, on 17 August, he moved resolutions condemning the 'aristocratical, irresponsible Foreign Minister' for his treaty with Russia, which was an insult to the French people, for whom he proclaimed his feelings of fraternity. Such treachery was yet another instance of the rotten nature of the House of Commons and of the need for its reform. These sentiments of fraternity for the French people were even more strongly voiced by Harney at an anti-war demonstration in Aberdeen on 8 October. He trusted they would hail as brothers the democrats of America, the republicans of France and the patriots of all nations. Several days later Julian Harney, now the Chartist candidate for Aberdeen, addressed a further meeting in protest against the threatened hostilities with France, and denounced all war unless undertaken for national defence.

The winter months were spent by Harney in Inverness and the northern counties, where he found the principles of the Charter to be 'as yet almost unknown'. The Highlands proved most disappointing, and after seven weeks of tramping he could not congratulate himself on having infused much enthusiasm there. He had met considerable prejudice, for which he blamed the editor of the *True Scotsman*, the lairds and the priests. Harney was delighted with the health and strength of the people there, and with the 'blooming cheeks and sparkling eyes of the bonnie lassies', but even in Inverness political knowledge was confined to a few, and the middle classes were divided between the Tories and the 'Whig Corn Law Repealers'. In Elgin he formed a Chartist association, 'strong in principle, if not in numbers', but elsewhere he considered it impossible to form associations and instead strove to establish clubs for reading democratic papers. In seventeen towns and villages of Aberdeenshire, Banffshire, Morayshire and Inverness he left behind agents, many of them shoemakers, to organise this work.[6]

By the autumn of 1840 the question of Chartist conduct at public meetings called by other organisations had become a matter of some controversy. It had been brought to a head by corn law repeal meetings, with which many Scottish Chartists had great sympathy, and others were deeply concerned over the disruption of meetings for other causes, such as slave emancipation. On 17 August James Moir announced that in future the Glasgow Chartists would intervene at "all public meetings which [diverted] public attention from the Charter, including anti-slavery meetings'. This obstructionist campaign had not been without its effect on the leaders of the repeal movement. In an 'Address to the Working Classes of Lanarkshire and Renfrewshire' in July, Archibald Prentice had appealed for toleration and support:

I do not ask you to cease agitating for the Charter, for ... I recognise the right of every man to be represented ... The Ballot, the extension of the Suffrage, short parliaments and the redistribution of seats are the means to great ends ... Repeal would be the very first act of a thoroughly reformed Parliament. But repeal must be advocated now if the nation will be ruined before we have thorough reform.

The matter was debated as one of the main items at the Glasgow convention in September, and it was agreed that in the event of any political party appealing for assistance, but refusing to recognise the principle of universal suffrage, it would be the imperative duty of every Chartist to go forward at all public meetings where such appeals were made and 'calmly, dispassionately, and fearlessly, meet and discuss with opponents the right of the productive classes to assert their political privileges'.

This resolution was carried into effect, especially in Glasgow, where, in November and December, there were intensified efforts to dominate anti-corn law, emigration, emancipation and all other public meetings. Disruption was the fate of meetings of the Emigration Society on 30 November, and of the 'Loyal Citizens of Glasgow' on the following day, when they met to present an address to the Queen on the birth of a princess. After the intervention of James Moir and the Chartists at 'an important House of Refuge meeting' at which they 'insulted and denounced the advocates of benevolence, the friends of humanity, and the most liberal dispensers of our local charities [because] pensions were given to the Kings of Hanover and Belgium', Peter Mackenzie of the *Scotch Reformers Gazette* advised the authorities to send the Chartists summarily, for at least sixty days, to hard labour in Bridewell prison.

The Chartist leaders by their outrages at such meetings [he complained] have now become the veriest pests of society ... They would object to enter Paradise itself, if opened to them, but move some counter amendment in favour of the Charter.

The achievement of a system of rapid communication and mobilisation of the Chartist forces in each locality was considered the greatest boon of the measures which had been adopted for 'more efficient organisation'. The peak of efficiency was believed to have been attained in Glasgow by the end of 1840.

So perfect indeed is the system of centralised organisation ... that any decision come to in the centre can be known through every workshop and factory throughout the city and surrounding villages in two or three hours. The summons goes forth like the fiery cross of the old time and thousands pour in at the call.

By these means the Chartists of Glasgow had been able for the previous twelve months to 'overthrow every other political faction' which had appeared before the public. Opposing parties were often amazed at the 'rapidity and certainty with which the Chartists could be brought to give their opinion on any subject, at all hours of the day, and in all parts of the city'. Through the operation of

this system of county organisation, under the direction of William Pattison, [the Chartists of Glasgow] have learned their real power, and the manner of using it; and all other parties have learned the important lesson that till they either concur in the demands of the operatives, or at least treat these demands in a civil and respectful manner, there shall be an end to public movements of every kind.

Eighteen months ago, concluded the *Scottish Patriot* in December 1840, such an assertion would have been laughed at. So long as the Chartists were content with petitioning and complaining, the middle classes had laughed and sneered. Now their policy of obstructing all public meetings was commanding attention.[7]

During 1840, therefore, there had been considerable vitality amongst the Scottish Chartists. Many associations had ceased to function, while many others were normally apathetic or paralysed by internal divisions. Nevertheless, out of almost 200 local associations which had been formed since the beginning of the agitation in 1838, about 125 were still functioning. Soirées and concerts were frequently organised to raise funds for organisational purposes in Dalkeith, Montrose, Stirling, Saltcoats, Dunfermline and several other places, while in Glasgow, Kilmarnock and Cumnock, at least, social meetings and concerts took place on a weekly or monthly basis, and the proceeds were sometimes substantial. Saturday evening concerts in the Glasgow Lyceum were 'a treat of no ordinary description', and were 'very popular'. They were 'one of the best projects entered into', since they were 'likely to be as useful financially as the Chartist Church'. In November 1840 the soirée committee of the Lanarkshire association reported a surplus of £23 2s 10d, and the weekly concerts in the Lyceum had realised £18, which enabled treasurer George Ross to report a most gratifying improvement in the finances of the association.

Amongst the other activities of the Lanarkshire Universal Suffrage Association was an attempt by 'the young friends of the cause' to bring the ladies more actively into the agitation, by starting a dancing class in Glasgow, which lasted throughout the winter. For more serious-minded adherents it made arrangements for a series of weekly lectures to be given throughout the winter 'on any plan or proposal that might be considered likely to aid or accelerate the Chartist cause, with the opening lecture devoted to a consideration of the ideas of William Lovett and John Collins'.

The cause of temperance, which had always been propagated by John Fraser and the *True Scotsman*, was embraced much more warmly within the Chartist ranks. Both the *Scottish Patriot* and the

Chartist Circular espoused the cause, and in the autumn of 1840 temperance was strongly advocated in the west of Scotland by Arthur O'Neill, and in the east by Henry Vincent and Henry Hetherington.

Some of the Chartists had been devoting most of their energy to the establishment of co-operative stores, and by the end of 1840 there were at least sixteen Chartist co-operative stores, in addition to those which were reported to exist 'in almost every village' in Fifeshire. In addition to renting shop premises, some associations rented halls for periods of six to twelve months, and a few claimed to be in possession of their own halls. In the newspaper press there was weekly advocacy of Chartism through the *True Scotsman*, the *Scottish Patriot*, the *Perthshire Chronicle*, the *Dundee Chronicle* and the *Scots Times*, in addition to the widely circulated *Chartist Circular* and *Northern Star*.

We may not be producing great effects upon the government [concluded the *Scottish Patriot*], but we are forming a character for the people which they have never before possessed—making them intelligent by instruction, and moral by inculcating the principles of total abstinence...Universal Suffrage has now been carried from the public arena into the domestic hearth of the working classes. It has become a part of the social character of the people. It is associated with their amusements. It has become identified with their religion.

It was perhaps this identification of Chartism with religion, and the growth of the Chartist church movement, that were the outstanding features of Scottish organisation in 1840.

One of the most remarkable features of Chartism in this part of the country [observed the *Glasgow Argus* in August 1840] is the number of places of worship which are opening in the various localities where their numerical strength is greatest. They have sermons regularly on Sabbaths in Glasgow, Hamilton, Lanark, Paisley, Greenock, Eaglesham, Kilbarchan and other towns in the neighbourhood; and in all these places, lay preachers officiate by turns. They regularly baptize children, and we understand that the sacrament was to have been dispensed by them yesterday in the town of Kilbarchan.

By the beginning of 1841, there were at least twenty Christian Chartist churches in existence in Scotland, when a delegate conference of Chartist congregations was held in Glasgow. In more than thirty localities Chartist services of worship were regularly conducted, and 'a Chartist place of worship is now to be found on the Lord's Day in almost every town of note from Aberdeen to Ayr'.[8]

NOTES

1. *True Scotsman*, 28 December 1839; 4 January 1840.
   Scottish Patriot, 5 October 1839; 15 February; 21 and 28 March 1840.
   Chartist Circular, p. 589.
2. *Scottish Patriot*, 8, 15 and 22 February; 7 March; 25 April; 16 and 23 May 1840.
   True Scotsman, 22 February; 25 April; 16 May; 13 June 1840.
   Northern Liberator, 6 June 1840.
3. *Scottish Patriot*, 7 and 21 March; 4 April; 16 and 23 May; 1 and 22 August 1840.
   True Scotsman, 7 March; 16 May; 11, 18 and 25 July 1840.
4. *Glasgow Chronicle*, 30 March 1840.
   True Scotsman, 12 September; 24 October 1840.
   Scottish Patriot, 19 and 26 September 1840.
5. *Scottish Patriot*, 19 and 26 September; 3, 10, 17 and 31 October 1840.
   True Scotsman, 26 September; 3, 10, 17, 24, and 31 October 1840.
   Northern Star, 3 October 1840.
6. *Northern Star*, 22 August; 3, 10 and 17 October 1840; 2 and 16 January 1841.
7. *Scottish Patriot*, 1 and 22 August; 26 September; 19 December 1840.
   Scotch Reformers' Gazette, 7 November; 5 December 1840.
   Glasgow Herald, 4 December 1840.
8. *Scottish Patriot*, 2 May; 7 June; 24 October; 7, 21 and 28 November; 26 December 1840; 27 March 1841.
   True Scotsman, 21 November 1840.
   Chartist Circular, 19 December 1840.
   Northern Star, 16 January 1841.

CHAPTER TEN

Chartist co-operation and total abstinence

Throughout the Chartist agitation there were incessant denunciations of monopolies, especially monopolies on food, and the 'shopocracy' received constant abuse. Even more than Ministers of the Crown, or ministers of religion, the shopkeepers were the scapegoats of local Chartist orators. It might have been expected, therefore, that the adoption of the principle of 'exclusive dealing' by the General Convention would have led to concrete discussion of the best means of putting this into practice, and that the system of retail co-operation would have found many advocates.

Yet while 'exclusive dealing' proved to be the most acceptable of the 'ulterior measures' recommended by the Convention, little thought was paid to the role which Chartist co-operation could play. A number of co-operative stores were, in fact, initiated by Chartists, but, except possibly in Fifeshire, they were not the result of any wide-reaching policy, and with a few exceptions, such as Hawick, they were short-lived enterprises. To some extent this was due to the fact that, despite wholesale denunciation of the middle classes and shopkeepers, the most influential of the Scottish Chartists never despaired of winning over these groups to the support of suffrage extension. They were regarded not so much as inveterate renegades but as fellow reformers whose appetites had been satiated and whose political consciences had been dulled. By judicious agitation, reason and patient remonstrance, they could again be converted—even if the shopkepeers might require some hefty material inducement or sanction.

For their part, the 'shopocrats' were generally willing enough, or fearful enough, to provide trifling support for the Chartist cause. When subscription sheets for Chartist funds were passed around, the shopkeepers could expect an early visitation, and they were usually able to delight, or appease, the Chartist collectors with quite modest contributions. Some shopkeepers went further and played an active part in the movement. These were rewarded with admiration and respect from their fellow Chartists, and one suspects that such a policy did not harm their businesses. At all events, few shopkeepers were ready to follow the example of many newspaper editors and openly invite the hostility of the Chartist masses. The Chartists were far too numerous for their custom to be lightly disregarded.

Exclusive dealing, therefore, was regarded by most Chartists not as a final declaration of war upon the shopocrats but as a warning shot across their bows. Some Chartists regarded exclusive dealing as savouring of persecution, and accepted the opinion of the majority only with reluctance. Even where exclusive dealing was put into operation, its effectiveness depended on the continued willingness, and financial ability, of the wives to support the arrangements. Many were too deeply in debt to credit-providing purveyors of groceries and drink to be able to choose where to take their custom. For most housewives, whatever future benefits might result from exclusive dealing, or co-operation, any change to cash dealing necessarily involved some immediate hardship.

In a few cases the implementation of exclusive dealing measures led directly to the establishment of Chartist stores. In July 1839 the Barrhead Chartists decided to establish a victualling society, and this apparently also happened at Alloa, Vale of Leven and Musselburgh, where fifty Chartists contributed 10s. each to set up an Exclusive Dealing Association. Elsewhere exclusive dealing practices were mainly limited to dealing with 'friends of the cause' among the shopkeepers, as in Dundee, Paisley, Partick, Stirling, Stonehouse and Strathaven. During the autumn of 1839, however, there were several efforts to establish Chartist stores. Early in September the Leith Universal Suffrage Association agreed to institute the Leith Chartist Provision Store, to effect exclusive dealing and to provide the necessities of life at the cheapest possible rate and at the best quality. The Leith store appears to have taken many months to materialise, but a similar decision at Hawick on 9 September resulted in the opening of the Hawick Chartist Provision Store on 9 November with a share capital of £13 10s 1d and some unexpected problems of keeping the butter free from coal dust. Possibly as a result of the Hawick example, a co-operative store was founded in

Galashiels, in which the leading Chartists William Sanderson and Alexander Johnston played the most active roles.

In Greenock a society of forty Chartists was formed which rented a shop 'in a very prominent place of the town'. Each member was admitted on payment of 10s, and the price of a full share, at £2, could be made up by instalments or by share profits on goods purchased. In Tillicoultry a co-operative society was started by Jordan Chadwick, the leading Chartist of the district, and sixty

Hawick Chartist co-operative stores: (1) the first shop,
opened in Silver Street in 1839

others, including one female. It is not certain that this was another Chartist foundation, but Arthur O'Neill regarded it as such on a lecturing and preaching tour through Fifeshire and Stirlingshire, when he proposed the formation of Chartist co-operative societies at Alva and Dunfermline. In Dalkeith a Chartist joint-stock provision store was established in December 1839.

From Forfar it was reported that four exclusive dealing stores were in active operation at the end of 1839, with fifty weavers employed on the manufacture of cloth. These were apparently controlled by Chartists but had been in existence for several years. In Cupar-Angus a co-operative society was formed in August or September 1839, which had a baking establishment, and appears to have been a Chartist-cum-Socialist venture.

It was a new and interesting feature of the movement, declared the *True Scotsman* on 28 December 1839,

to see working men trying their own strength, estimating their own capabilities and combining and directing their own energies for their own benefit... Victualling societies are springing up throughout the country, under the management of working men, by which they can secure provisions from 12 to 15 per cent cheaper than they can at the common stores and groceries.[1]

Hawick Chartist co-operative stores:
(2) the branch at Sandbed, opened in
1842

Neither John Fraser nor any of the other leading Chartists, however, seemed to regard co-operation as having any direct contribution to make to the Chartist cause. It was regarded as being good in itself and useful to the movement indirectly, in so far as it might ease the financial burden on Chartist families. They regarded it chiefly as an extension of exclusive dealing, and as exclusive dealing did not produce any valuable acquisition of new strength to the agitation, enthusiasm flagged for this method of achieving the millenium.

The excitement at the beginning of 1840 over the trials of John Frost and his colleagues, and the energy expended on protest meetings and petitioning, must have reduced whatever prospects existed that exclusive dealing would develop into a strong Chartist co-operative movement. Nevertheless, throughout 1840 there were occasional reports forthcoming which indicated that interest in the subject had not completely lapsed.

In January a Chartist store was opened at Lochee. Another started in business at No. 17 Niddry Street, Edinburgh, on 15 February. Shares in it cost 10s, with no individual being permitted to hold more than five shares and one vote. As at Hawick and several other Chartist stores, one of the standing rules was 'that no intoxicating drinks be kept in the store, nor any of the society's business to be transacted where they are sold'. In Gorbals an appeal from Robert McLardy, their president and a director of the Lanarkshire Universal Suffrage Association, moved the Gorbals and Chartist Boot and Shoemakers' Association to support the co-operative society being established there in April 1840. The 'imminent establishment' of a Chartist provision store at Luthermuir was announced in May, while in June it was reported that co-operative stores had been 'set a-going' by the Chartists in Inverleven and in almost every village in the 'Kingdom of Fife', and that these were well supported.

Only four Chartist co-operatives seem to have been formed in the second half of 1840. These were at Calton and Mile-end, where the 'shopocracy were keeping prices too high', and at Newmilns, Darvel and Galston in Ayrshire. From Newmilns it was reported in August that

this town was the first in Scotland for energy and determination, but after the Convention of the working classes broke up, the great exertions which the people had made seemed to paralyse them for a time, and during the time the country has been slumbering, we turned our attention to the erection of an economical Society . . . It has now been in existence three months and is doing well, with between two and three hundred members.

In contrast, the neighbouring society at Darvel was organised by nineteen handloom weavers, who could find only seventeen others to join them in the promotion of a store. In July a second store at Greenock was in preparation, and another was in the 'final stages of organisation' in Tradeston and Hutchesontown. There were probably several other attempts to establish Chartist co-operatives with as little success as the Tradeston project, for which, after twelve months, the committee had succeeded in raising only £15 of share capital.[2]

The subject of the formation of Chartist co-operative stores was taken up by the directors of the Lanarkshire Universal Suffrage Association on 10 April 1840. Without much discussion, agreement was reached on the principle of the matter, and a committee consisting of W. C. Pattison, William Thomson and Walter Currie was appointed to prepare plans for submission to the next general meeting of the association. No plans were forthcoming, but on 22 April Thomson made an interesting report based on his past activities as a co-operator.

Many co-operative stores had been formed in recent years, and some had failed. If the causes of failure were investigated, however, it would be found in each case that this was due to inefficiency or mismanagement on the part of the conductors of the societies. He believed this to be a most important subject, which could embody the principle of exclusive dealing, and he urged the establishment of stores in every locality where the shopkeepers would not support the Charter. This was one part of the vast power which the people possessed within themselves. He himself had first approached the subject in 1832, but although he was keenly interested in it he had dropped it as the reform agitation reached its climax. When, however, the shopkeepers, whose interest the people had helped to advance in 1832, showed their dishonesty, he had taken up the subject of co-operation once again. Within a short time he had started about seventy victualling stores on co-operative principles in the west of Scotland, including one in his own little village of Parkhead. Had he not been taken away from this work he was confident that there would have been one in every village in the county.

Thomson postulated a choice between three types of co-operative society. He did not greatly approve of the system whereby members received an annual dividend based on the expenditure noted in their pass-books. As for those victualling societies which were joint stock ventures, with the object of making a profitable return on the money invested in them, such societies generally lost the benefits of having a ready-money capital, by giving credit to the amount of the shares deposited. That seldom produced the effect really aimed at by co-operation, namely the cheapening of provisions. He proposed the system which he called the 'economical society', in which each member initially paid a given sum, then drew no dividend until the capital had accumulated to another fixed sum, when each shareholder would receive his proportion of profit. There would be neither giving nor taking of credit.[3]

Thomson's speech helps to indicate the relative importance attached to co-operation, the reform agitation of 1831–32 and Chartism by a person who was deeply bound up with all of these. Here, the secretary of the Central Committee and editor of the *Chartist Circular*—which makes only occasional mention of co-operation—speaks, apparently for the first time in the Chartist period, of his past connections with co-operation. As if to emphasise the relative unimportance placed on co-operation, the meeting immediately proceeded to a discussion of Feargus O'Connor's most recent proposals. By the end of 1840 the matter had not been raised again, and the Lanarkshire directors had passed on to the subject of total abstinence.

Along with 'exclusive dealing', total abstinence was considered by the Scottish Chartists to be the most judicious and practicable of the ulterior measures proposed by the Convention. Previously, total abstinence from alcohol had been constantly advocated by John Fraser, ever since the publication in July 1838 of his *Monthly Democrat and Total Abstinence Advocate*. Dr Taylor's plan for D'hurna societies in 1838 had also required abstinence from duty-paying drink, but these proposals were never taken seriously by their Chartist colleagues until abstinence was recommended by the Convention. Even this recommendation failed to please Fraser, for he objected to the use of teetotalism as a mere political expedient. The Radicals would not derive from that the inspiration required to carry it out. There was probably some truth in this, as, apart from decisions by the Bridgeton, Galston and Bathgate associations to carry total abstinence into effect, little resulted from all the lip-service paid to it in the summer of 1839.

Considerably more determination to adopt total abstinence was shown in the first half of 1840. In January a Chartist total abstinence association was formed at Greenock, and during the following months the question was seriously considered by several associations. The possibility of union with existing teetotal associations was explored, but apparently always rejected, as few of these societies would tolerate any political discussion. At Partick, total abstinence was reported to be going 'hand in hand' with Chartism, and

Chartist total abstinence associations were formed at Calton in April, at Luthermuir in May, and at Alva and Tradeston in June.[4]

At the monthly meeting of the directors and delegates of the Lanarkshire Universal Suffrage Association on 1 May, all the directors 'seemed impressed with the propriety' of total abstinence. Letters were received from East Kilbride, Hamilton, Stonehouse, Strathaven, Shotts and Uddingston which expressed 'the strongest concurrence' in the principles of total abstinence, and all the delegates present expressed willingness on the part of their constituents to refrain from the use of excisable liquor. Several associations were reported to have already taken this resolve, following the recommendation from Feargus O'Connor to adopt total abstinence for three months.

The debate produced considerable division of opinion, and a 'long and desultory conversation' ensued over the most practicable method of putting these principles into effect. Walter Currie and James Hoey, the leaders of the Gorbals association, thought that the teetotallers had done more than the Chartists to weaken the government, and wanted to have total abstinence inserted as a rule of the county association. Currie was impressed by the potential benefits to Chartists' family relations from temperance. By continually adjourning to public houses to discuss Chartist matters, they had raised the ill-will of their wives against Chartism, and led them to associate it with late hours and habits of intemperance.

This policy was strongly supported by James Hamilton of Stonehouse, the chairman, who feared both the anatomically destructive power of liquor and the sinister designs of the government, which sought to enslave the nation through the demoralisation resulting from the reduction of the excise duty on spirits. It was, however, strongly opposed by W. C. Pattison, John Rodger, Malcolm McFarlane, Robert Malcolm jun. and James Jack, the county secretary, who all wished to confine action to recommendations to individuals to abstain as much as possible. Jack argued that there was no power vested in the directors to go beyond this on such an issue. McFarlane deplored any move to narrow the basis of Chartist associations, and Pattison went so far as to deplore teetotal societies. He could not endure their intolerance towards the discussion of political questions, and averred that Chartists who ventured into their meetings were liable to be manhandled. The large majority of their members were a set of 'priest-ridden' men, who were averse to the cause of political freedom, and 'of that stamp, who bent before the will of the ministers and the employer'.

Agreement was eventually reached on a motion proposed by Pattison and Thomson 'that the Directors recommend to the Chartists throughout the county to adopt the principles of Total Abstinence from all spirituous liquors, and appoint a committee to arrange measures to carry the recommendation into practice'. As the committee which was appointed consisted of Thomson, Rodger, Jack and Pattison, there was little likelihood that any far-reaching measures would be forthcoming. The meeting also decided to request the Central Committee for Scotland to take up the question, and so, once again, the matter was left in safe hands.

John Fraser, however, was highly optimistic:

At last [he proclaimed in May] this glorious principle is beginning to excite the masses ... it is a principle that must be adopted before society can be purified to the extent which the patriot desires ...
Drinking radicals is a contradiction in terms. Radicalism has been made a laughing-stock throughout the country by reason of the drinking and drunken habits of many of its advocates. Pot-house politicians hiccuping for liberty [are] a revolting spectacle ... Will the men who are so fond to die for liberty, not prefer living to enjoy it, by taking this very simple and safe method of putting down tyrants ...

On the same day the *Scottish Patriot* also spoke of the benefits accruing from habits of temperance, though in rather more sober tones:

It is by no means insinuated that the Chartists are addicted more than others to habits of intemperance, but the money spent in spiritous liquors, could be otherwise laid out with far greater benefit to themselves, and to society.

Little further interest was evinced in abstinence until November, when Arthur O'Neill made a tour of Ayrshire, lecturing on Chartism and teetotalism. This ended with a series of lectures in Ayr on 'Mind, metaphysics and matter', which concluded with 'impressive exhortations 'on the propriety of every non-elector being sober. Twelve miles away, Abram Duncan was lecturing to a Kilmarnock audience on 'Harmony between Chartism and teetotalism'. If connected with the Chartist churches, teetotalism might do much good, but it ought to be used more as a political, and less as a superstitious, measure. The tendency of many teetotal societies had been 'to keep the human mind in darkness respecting the rights of man'. In Cumnock social meetings were now held jointly each month by the Chartist and the temperance associations, while in Dalkeith, where the majority of the members of the Radical Reform association had signed the teetotal pledge, William Taylor, its secretary, was lecturing on the inconsistency of Chartists who partook of strong drink. But a declaration in favour of temperance from Henry Vincent and Henry Hetherington in Dundee passed virtually unnoticed.[6]

At the new year in 1841, an appeal signed by 100 well known Chartists was published in the *Chartist Circular*, asking Chartists to adopt total abstinence. Among the signatories were Brewster, Fraser, O'Neill, Ross, Cullen, Thomson, Pattison and Abram Duncan. The list contained all the office-bearers and almost all the members of the Central Committee and of the Lanarkshire Universal Suffrage Association. All the senior office-bearers of the Airdrie, Campsie, Girvan, Hawick and Stonehouse Chartist associations signed, along with at least two senior members, usually the president and secretary, of the associations in Dundee, East Kilbride, Kirkintilloch, Kirkcaldy, Kilmarnock, Markinch, Maybole, Perth, Paisley and Stirling. Other signatories included leading Chartists in Aberdeen, Alloa, Arbroath, Bathgate, Falkirk, Forfar, Galston, Newmilns, Strathaven and Selkirk.

Meanwhile in the borders, on new year's day, a delegate meeting of the border Chartist associations took place in Jedburgh. It was decided that they should form themselves into Chartist total abstinence societies, and that these should form a Border Union. Alexander Hogg, of Selkirk, would be the general secretary, and to him would be sent monthly lists of members, who would be pledged to abstain from all intoxicants for at least one year.

These decisions and appeals were followed in the early months of 1841 by the formation of Chartist total abstinence societies in Selkirk, Hawick, Glasgow, Linlithgow, the Vale of Leven and Edinburgh. The Glasgow society was formed on the motion of William Thomson of the *Chartist Circular* at a meeting in the Chartist church, presided over by William Pattison, who now seemed determined to redeem the shortcomings of which John Fraser had accused him—'of trifling with the pure and great principles of Abstinence'. The Edinburgh society was formed by Robert Gourlay and James Grant. Its rules contained a pledge of abstinence, except under medical prescription or at religious ordinance. All discussion on theological questions was prohibited, and the sanction of expulsion existed against any member persistently using violent language or recommending illegal proceedings.

Little further progress, however, was reported of this movement for 'moral reform' on which Fraser had placed so much hope. He now complained that while the *True Scotsman* had invoked the loathing of the very large class of 'occasional tipplers', it had not been supported by teetotallers for upholding strong total abstinence views. Many of them were narrow-minded, dominated by reactionary priests and totally indifferent to the question of political rights.

A vast number of teetotallers [concluded Fraser] are bigots; and scowl at their views being supported in a Chartist newspaper. This fact is very well known; and it is also very well known that comparatively few of this class will give any support to a Moral Reform newspaper.

There was no encouragement for advocating abstinence and the only reason for doing so was that

some one must break the silence of the press ... We have done this ... The industrious classes, once sober, will shame all others out of the opposite practice, and introduce an era of morality, prosperity, and joy such as the world has hitherto never seen.

This lack of support for the *True Scotsman* which so sorrowed John Fraser proved fatal. It ceased publication on 27 March 1841, and both the Chartist and temperance movements lost a valuable, though voluble, ally.[7]

NOTES

1. *Scottish Patriot*, 20 and 27 July; 17 and 24 August 1839; vol. i, p. 329; vol. ii, p. 294.
   True Scotsman, 17 August; 23 November; 14 and 28 December 1839; 25 January; 22 February 1840.
   Hawick Co-operative Store Company, jubilee *History*, 1889, pp. 16–19.
   New Moral World, 15 August 1840.
   Northern Star, 14 September; 2 and 23 November 1839.
2. *True Scotsman*, 25 January; 22 February; 16 May; 11 July; 7 November 1840.
   Scottish Patriot, 27 April; 1 August; 19 September 1840.
   Northern Star, 22 August 1840.
   Chartist Circular, p. 286.
   The Reformers' Gazette, 7 August 1841

3. *Scottish Patriot*, vol. ii, p. 262. (For an earlier, but similar, account of Thomson's co-operative activities, see *Glasgow Argus*, 14 August 1834.)
4. *True Scotsman*, 1 February; 16 May 1840.
   Scottish Patriot, vol. ii, pp. 233, 265.
   Northern Star, 20 June 1840.
5. *Scottish Patriot*, vol. ii, pp. 307–8.
   True Scotsman, 16 May 1840.
6. *True Scotsman*, 14 and 21 November 1840.
   Scottish Patriot, 12 September; 28 November 1840.
   Chartist Circular, 19 December 1840.
7. *Chartist Circular*, 9 January 1841.
   True Scotsman, 9 and 16 January; 13 and 20 February; 20 March 1841.
   Northern Star, 16 January 1841.

CHAPTER ELEVEN

Christian Chartism

Religious roots were deeply implanted in the men who established Chartism in Scotland. 'Appoint only moral men, who have the fear of God before their eyes' was the annual admonition of John McKerrow, the treasurer of the Gorbals Chartist association. Many of the Scottish Chartists were sceptics in certain religious matters, but not in regard to the Scriptures or Christian belief. Almost universally they were devout, God-fearing men, whose scepticism was confined to the behaviour of 'false pastors'. One Chartist newspaper went so far as to declare

The man who is not a Chartist is not a Christian, otherwise than in name ... Practical Christianity can never be reconciled to narrow selfish systems of politics ... Real Chartism seeks to do justice to every man without exception. It is therefore a holy and sacred principle—a principle which must be engraved on the heart of any man who loves justice, who loves humanity, who loves the Christian religion.

Faced with prevailing social distress, the Chartists found it difficult to reconcile their belief in a 'God-ordained brotherhood of man' with existing practice. 'In the midst of national abundance', read the memorial of the Central Committee for Scotland to the Relief Synod, 'there exists a vast portion of the working classes doomed to struggle with almost perpetual famine—ill-clothed, ill-lodged, ill-educated, deprived of the means for mental and religious improvement.' All efforts to remedy such abuses, therefore, must surely be part of the fulfilment of God's will, and the Chartist movement became for its participants in Scotland merely a continuation of the age-long struggle carried on by their forefathers for civil and religious liberty. As in the days of the Covenanters, they were on God's side, and they had not the slightest doubt that God was on theirs.

'Study the New Testament,' exhorted the *Chartist Circular*. 'It contains the elements of Chartism.' Its message was the brotherhood of man, and the mission of Christianity was that of coupling freedom with social justice. One's duty, and the 'only possible basis of social and political justice', was to love one's neighbour as one's self, and to do one's utmost to advance his cause. Universal suffrage was clearly based 'on the revealed word of God', and 'a simple democracy was the only true order of government instituted by God'.

Little of this was new. Indeed, a great part of the strength of such doctrines among the Chartists lay in their very familiarity. The editor of the *Chartist Circular* was making not a complaint but merely what he considered a plain statement of fact when he wrote that

the people of Scotland are proverbially slow in adopting new opinions. They have a national reverence for the deeds and opinions of their fathers—they love every mountain and valley consecrated by the resistance to tryanny.[1]

Within recent years many of their ministers had encouraged them to play their part in the struggle for the Reform Bill. Even more recently, when the Established Church was convulsed over the questions of the 'Veto Act' of 1834 and of 'non-intrusion', interest in Church patronage and spiritual independence was not confined to the ranks of the Church of Scotland, nor to any narrow section of the Scottish people.

It therefore required little judicious prompting by the missionaries of the political unions to persuade many Scotsmen of the connection between Christianity and the struggle for social and political freedom. And since no true Christian could fail to sympathise with the Chartist cause, it was hardly surprising that, in the early stages of the movement, the Chartists should have looked confidently to the Churches for support and leadership. Most of the Chartist committees quickly appointed deputations to wait upon the ministers of their parish and solicit their support. In February 1839, for instance, the Glasgow Universal Suffrage Association applied in this fashion to no less than eighty-three clergymen—and got one sympathetic reply. Encouragement and wise guidance were, at first, sincerely hoped for, but later canvassing efforts were usually designed to 'expose' the 'inhumanity' of the clergy for propaganda purposes, or else to obtain their help for specific 'humanitarian, non-political' projects.

From the clergymen of the Established Church, however, no co-operation was ever expected. They were known to be anti-democratic, honest opponents of reform. It was from the Dissenting clergy, especially the ministers of the United Secession Church and of the Relief Synod, that support was confidently anticipated. The response was a profound and bitter disappointment to many devout Chartist Dissenters. From the outset almost all clergymen showed the greatest diffidence about committing themselves to the Chartist cause, and approaches to the Relief and United Secession synods were invariably rejected on account of the political character of the memorials.

Even clergymen who were well known locally for their reforming zeal found paltry excuses for refusing to sign the National Petition, and their rather less paltry excuses for refusing to preach sermons, at which collections might be taken for the defence of insurrectionary Chartists, were regarded with even greater astonishment and indignation. Despite this, much valuable assistance was forthcoming in the provision of church halls for Chartist meetings; at Airdrie, Kirkintilloch and West Kilbride, Chartist meetings normally took place in the Secession churches, while at Hawick, Hamilton, Tollcross, Colinsburgh and several other places the Chartists were permitted to use the Relief churches.[2]

The Chartists were loath to come to the conclusion that substantial support was not going to be forthcoming from their ministers. It might take some time before their own honest and laudable motives were understood, and before the prejudice against Christians 'meddling in politics' was overcome. There were, moreover, several notable exceptions amongst the clergy to this mode of behaviour. In particular there were the outstanding examples of the Rev. Patrick Brewster, of Paisley Abbey parish, who defied the prejudices of his colleagues in the Established Church by his advocacy of total abstinence, poor law reform and Chartism, and the Rev. Archibald Browning, of Tillicoultry.

Ministers who condescended to lecture to Chartist associations were assured of attentive and admiring audiences. If they wished to become local heroes, ministers had only to say a few words in support of the principle of universal suffrage. Even this became increasingly difficult for them, as Chartist admiration could be embarrassing for the recipient, and the Rev. George Campbell found it necessary to persuade the *Scottish Patriot* to correct the impression given by the report of some 'well-meaning Strathaven Chartist' who had hailed him as 'a staunch advocate of Universal Suffrage ... and one of the most acute and original thinkers of his age. 'Some ministers who had been sympathetic to the Chartists in 1838 cooled off as newspaper opinion hardened against Chartism in 1839.

Like the Established Church ministers, the Baptists were seldom sympathetic, and in some Baptist congregations 'intolerance' was shown to Chartist members. Several numbers of the *Scottish Patriot*, the *Scottish Vindicator* and the *Chartist Circular* contained attacks upon the 'hypocritical' and 'narrow-minded intolerance' of the Baptist faithful.

Towards their much abused brethren, the Irish Catholics, there was a good deal of fellow feeling amongst the Chartists, but this feeling was seldom reciprocated, and it was only in the later stages of the movement that the 'Irish' Catholics played any significant part. In the early stages of the agitation Dr Donnelly, with his 'mellifluous brogue', was well known in Greenock and the west of Scotland, and was in constant demand as a lecturer. It was clear from the numerous debates between the Glasgow Chartists and the Glasgow O'Connellites, especially in 1840, that the decisive factor in determining the conduct of the 'Irish' Catholics was always the current attitude of Daniel O'Connell, who remained one of the best-hated men in the eyes of the Chartists ever since his condemnation of the Glasgow cotton spinners and trade union activities. Few members of the Roman Catholic Church, even in Glasgow and the west of Scotland, appear to have taken any real interest in Chartism; those who did so, such as Con Murray, who became a leader of the O'Connorite faction in Glasgow, had to reckon with expulsion from Catholic societies. Nor did Chartism ever take root in the Western Isles and the Highlands, where, in addition to any religious difficulties, there was virtual isolation of the Gaelic-speaking population.

The spectacle of defiance of the State by the Established Church delighted the Chartists. Those people who had most abused them as revolutionaries had no scruples about defying the government, about setting aside the judgments of the Court of Session, nor about refusing to submit to the law of the land. The Chartist newspapers frequently entered into the non-intrusion controversy, normally for the sake of scoring points over their opponents. But many Chartists showed real concern over the points of doctrine which were at issue, and Robert Malcolm of the *Scottish Patriot*, at least, saw that even more harm might be done to freedom and democracy by the party led by Dr Thomas Chalmers.

> The great struggle they maintain [he wrote in March 1840] is to transfer the power of Ecclesiastical legislation from the State to the Church Courts. Let that object be accomplished, and the Church Courts may do with the people what they please ... If the claim of exclusive legislation is well-founded, the Church has the absolute power of depriving the people of any voice in the election of their pastors. This power, at present, they do not exercise. But we challenge the party who call themselves non-intrusionists to deny that, according to their ideal of ecclesiastical power they possess it.[3]

It was this danger which the Rev. Patrick Brewster offered later as his reason for refusing to leave the establishment. There might still be more freedom and less intolerance within the State Church than in the Free Church.[4]

By March 1840 an important secondary movement was beginning to emerge from within the framework of the Scottish Chartist movement. In many parts of the country Chartists were now organising religious services every Sabbath, and in some places permanent congregations had been formed which designated themselves the 'Christian Chartist Churches'. This movement had grown out of the application, especially since the autumn of 1839, of 'exclusive dealing' against clergymen. The idea had been first seriously voiced in April 1839, when James Moir warned his fellow churchmen, the 'Voluntaries', that if they did not give greater support to the movement for the Charter there would be no alternative but to found a new religious denomination, which would embrace the principles of Christianity and Chartism.

The Chartists of Hamilton 'set up on their own account' in religious worship in May 1839, and throughout that month they had regular attendances of eighty to a hundred persons at their services. In Paisley also, about then, the Chartists adopted the practice of conducting their own religious services, and conventicles were held every Sabbath in Millerston and Charleston. The *Scotch Reformers' Gazette* observed of these happenings:

> The greatest curiosity in the whole mania ... is the idea of preaching

which has got amongst the Paisley Chartists . . . The blue sky of heaven is their vaulted sanctuary, and the scene presents one of the finest landscapes in Scotland; it is, therefore, a concentration of the sublime and the ridiculous.

These events were widely publicised as a result of the Scottish convention of August 1839, and thereafter there were numerous reports of similar developments. At a meeting of the Bridgeton Radical Association on 4 September, a typical discussion on the inconsistency of Churchmen and Dissenters in their professions of regard for the spiritual welfare of the people, whilst they stood in the way of changes which would ameliorate their temporal condition, concluded in a decision to open the Universal Suffrage Hall for Sabbath worship services.

This experiment began with a sermon on 15 September—on the text 'How long shall the wicked triumph?' The success of this venture was reported by John Rodger, president of the Bridgeton Radicals, at a meeting of the Glasgow Universal Suffrage Association on 24 September, when he proposed that the hall of the Glasgow association should also be opened on Sundays for public worship. This proposal was adopted, and without the slightest delay the first of the religious services in the Universal Suffrage Hall, in the High Street, was given on Sunday 29 September 1839. In the forenoon Malcolm McFarlane, a cabinet-maker and one of the vice-presidents of the Glasgow association, delivered a discourse from the fourth verse of the fourteenth psalm: 'Have all the workers of iniquity no knowledge? who eat up my people as they eat bread, and call not upon the Lord'. In the evening McFarlane passed on to the fifth verse of the same psalm, dealing with the text 'They were in great fear, for God is in the generation of the righteous'. Meanwhile the congregation had gone through 'other devotional exercises' in the afternoon, when directors of the association 'read and expounded the Scriptures'. The collections for that day were devoted to the funds of the Central Committee for Scotland, and on the following Sunday they were to be given to the fund for the support of wives and children of patriots suffering in the cause of freedom.[5]

There was seldom, at this time, any firm intention of introducing Chartist services as a substitute for the older forms of organised religion. For several months yet, the intention was partly to influence clergymen, by boycotting churches where hostile ministers indulged in frequent abuse of the movement, partly to provide a place of worship 'for those who had been expelled from their congregations for advocating the People's Charter' and for those Chartists who had been made to feel uncomfortable in their own churches.

The Glasgow Universal Suffrage Association heard its first interim report on the scheme on 22 October, when Thomas Mair presented the findings of the religious worship committee. On all occasions the hall had been crowded with respectable people, and they were satisfied with the talents of those who had officiated, though it was disappointing that only three of the six members of the committee had officiated. The committee had already a 'considerable amount of money on hand', and they recommended the purchase of a suitable Bible. Some remuneration should also be made to the precentor, who was 'a poor workman'.

By the end of October, Chartist Sabbath services were being held regularly by the Glasgow, Bridgeton, Gorbals, Paisley and Hamilton associations, and the experiment was beginning to spread rapidly. At the end of December 1839, Shettleston could claim to be merely following the 'example of the other towns and villages throughout the country' in worshipping God 'according to their conscience—having set up on their own account'.

Sometimes the religious service committees managed to secure the services of reverend gentlemen. Whenever this happened it was accounted a major success for the committee—as when the Rev. Mr Calder preached to the Glasgow Chartists on 6 October, or when the Rev. Mr Percy preached to the Bridgeton Chartists on 27 October. Normally, however, they had to rely on lay preachers, several of whom became very popular. In particular, Andrew Cassels of Partick, William Tait of Auchinearn, Charles McEwan of Gorbals, and Arthur O'Neill of Maryhill were in constant demand, and were required to preach on most Sundays.

O'Neill, the youngest member of the Central Committee for Scotland and a former student of theology, quickly became the most energetic and popular of the lay preachers. On 13 October, when he preached in Glasgow, the Chartist Hall was 'packed to suffocation', and hundreds were refused admission. On 27 October, when he preached the first Chartist sermon to be heard in Campsie, the hall was crowded to excess. 'A large proportion of the fair sex' was present to hear this young man with a growing reputation, and the neighbouring village of Milton was 'almost completely forsaken'.

At Shettleston, where 'large and attentive' audiences had attended every Sabbath since the inauguration of services there, O'Neill preached to the largest meeting, on 26 January 1840, when 'many females' were again to be found in the congregation. From a lecturing-cum-preaching tour in Fifeshire in November, O'Neill had already reported that

Chartist congregations, to become general in every corner of the land [required] only Chartist preachers—men who would tell the truth, and the whole truth, and who would not scruple to raise their voices against any voice, whether in Church or State ... [6]

During 1840 the practice of conducting their own services spread to at least thirty localities, and in twenty of these places the further step was taken of formally establishing Christian Chartist congregations. This final step was usually approached with considerable caution. Difficult questions of doctrine, and of dispensing the outward ordinances of religion, such as baptism and marriage, were involved. In this matter, leadership was provided by the Glasgow Worshipping Assembly, which on 28 February adopted a committee report on the rules and ordinances to be followed by that body, which would thereafter be called 'The Christian Church'.

Marriage ceremonies were to be carried out by the acting chairman or vice-chairman of the church. The parties to the union must be 'of proper age' and attested by two witnesses to be 'free'. Baptism could be performed at any age, since the Scriptures indicated no particular age. Neither could any illusion be found in Scripture to the frequency with which communion should be held, so that decision would be left to the members who would 'assist each other at this solemn service'. All members would be required to act in turn as chairman and vice-chairman of the church. The former would open, and the latter would conclude, the service of the day, which would also include a sermon from a preacher. The same procedure, within the limits of those who had an understanding of music, would be followed for conducting the Psalmody.

All would be welcome at their services, with no distinction between rich and poor. Seat letting was an unnecessary evil, and the only overriding rules would be the Bible and the advice of the Apostle Paul, to 'let all things be done decently and in order'. For the funds of the church, they would depend entirely on the free and voluntary offerings of the people. Part of these funds would be appropriated to the relief of the poor, who had always been the peculiar care of Christian Churches. Part might also be drawn upon to finance missionaries, who would be sent out to explain their views, and where possible to create churches.[7]

The new arrangements in Glasgow were entered into by 'The Christian Church' on 1 March 1840, when three sermons were preached, three baptisms were held, and sixty-five people were enrolled as members. Their meeting place was the Mechanics' Hall, Tontine Close, which became the focus of Christian Chartism in the Glasgow area. Within a few weeks an address issued by the committee announced that the field of operations was fast widening —faster, indeed, than they could supply instructors. Those already engaged in the task were doing their utmost, but the work was too great for them to accomplish without further physical help. In Glasgow they had raised the 'standard of universal peace', but they needed fresh talent.

Twelve months previously such a proposal would have met with considerable suspicion from many 'respectable Chartists', but by March 1840 the project was already palatable. Mainly this had been due to the remarkable success of the Chartist lay preachers, coupled with the growing hostility of the clergy. Many who had remained lukewarm to Chartism were roused to indignation by the attitude of their Voluntary clergymen preaching openly against Chartism, or trying to deny Chartists access to their services or the use of their church halls. An interesting case took place in Newburgh, where fifty or sixty members of the Secession church seceded when the church committee refused the Chartists the use of the hall. Half the seceders formed a Christian Chartist church, while the remainder formed an independent church.

The success of the Chartist church movement was beginning to alarm some clergymen, even some of the most hostile of the Dissenters, into a more sympathetic or neutral attitude. At the United Secession Church synod in December 1840 the Rev. Andrew Marshall, of Kirkintilloch, who had been a favourite target of the *Chartist Circular* and who believed that there were few clergymen more obnoxious to the Chartists than himself, proposed that in view of the growing alienation of the working classes from the Dissenting Churches it should be the duty of ministers to save the masses to the Churches by showing some sympathy to the efforts of the people for an extended franchise. While ministers should not participate in political agitation for the Charter, they should avow on 'all proper occasions' that they were in favour of a more extended franchise.

Amongst the ministers who changed their minds about Chartism was the Rev. Mr Harvey of Calton parish, several of whose parishioners had left his church because of his violent denunciations of Chartist principles. Yet at the time of the Leeds Household Suffrage Conference in January 1841, Harvey was to be found lecturing on 'Universal Suffrage' in a series of lectures showing the duty of the middle classes to assist the unenfranchised in gaining the vote. He spoke of the groundlessness of the fears regarding the consequences of universal suffrage, and further redeemed himself in the eyes of the Chartists by declaring, in Perth, that the party led by Dr Chalmers was ten times more guilty of revolution than had been John Frost and the Welsh Chartists.[8]

Encouraged by the success of their policy of placing the Chartist churches on a more permanent basis, several Chartists now began to envisage the establishment of a Chartist Synod, a universal Chartist Church, embracing all the local Chartist churches. By January 1841 it was considered opportune to hold a delegate conference of the Chartist churches of Scotland to consider how best they could assist each other, and whether any central or unitary association should be formed.

At this time there were about twenty Chartist congregations organised on a fairly permanent basis. Around Glasgow, these existed at Bridgeton, Gorbals, Shettleston, Partick and Pollockshaws. Slightly farther away were congregations at Campsie, Eaglesham, Greenock, Lanark, Alexandria, Hamilton, Kilmarnock, Kilbarchan and Paisley, while in the east of Scotland churches had been formed at Arbroath, Alloa, Dundee, Inverleven, Linlithgow, Newburgh and St Ninians. In addition to these congregations, Sabbath worship was conducted fairly regularly under Chartist auspices in Aberdeen, Ayr, Anderston, Arbroath, Bannockburn, Dalkeith, Larkhall, Leven, Montrose, Saltcoats, Stonehouse, St Rollox and Tollcross. Several of these may have been organised as Chartist churches, and there seems to have been a Christian Chartist church at Johnstone for some months in 1840.

'A Chartist place of worship,' declared the *True Scotsman* on 2 January 1841, 'is to be found on the Lord's Day in almost every town of note from Aberdeen to Ayr.' Surprisingly, however, there was no evidence of Chartist worship at that time in Edinburgh, Dunfermline, Dumfries or Perth, though during 1841 Chartist services spread to Perth, Edinburgh, Forfar and Strathaven, and three new Chartist churches were established at Arbroath, Anderston and Cupar.[9]

Only a few of the Chartist churches owned their buildings. This was apparently the case at Arbroath, Kilbarchan, Greenock and one or two of the Glasgow churches. Usually it was announced that congregations met in their 'Chartist Hall of Worship', but normally these were premises rented by the local Chartist association. At Arbroath, the congregation progressed from a wooden erection, covered by canvas, to a rather more imposing building which remained in post-Chartist days as St Ninian's Chapel. In Glasgow the Chartists acquired St Ann's Church (the 'Noddy Church') in Great Hamilton Street, which had belonged to the Established Church of Scotland.

While the enrolled membership of these churches might remain small, the number of fairly regular adherents was substantial, and was often limited chiefly by the size of the hall. At St Ninian's, where there were a hundred adherents, only thirty were members. The Newburgh Christian Chartist church must have been the smallest, having only twenty members. At Campsie, the average attendance, for several years apparently, varied between 150 and 200, while at Kilbarchan, which was one of the strongest churches, there were 120 members by the end of 1840.[10]

Once Chartists had established a local reputation as preachers, they would receive numerous invitations to preach at neighbouring towns and villages. If they were greatly appreciated, the Chartist Church Committee might offer to engage them and they would be 'given a call' as regular preachers. Offers of permanent employment were also made, on occasion, to Chartists on lecture tours, and there was some degree of competition amongst the democratic church committees in their efforts to obtain the services of the best Chartist preachers. Amongst the 'pastors' with regular employment were three members of the 1839 General Convention: John McCrae at Kilbarchan, Strathaven, Hamilton and Dundee—over a period of seven years—William Thomason at Alexandria, and Abram Duncan at Arbroath, Alloa and Falkirk. Whereas McCrae migrated in response to more attractive offers of employment, Abram Duncan was forced to move because his flock could no longer afford to pay him.

Thomason, McCrae and most of the other pastors acted as school-masters to the children of Chartists, and their meeting-place served as church, day school, evening school, committee room, concert hall and public meeting place, according to the needs of the moment. Chartist schools with over a hundred pupils were conducted in Alexandria, Arbroath, Greenock, Gorbals, Strathaven and Hamilton.

At several churches where regular pastors were appointed, objections were raised to payment for such duties. To many Chartists the practice of paying clergymen savoured of impropriety, and the compromise was often adopted of paying not for preaching but for teaching duties in the Chartist school. At the conference in January 1841, it was agreed that lay preachers should receive a fair rate of compensation for time lost from their work. Missionaries and visiting preachers should receive, in addition, travelling expenses.

The procedures followed in establishing congregations, and in appointing pastors, occasionally met with some criticism. John Fraser believed that some of these congregations had been formed too hastily, without due consideration of 'the principles of Christian Union', and without sufficient information as to the Christian character of the members. Some pastors had been chosen more on account of their qualifications as political lecturers than because of appropriate character or talent for the pastoral office. Such criticisms of the Chartist churches were certainly valid, and 'mistakes' such as Fraser alleged were made. Yet there is no evidence to suggest that those who fell into such 'error' did not do so quite deliberately. The whole spirit of such criticism was foreign to the messianic spirit in which this politico-religious development was carried out.

Despite an increase in number of Chartist congregations in 1841, there was no further attempt to unite them in any wider organisation, and no further delegate conferences of the Christian Chartist churches took place. After 1841 there appears to have been a steady decline in the number of localities where Chartist services were held, but the stronger congregations continued to exist for several years, at Alexandria, Campsie, Dundee, Gorbals, Glasgow, Kilbarchan and Paisley; when the Rev. William Hill, the editor of the *Northern Star*, toured Scotland in August 1843, he found that the chief strength of Scottish Chartism now resided in the Christian Chartist churches.[11]

The Chartist church movement was a manifestation of the deeply religious spirit which pervaded the Scottish Chartist agitation, and throughout the latter years of the movement provided it with a backbone whose strength remained considerable during the periods in which Chartism was at an almost complete ebb in England.

NOTES

1. *Chartist Circular*, pp. 1, 9, 222, 433.
   Scottish Patriot, vol. i, p. 373; vol. ii, p. 168; 23 May 1840.
2. *True Scotsman*, 15 December 1838; 30 March 1839.
   Scottish Patriot, 8 February 1840.
3. *True Scotsman*, 6 April 1839.
   Chartist Circular, pp. 374, 572.
   Scottish Vindicator, 2 November 1839.
   Scottish Patriot, 17 August; 28 September 1839; 11 January 1840; vol. ii, pp. 57, 107, 161, 170, 294, 405–6.
4. P. Brewster, *Seven Chartist and Military Discourses*, 1843, appendix.
5. *Glasgow Argus*, 25 April 1839.
   Scotch Reformers' Gazette, 20 July 1839.
   True Scotsman, 18 May 1839.
   Scottish Patriot, 17 August; 7, 21 and 28 September; 5 October 1839.
6. *Scottish Patriot*, vol. i, pp. 233, 256, 278, 281, 329; vol. ii, p. 294.
   J. Cameron, *The Parish of Campsie*, 1892, pp. 116–18.
7. *Scottish Patriot*, vol. ii, p. 153.
8. *Scottish Patriot*, vol. ii, pp. 345, 360; 7 March; 26 September 1840.
   True Scotsman, 16 May 1840; 9 and 30 January; 6 February; 13, 20 and 27 March 1841.
   Northern Star, 3 October 1840.
9. *True Scotsman*, 2 January 1841.
   Northern Star, 16 January 1841.
10. *Scottish Patriot*, 27 March 1840.
    True Scotsman, 6 June; 1 August 1840; 13 March 1841.
    Cameron, pp. 116–17.
    McBain, *Arbroath, Past and Present*, 1887, pp. 54–5.
11. *True Scotsman*, 20 March 1841.
    Scottish Patriot, 27 March 1841.
    Northern Star, 9 and 16 January; 19 February; 11 September; 23 November 1841; 29 January 1842; 2 September 1843; 19 April 1844.

CHAPTER TWELVE

Corn law repeal and middle class union

An issue which the Scottish Chartists were never satisfactorily able to resolve was their attitude to overtures from middle class reformers, especially in relation to corn law repeal and suffrage extension. Most of the Scottish Chartists regarded the corn laws in much the same light as their brethren in the north of England regarded the new Poor Law Amendment Act—as the prime example of perverse class legislation—but with the important difference that it was the Tories and aristocracy who were regarded fundamentally as the enemy of the working classes, no matter what 'trickery' the Whigs might attempt.

Most of the Scottish Chartists regarded themselves as 'out-and-out Repealers', and it was axiomatic that corn law repeal would be the first legislative measure of a Parliament elected on a universal suffrage basis. In view of the long history of working class hostility to the corn laws, it was hardly to be expected that one movement should regard the other as a rival. In many districts the rank and file of the repeal agitation overlapped, in 1838 and 1839 at least, with that of Chartism. Many of the local Chartist leaders quoted with approval from the *Anti-Corn Law Circular*, and appreciated the way in which the missionaries employed by the League reflected the social grievances of the people. Corn law repeal received prominence on Chartist banners and platforms, and it was enumerated in the lists of objectives in the policy declarations of such papers as the *Ayshire Examiner*, the *Scottish Patriot* and the *Glasgow Saturday Post*. Many of the Chartist leaders, such as James Moir, Dr John Taylor and William Pattison in Glasgow, and William Carnegie in Dunfermline, had been directors of anti-corn law associations in the 1833–36 period.

Somewhat surprisingly, it was the Birmingham Radicals rather than Feargus O'Connor who first ruffled this relationship. During the summer months of 1838, when the efforts of William Weir of the *Glasgow Argus* were resulting in a crop of repeal associations being formed in the west of Scotland, the *Birmingham Journal* deprecated all unions which held out symptomatic grievances as the prime object of attack. The people of Kilmarnock and the west of Scotland were advised to leave such 'little goes as anti-corn-law associations' to the less clear sighted patriots. The *Northern Star*, on the other hand, was understood to be advocating immediate repeal. The Birmingham lead was followed by John Fraser and Abram Duncan, who made efforts, in the east and south of Scotland in the autumn of 1838, to expose the repeal agitation as a Whig plot to divert the support of the people from Chartism. In Glasgow, Bailie Alexander Hedderwick, who was about to be elected a director of the Glasgow Anti-Corn Law Association, lost the election as member of the General Convention because he refused to give sole priority to Chartism, while Alexander Purdie, secretary of the Glasgow Chartists, was attacked for his close relationship with the Anti-Corn Law Association. In Ayr, Dumfries, Dalkeith, Campsie, Edinburgh, Kilmarnock, Kilsyth, Kirkintilloch, Leslie and Newmilns, Chartists took an interest in repeal meetings, but only in a few places were their associations definitely hostile to repeal. Nor was there any readiness to interpret the declaration of the General Convention on this issue as a declaration of war on the repeal agitation.

From March to November 1839, the Chartists took little notice of the repeal movement. In Forfarshire and Perthshire, where George Troup was active on behalf of repeal, there were debates and discussions between Chartist and League supporters, and in Glasgow, in July, the *Scottish Patriot* appeared as the organ of the Chartists, promising to advocate repeal of the corn laws as one of the most important points in its policy. Opinion, however, was hardening in Chartist circles against the leading members of the League—a dislike which was largely due to the insinuations of Feargus O'Connor, and which seemed to grow in proportion to his increasing influence over many sections of Scottish Chartism. Partly it was due to disappointment with the attitude of leading repealers towards Chartism. Many of them seemed to prefer to make denunciations of Chartist leaders rather than to propose plans for collaboration between the two movements, and the fading away of much of the middle class support which had been forthcoming in May 1838 deeply aggrieved the Chartists.[1]

The intensification of the anti-corn law campaign, in the autumn and winter of 1839, raised one of the most difficult problems which the Universal Suffrage Central Committee had to face. When it tried to define its policy towards the repeal movement on 14 November, its discussions ended in stalemate. Matthew Cullen, the joint president, urged denial of Chartist support to any party which refused to promote the principles of universal suffrage. The Committee should declare that it was the duty of every true Chartist to attend all public meetings and assert the political rights and privileges of the productive classes. Chartist amendments, therefore, should be moved at all public meetings. Against this attitude, Pattison and Thomson argued that the middle classes had now joined the working classes in the struggle for repeal, and that it was impossible to prevent the people from supporting the repealers. The working classes by themselves could not carry the Charter, while the middle classes could not by themselves repeal the corn laws. According to Pattison, some Trades discussed only repeal, and great numbers of the working classes were decidedly in favour of both agitations. Arthur O'Neill reported from a lecture tour in central Scotland that he had been converted from opposition to the repeal agitation 'by my brother Chartists ... everywhere', and he was convinced that the corn law agitation was doing the Chartist cause much good.

When the debate was renewed a fortnight later, Cullen's proposals were adopted, by a single vote, and the new policy was tested, on 21 December, at 'one of the largest public meetings ever held' in the Glasgow town hall. This was a repeal meeting which was to open the Scottish campaign, and was attended by the two Glasgow members of Parliament, in addition to many bailies and councillors. Lord Provost Mills presided over the meeting, which ended in the election of a Chartist chairman, confusion, the hurried departure of the platform party, and the passing of Chartist resolutions.

After this setback, the Anti-Corn law Association decided that if they could not pass their resolutions at public meetings without Chartist interference, they would grant admittance to their Glasgow meetings only to electors. Even this, however, did not ensure an easy passage for their resolutions, and when the repealers resumed their disrupted meeting, on 27 December, the Chartists were still present in some strength, insisting that universal suffrage was the only way to repeal the corn laws. Confusion again ensued when the chairman declared the repeal motion carried without putting the Chartist amendment to the vote; and the meeting ended with the police superintendent, and a posse of police, threatening to put out the gas if the meeting did not disperse quietly.[2]

These meetings were noticed by Chartists and repealers far from Glasgow. The *Champion* was again full of praise for the Scottish Radicals, and was highly delighted with the disruptive proceedings in Glasgow. Letters expressing sorrow at Chartist tactics were received by Allan McFadyen, the secretary of the Glasgow Chartists, who hailed them as 'an earnest of a better spirit on the part of the middle classes'; and the *Glasgow Argus* perceptively observed that 'the Chartists are perhaps less moved by their love of Universal Suffrage as an abstract proposition than by the slighting indifference which the middle-class exhibit towards the general welfare'.

Elsewhere, local associations had also been faced with the growing urgency of deciding their attitude to repeal. Abram Duncan reported distress amongst the unemployed in Dundee, where 2,500 men and women were starving. Many mill owners were on the list of bankruptcies; trade was believed to be on a worse footing than in any other town in the country; and the Anti-Corn Law Association was making strenuous efforts to persuade the people that repeal was the remedy. He and Robert Lowery were counselling the Chartists in Fifeshire and Forfarshire against opposing the repealers. The people should sign all the anti-corn law petitions, though it would do them little good, as repeal would not be gained without bringing the country to the brink of revolution.

Within a few weeks the Glasgow policy had been followed in many parts of Scotland. Carefully organised repeal meetings were *subjected* to control or disruption, and the preparations of the repealers for the election of delegates to the anti-corn law dinner in Manchester on 13 January 1840 led to several sharp conflicts. From Dumfries, Edinburgh and Paisley came complaints that the supporters of the League were attempting to hold public meetings without either informing the public or allowing these meetings to appoint their own chairman. In Edinburgh, where they tried to exclude the Chartists by charging a 6d admission fee, a physical struggle resulted from the election of the Chartist nominee and the successful attempt to instal him in the chair in place of the Lord Provost.

In most places, as in Edinburgh, Markinch and Ayr, the proceedings followed a fairly simple pattern, with the Chartists imposing a chairman, or a set of resolutions, or both, upon the meeting. Sometimes, however, the position was rather more confused. At Greenock the Chartists failed to elect their nominee to the chair but were able to carry their amendment. At Dundee the 'Whig tricks' of the chairman succeeded, and the Chartists were left full of wrath and benumbed. In Paisley, Provost Bissett, formerly vice-president of the Renfrewshire Political Union, and the Rev. Patrick Brewster were appointed delegates to the dinner, at a meeting which rejected a Chartist amendment proposed by Robert Cochran and Samuel Miller, of the moderate section of the Paisley Chartists. Brewster declared himself a Chartist at heart, and that 'I never will devote my time or money to any purpose other than Chartism', only to be denounced by the extremist faction, led by Edward Polin, as a corn law repealer and an 'expediency Whig'.

Another curious meeting was held at Dumfries on 2 January, where the opposition to the organisers of the meeting, the provost and the editor of the *Dumfries Times*, was led not by the Chartists but by a lawyer, Mr Johnston, who objected to the way in which the meeting had been called. He moved a long resolution which coupled total abolition of the corn laws with the National Petition. The Dumfries Chartists were not willing to be wooed in this way, and defeated Johnston's resolution with one declaring the imprudence of turning aside from the Charter.[3]

These tactics infuriated the Whig and liberal press, which rained storms of abuse on 'these Chartist vagabonds' who outraged every public meeting. Such tantrums, however, only encouraged the Chartists once they had embarked on their moderately exciting course. By this stage of the movement, they found it preferable to have their 'infamy' highlighted in the public eye than to be ignored. It could not be disguised, however, that most of the middle class supporters of universal suffrage were alarmed by the reports of Chartist conduct in the non-Chartist press. In a letter to the *Sun*, W. S. Villiers Sankey, the former Member of Convention for Edinburgh, hoped to allay such middle class misgivings.

The operatives [he declared] have at present but one really influential right of freemen left them, namely that of taking a part in public meetings. Were they, however, to use this right only in accordance with the views of the enfranchised, it would be worth nothing to them...They should use their present sole privilege as a wedge, and continue to drive it home, till the necessity of granting them the franchise be admitted. The right of constitutionally stopping all proceedings at public meetings is to them what the right of stopping the supplies was to the House of Commons.

Offers to compromise were sometimes made by the repealers, and on a few occasions from the Chartist side. Such offers were usually spurned, but the pattern of Chartist intrusion at repeal meetings was still not one of universal hostility. At Strathaven both sides adopted a petition for repeal, accompanied by a prayer demanding universal suffrage, which was moved by James Currie Esq., of Turnlaw, and the Rev. George Campbell. At Denny, farmer Rea agreed with the principles of the Charter and successfully appealed for the appointment of a joint committee to modify the repeal petition to placate the Chartists. In Crieff the repeal leaders found interference by the Chartists out of place at a repeal meeting, but agreed to support a further meeting which would be in favour of the Charter. At these and other meetings in Markinch, Dalry, Lochwinnoch, Pollockshaws and Kirriemuir, the Chartist party showed a willingness to compromise, so that joint petitions could be adopted. Out of such meetings arose a revived belief in the practicability of a middle and working class alliance, and in the benefits of conciliation for both movements. These feelings were expressed in Stirling, Dunfermline, Perth and Auchterarder. Faced with a by-election in April 1840, the reformers of Perth agreed to unite on repeal and household suffrage, while in nearby Auchterarder the electors and non-electors agreed to form an association which would couple their principles.[4]

This evidence of mutual co-operation between Chartists and repealers was beginning to cause some dubiety about the advisability of the general Chartist tactics. 'New Light Quaker' of Dunfermline was probably speaking for many others when he voiced his disapproval of disruptive tactics in a letter to the *Scottish Patriot* in April 1840:

This time last year, when we were in full organisation...we were excusable in kicking every minor agitation out of our way...But matters are now very different. Our movement is broken in pieces. We have no organisation, no union...no leaders or such leaders as are more dangerous to those that are with them than to those that are against them. Why then should we endeavour to nullify the efforts of others for a general good? ... We ought not only, not to oppose the repealers but we ought to back them unitedly and singly.

At this stage, the question of repeal and the Chartist attitude towards the middle classes became bound up with that of household suffrage, and whether the Chartists could be satisfied with the promise of any extension of the suffrage which was less than universal manhood suffrage. For several years the main current of Chartist discussions on repeal was to be inextricably bound up with the issues of household suffrage and complete suffrage.

The danger of this growing division of opinion in the ranks of the Chartists was pointed out by the *Scottish Patriot* on 11 April, when an editorial counselled the immediate discussion of this question in every district. If necessary, a delegate conference should be held to assess Chartist feeling, and to decide Chartist policy in the event of 'the middle classes coming out upon an unqualified household suffrage'. The most important consideration was that 'whatever course is to be adopted, must be done by the Chartists as a whole, the minority yielding to the majority. If this is not done, the most serious results are to be apprehended.'

This appeal seemed opportune at a time when the Anti-Corn Law League was deciding to combine a programme of parliamentary reform, including suffrage extension, with its free trade programme. But even before this policy had been officially enunciated by the League, Julian Harney, Feargus O'Connor and other Chartist leaders were busily confusing these issues and trying to sink the new proposals in a sea of obloquy, as mere deviations and tricks. Chartist lieutenants were quick to denounce this new move by the repealers, and at Old Cumnock, Mauchline and other parts of Ayrshire, during April and May, Julian Harney denounced the 'Household Suffrage Humbug' and exposed 'the real nature' of anti-corn law motions.

Harney, O'Connor and their Scottish admirers were determined to destroy any possibility of co-operation between the League and the Chartists on any programme of suffrage extension and free trade. Yet it is doubtful whether they would have succeeded in making this view prevail had it not been for the unhelpful existence of Daniel O'Connell. While Pattison and several of the Glasgow leaders could be expected to favour compromise, their position with the rank and file was always liable to be undermined by English demagogues and Irish demi-gods. They could seldom afford an incautious move, and, at this period, the most fatal of all possible moves was to appear to be in alliance with Daniel O'Connell. Their dilemma became more acute when O'Connell indicated that he regarded himself on the side of the operative classes on the question of parliamentary reform. It seemed too good to be true that the politician who had been most vehement in his diatribes against the trade unions, and in his encouragement of governmental action against them, should now be publicly stating that

all the political evils that afflict this country flow from the want of adequate representation in the House of Commons; from that house not being the organ of public sentiment; from that house representing but a class, and that class but a small one of the British people ... Above all there is not the slightest possibility of repealing the bread tax, without a further reform in which the operative classes will obtain votes, and be enabled to exercise constitutional influence over the representatives of the people.

Once O'Connell had involved himself in the issue of suffrage extension, and whether or not he was associated with the Anti-Corn Law League, the whole question, so far as the Chartists were concerned, revolved on his trustworthiness towards the working classes.

On this fundamental issue the *Scottish Patriot* was again cautious, and quoted from the *Statesman*:

There is no man of the present day so fit to be a popular leader; of audacity so dauntless, caution, so profound, and such consummate tact; but as regards the English Radicals, they have lost all faith in the leadership of public men. They have been used to serve the ends of a faction too often, again to trust those who have appeared to be parties to their deception; and amongst these, Mr. O'Connell stands conspicuous.

The *True Scotsman* was, as usual, more outspoken. Why had O'Connell failed to indulge in a similar display of energetic Radicalism 'when the people were high in hope, and unswayed by violent counsels'? Why had he delayed until he had been infuriated by Lord Stanley's Bill for the registration of voters? John Fraser's misgivings on the trustworthiness of O'Connell were increased by the latter's new formula, 'the extension of the suffrage upon a principle which should include as many as practicable of the middle and working classes'. This sounded very promising, and yet

Mr. O'Connell, if sincere, ought most religiously to have avoided the word 'practicability'. It is of Whig origin, and doubtful meaning in the hands of a double dealer. That Mr. O'Connell has been both a shuffler and a doubledealer, the working classes have too good reason to be well assured. They remember that he was an author of the Charter, in which there was not one word about practicability.[5]

Amongst the Glasgow Chartist leaders, opinion about O'Connell was unanimous, and almost all of them had participated in a series of debates on this subject with the admirers of 'The Liberator' resident in Glasgow. But on the conclusion that his touch must spell death to any prospect of union with the middle classes there was deep division. One group, headed by James Moir, Matthew Cullen and Thomas Gillespie, failed to see how any Chartists could be willing 'to trust the Whigs once more'. This group was determined to 'relax no effort to get the Whig ministry kicked out of office' even if this involved putting the Tories in their place.

The comparatively weak opposition to this view was led by W. C. Pattison, Robert Malcolm jun., John Rodger and Malcolm McFarlane, who could see no prospect of immediate success for the Chartist cause. While the principles of liberty and political knowledge were 'spreading like wild-fire', thousands were 'absolutely sick' of exertions to which they could see no end. Since the Chartists could not carry the Charter without middle class assistance, and since they could not force the middle classes to unite in the agitation for the Charter, the Chartists should meet the repealers in some genuine compromise, possibly upon the Durham programme of 1834, and not seek complete surrender from the corn law repealers. In their view, household suffrage was to be regarded merely as a stepping stone to universal suffrage. While the Chartists must still remain a distinct body demanding a long-term programme, they could 'assist in raising the cry for a measure which is nine-tenths of the whole demand'.

The speeches at the Chartist anniversary meeting on Glasgow Green on 21 May 1840 reflected only the uncompromising outlook. James Moir led the attack on 'quack-politician Daniel O'Connell, who was swearing by all the saints that he was now in earnest and no mistake'. The agitation for the Charter was exposing many quacks. Even the teetotallers would not turn Chartists, and the Voluntaries, who were much more than Chartists in Church affairs, were not Chartists in civil affairs. The extravagance of the Whigs was worse than the most extreme Tory profligacy, and the sooner the Tories were back the better. Moir trusted that the Chartists would never change their universal suffrage colours for those of household suffrage. They should never relax their opposition to the Whigs while helping the Tories into office.

No speeches favourable to middle class union were reported, and Rodger kept to safe ground with an attack on the clergy, and another on the Ministry for its cruel treatment of O'Connor and other political martyrs. Only a few of the Committee of Management attended, and, apart from the Springfield Works Band, Moir's chief support came from two west of Scotland 'physicals', who had never previously been honoured by the Glasgow Chartists. William Halliday of Greenock, editor of the short-lived Chartist newspaper *The Ayrshire Democrat*, dealt with the behaviour of the Whigs to the Irish, with their 'Coercion Bill', to the Canadians, with repression and bloodshed, and to the Scots with persecution of the Operative Cotton Spinners. John McCrae, formerly member of Convention for Ayrshire, indulged in one of his usual panegyrics about the better conditions enjoyed in previous centuries by serfs and vassals, who had apparently been comfortably lodged, clothed and fed, yet who had stained 'many a heathery hill with their best blood'.

The prevailing temper of the Glasgow Chartists seemed to be set against any compromise, and even the *Scottish Patriot*, which had been exhibiting schizophrenic tendencies in recent weeks, was able to make up its mind on the issue:

We are fully aware that repeal ... at present would be one sided, wholly for the masters' benefit, and the poor workmen would have to submit to a complete reduction of wages, and would have no power of redress. We have therefore resolved to take no part in a repeal agitation till we have got a sufficient control over the Parliament, which shall repeal not only the Corn Laws, but every other iniquitous law.[6]

Joseph Hume, Roebuck, O'Connell, Sharman Crawford and other leading Radicals did seem to be coming to the conclusion that a union of the middle and working classes ought to be effected, but they were taking such a painfully long time to show their hand that the possibility of such a union was being gravely prejudiced. Despite the efforts of a few perennial optimists, such as O'Neill and Pattison, who stubbornly refused to set their faces against the possibility that the middle classes might never be won over to the people's cause, the time was passing in which any middle class compromise might be acceptable to the Chartists. The ascendancy and influence of Feargus O'Connor was rapidly becoming absolute over the rank and file of the movement, and by the autumn of 1840 the most influential sections of the Scottish Chartists seemed to have decided that little was to be gained by union with doubtful reformers.

Little prompting was required from the *Northern Star*, in December 1840, to make many of the Chartist associations laugh at the efforts of the Leeds Reform Association to effect a union of reformers on the basis of household suffrage, and take up the Leeds invitation in a spirit of destructiveness. If O'Connell attended the Leeds conference he must be assured of an appropriate welcome, and even the Glasgow Christian Chartist church donated £1 towards the 'Welcome to Dan'. James Moir, who was elected the Glasgow delegate to the Leeds meeting, was instructed to express the determination of the Chartists of Glasgow 'not only not to countenance, but to oppose any agitation for any extension of the suffrage, short of that commonly called Universal Suffrage, as defined in the People's Charter'.

The *True Scotsman*, which had shown a more conciliatory tone towards O'Connell during December, considered the Leeds meeting a step in the right direction, which should be welcomed. The chartists were in a more advanced position than the Leeds reformers, and it would be madness for them to compromise their demands. Nevertheless, the Leeds Association deserved respect, not ridicule, and encouragement to 'hasten onwards'.

We have no right [explained Fraser] to abuse its members because they do not go as far as ourselves. We want the co-operation of the other classes ... If, when they begin to move, we begin to frown and scold, we act the part of fools ... We want no more than a clear stage and fair play to plead our holy cause.

Fraser rejoiced in the adoption of the resolution moved by Joseph Hume and seconded by James Moir, 'that the united efforts of all reformers ought to be directed to obtain such a further enlargement of the franchise as should make the interests of the representatives identical with those of the whole community'. Now, for the first time, concluded Fraser, the Chartists have 'got their case opened in the ranks of the middle classes'.[7]

Despite the conciliatory moves of Hume and Moir at Leeds, and the apathetic condition of Chartism in England, the tide of Chartist opinion in Scotland continued to veer away from reconciliation with middle class reformers. In March 1841 there was a wordy controversy in the *Scottish Patriot* between Robert Malcolm jun., the nephew of the editor, who had been demanding a more tolerant attitude to Joseph Hume, and those who regarded it as ridiculous to consider Hume a 'friend of the poor'. Malcolm was also laughed at when he concluded a lecture on 'Class Legislation' in the Glasgow Chartist church by proposing a union with the middle classes, and recommending the avoidance of all offensive language. Cullen, Colquhoun and others maintained that the Chartists had done everything possible to get the middle classes to co-operate, but they had found them hopelessly divided. They were Whigs and Tories, Corn Law Repealers, Undefined Extension of the Suffrage Men, Household Suffrage Humbugs, Voluntaries, Non-Intrusionists, Church Endowment Men and Black Slave Emancipators.

The need for a fresh approach to the whole problem was stressed in one of the last issues of the *True Scotsman* by John Fraser, who regretted this spirit of hostility against what was called 'a union with these men'. Generous, lofty-minded and Christian men such as John Collins and Arthur O'Neill were not betraying the cause of Chartism by encouraging such a union, if they were asking the middle classes to accept Chartist principles.

During the last two years [declared Fraser] the Chartists have been sowing the seeds of great principles, and not in vain for they have taken deep root in the public mind, and cannot now be eradicated ... We can hardly open a newspaper without finding a record of Chartist proceedings, or criticisms on its character and tendencies ... [But] having sown the seed, how are we to reap the harvest? Teaching the doctrine of political equality will not secure it. Three cheers for the charter at every meeting will not make it the law of the land. Many run to and fro and give a knowledge of its nature ... Societies may be organised, meetings held weekly and monies collected to pay their expenses; but all these things make no conquest to us of the charter. We may preach peace, charity, and goodwill to the middle and upper classes, but the goodly work will not secure for us the prize we want. Violence has failed to win it, and so even will mere peacefulness of conduct ... Public opinion may sanction the Charter; but that does not make it law. It can only be made law by a revolutionary declaration of a majority of the people in its favour, or by the decision of a majority of the members of Parliament to the same purpose. The former step is now but little contemplated by the people; we have therefore no alternative left but to promote the last ... So long as the two rotten factions are left to play their wonted tricks and games at the Poll, so long will the Charter be despised ... We call on the Chartists, then, to direct their attention to elections, and make their power felt on all these occasions.[8]

By the time of the general election in July 1841, considerable attention had been given to possible Chartist tactics in these elections. For several months James Moir and several other local leaders had been avowing their determination to destroy the power of the Whigs, even at the cost of supporting the Tories. The Glasgow Chartists were split between this 'Down with Whiggery at all costs' school, led by Moir, Ross and Proudfoot, and the supporters of Malcolm and Pattison. Private meetings between the factions found them unable to reach 'a proper understanding', and the rift was widened in public at a meeting on 21 June which was intended to provide a final decision on Glasgow Chartist policy. Robert Malcolm jun. 'condemned in unmeasured terms' those who intended to vote Tory, and was promptly castigated by Proudfoot for trying to saddle the charge of dishonesty on men exercising their conscientious opinion. Ross declared that he would not vote for a Whig, but might vote for a Tory, whatever Pattison and any others of the opposite party might say. Cullen defended Moir's attitude to the Whigs as necessary to prove to the latter that the Chartists held the balance of power, and accused those who advocated the opposite course of having been loudest in support of the Tory foreign policy. James Moir, who had 'so long stood high in the estimation of the Chartists, was hissed and hooted, and declared to be no Chartist, because he refused to give up his vote to the decision of a public meeting'. Walter Currie moved that the Chartists should offer to split votes with a Whig or Tory in return for support for a Chartist candidate, but this received only thirty votes, and the author of *Willie White's visit to the infernal regions* thought it infernal that Chartist electors should go to the poll at all. Eventually it was decided that the Chartist electors should be left to decide for themselves, unless the Chartists brought forward two candidates, but the meeting was quite unable to decide who those candidates should be.

On the eve of the election, great excitement prevailed throughout the country. Letters 'poured' into the *Scottish Patriot* office, demanding candidates to stand at the nomination ceremonies and deputations arrived in Glasgow seeking Chartist orators. In Perth, Ayr, Fifeshire, Kilmarnock, Stirling, Edinburgh and Glasgow the names of prospective Chartist candidates were announced, and once the policy of Feargus O'Connor became known, his supporters chorused the catch phrases 'Down with Whiggery', 'Avoid all tampering', 'Be not gulled by corn law quacks'. From Paisley 'a Chartist Alliance with the Monopolists' was headlined by the *Renfrewshire Reformer*. In Edinburgh *The Scotsman* found it gratifying that the Chartists generally 'have not so far forgotten their own interests . . . as to adopt any step calculated to help the Tories into power'. By a

cordial union at this time with the middle ranks, headed by the most enlightened of the aristocracy, the Chartists could break down the monopolies which now press so keenly on the industry of the country . . . [but] let the Chartists throw their weight into the Tory scale and they at once defraud themselves and the country, and show that their aim is not good government, but revolution.

Almost all the prospective Chartist candidates went to the hustings, where they made speeches in favour of the Charter. Almost all received the majority in the show of hands, but hardly any went to the poll. In Ayr, James Jack ventured to make his speech only after the proceedings were officially concluded, probably for fear that he might suffer the same fate as William Thomason, who, despite a declaration that he had no intention of going to the poll at the Paisley election, a week earlier, was ordered by the Sheriff of Renfrewshire to pay £15 as his share of the expenses. In Edinburgh, Colonel Perronet Thompson and Robert Lowery, the Chartist candidates, won on a show of hands over Macaulay and Gibson Craig, but forthwith retired. So also did James Moir in Glasgow, Andrew Wardrop in Dumfries, John Duncan in Cupar, Abram Duncan in Dollar, and John McCrae in Greenock. At Perth, R. J. Richardson failed to win a majority over Fox Maule at the hustings, and in the Roxburgh election John Fraser was received with considerable cheering but also failed to win the show of hands. At Aberdeen, Robert Lowery polled thirty votes.

Only in Glasgow was there any clear evidence of an agreement between the Chartists and the Tories. Here, after the withdrawal of Moir at the hustings, Chartist candidate George Mills, son of the Lord Provost, went to the Poll and obtained 355 votes, many of which were cast by Tories. A handful of Chartists voted for the Lord Provost, who was the single Tory candidate, and the incident was exposed by the *Scotch Reformers' Gazette* with infinite relish and venom. Even a paper normally so sympathetic to the cause of universal suffrage as the *Glasgow Chronicle* felt outraged. 'Of the conduct of those persons, calling themselves Chartists, who have lent themselves to the Tories, we can neither think nor speak but with feelings of unmitigated disgust.[9]

The general election, however, did not destroy the possibility of 'a cordial union' being yet established between the middle and working class reformers. The *Scotch Reformers' Gazette* might lament that 'in no place in the kingdom did the Chartists come forward to contest the election with, or oppose the return of, any Tory', and the *Perth Advertiser* might complain that there was proof of a sympathetic bond between Chartists and Tories; but there were comparatively few recriminations against the Chartists in Scotland for any part they might have had in the defeat of the Whigs. In many parts of the country the Chartist cause profited from the revival of exuberance at hustings demonstrations and processions. The principal result, however, was that in Glasgow the election had brought to the surface deep divisions of opinion, which were never again healed, and which foreshadowed the eventual splintering of the movement.

NOTES

1. *Glasgow Argus*, 3 March 1834; 26 December 1836; 3 and 24 January; 14 February 1839.
   Northern Star, 24 March 1838.
   Birmingham Journal, 28 July; 15 September 1838.
   True Scotsman, 20 and 27 October 1838; 19 January 2, 16 and 23 March 1839.
2. *Scottish Patriot*, 16 November 28 December 1839; 11 January 1840.
3. *Champion*, 29 December 1839.
   Glasgow Argus, 23 December 1839.
   True Scotsman, 16 and 23 November; 28 December 1839; 18 and 25 January 1840.
   Scottish Patriot, 11 and 18 January 1840.

4. *True Scotsman*, 18 January 1840.
   Scottish Patriot, 25 January; 13, 20, and 27 March; 11, 18 and 25 April 1840.
5. *Scottish Patriot*, 11 and 25 April; 2, 9 and 16 May 1840.
   True Scotsman, 9 and 16 May 1840.
6. *Scottish Patriot*, 2, 16, 23 and 30 May 1840.
7. *True Scotsman*, 12 December 1840; 30 January 1841.
   Northern Star, 2 and 16 January 1841.
8. *True Scotsman*, 13 February 1841.
   Scottish Patriot, 27 March 1841.
9. *Scotsman*, 19, 26 and 30 June; 3, and 10 July; 21 August 1841.
   Northern Star, 26 June; 3 July 1841.
   Glasgow Chronicle, 28 June; 6 September 1841.
   Scotch Reformers' Gazette, 3 July; 7 August 1841.
   C. Dod, *Electoral Facts*, 1853.

CHAPTER THIRTEEN

King Feargus and Complete Suffragism

Feargus O'Connor never lacked enthusiastic admirers in Scotland. Although during the early months of the Chartist agitation he had been eclipsed by the leaders from Birmingham, he had endeared himself to large sections of the working classes by his panegyrics on behalf of the Glasgow cotton spinners. In his Scottish tour, he demonstrated great ability to gain the wholehearted support of those who applauded the plainly expressed physical force ideas of his friend, Dr John Taylor, while maintaining discreet reserve in his own choice of language. The measure of this ability to represent himself as the honest embodiment of Radical aspirations and the defender of the unity of the movement—which, secure in its possession of latent physical power, need employ no more than 'moral means'—was shown in his triumph over Brewster and Fraser in the battle over the Calton Hill resolutions.

After that affair, O'Connor clearly regarded himself as the presiding genius of the Scottish movement. He flattered the Scottish leaders, and eulogised their organisational efforts in his Scottish tours. Yet, apart from John Taylor, there were few Scotsmen whom O'Connor seemed genuinely to respect and trust. He could rely on James Moir, James Proudfoot, John McCrae and George Ross, on each of whom he showered constant praise, but there was never any mutual love between O'Connor and many of the local leaders. He showed considerable reserve towards men with ideas of their own, which they might wish to promote, and in particular he seemed distinctly uneasy over the social reformist tendencies of such men. They were difficult to control, but though they were occasionally stigmatised in general terms as 'leaders', O'Connor was usually willing to allow them more scope for independent action than he liked. He even found himself forced to withdraw his proscription on certain types of agitation, such as 'Bible Chartism' in

167

Scotland, because of the appeal which they exercised over the rank and file of the movement.[1]

Even the most important of the Scottish leaders, however, were soon made to realise that estrangement from O'Connor was equivalent to leadership without any followers, and possibly proscription from the mainstream of the movement. Yet it was not merely fear of suppression which bound almost all the local leaders of note to O'Connor. Probably more important was the element of mutual usefulness. Not merely did many of them enjoy adulation in the columns of the *Northern Star*, but the more practical of them realised the value which O'Connor's blessing could confer on their projects. There was, moreover, a considerable degree of tolerance observed in the relationship, which made possible the preservation of the agitation on a mass basis; only those who became reckless of the unity of the movement, as well as of their own position, could think of flaunting O'Connor's authority.

This ascendancy which Feargus O'Connor had gained over the Chartists of Scotland, and the consequences of independent action, were well demonstrated in April 1841 by his success in completely shattering the 'new move' of William Lovett and John Collins. Many of those who signed the 'Address of the National Association to the Political and Social Reformers of the United Kingdom' were forced to have second thoughts about their support for the 'new move', or were forced out of office. John McCrae, now pastor and Chartist schoolteacher at Kilbarchan, was one of the first to beg for forgiveness, and this was readily granted. James Jack and William Pattison resigned their offices as secretary and vice-president of the Lanarkshire Universal Suffrage Association, and their places were taken by O'Connorites, who almost immediately began to plan a demonstration and triumphal tour of Scotland for O'Connor on his forthcoming release from 'martyrdom'.

Let the people of England know that Feargus O'Connor is the admiration of the people of Scotland [wrote William Brown, the new secretary of the Lanarkshire association]. Such is the testimony of public opinion towards your patriotism that on all public occasions you have been brought forward as the lion of our cause—no meeting concludes here without the name of Feargus O'Connor coupled with the Charter, receiving three cheers.[2]

In August 1841 a scene of 'great enthusiasm and excitement' was reported from Glasgow on the news of O'Connor's liberation, and of his acceptance of the invitation to visit Glasgow. A delegate meeting was called to make the arrangements for the visit, and to ensure that—especially as this was the first time the Chartists of Glasgow had sent him a special invitation—the demonstration and soirée would be a fitting tribute to the liberated hero. Through the good offices of Captain Miller, the superintendent of the Glasgow police, the Chartists obtained the permission of the Lord Provost to use the new large hall beside the Bazaar for the soirée. This could accommodate over 4,000 people and was 'the largest and most splendid in Britain and Ireland, Birmingham excepted'. From Dumfries to Aberdeen appeals were eagerly addressed to O'Connor to favour a multitude of localities with a visit, and possible itineraries were suggested so that a maximum number of places could be satisfied.

O'Connor was delighted with his Scottish tour in October and November 1841, with the Scottish people, whom he would uphold 'in all my speeches as the stronghold of democracy', and with the 'nearly fifty large meetings' which he over-optimistically claimed to have attended. The *Scotch Reformers' Gazette* reported the O'Connor demonstration on Glasgow Green as 'the smallest outdoor meeting' ever held by the Glasgow Chartists. Its estimate of 4,000–5,000 people was strikingly at variance with the report in the *Northern Star*, according to which 200,000 were on Glasgow Green to welcome O'Connor on his arrival by steamboat from Greenock on Monday 11 October. James Moir, who was chairman at the demonstration and who was not easily satisfied on such occasions, was, however, 'glad to have this proof, with the aid of this spectacle, that Chartism was very much alive'. Delegations were present from Airdrie, Hamilton, Stonehouse, Kirkintilloch, Eaglesham, Paisley, Greenock, Pollockshaws and the Vale of Leven. Notwithstanding the advice of the *Scottish Patriot* to the working men of Glasgow not to leave their work, since they could see O'Connor in the evening,

such was the electric effect of Mr. O'Connor's presence and the deep-rooted love of the people to the principles of the Charter, that we believe there was scarcely a workshop or factory in or around the city that did not contribute to the immense gathering.

The Glasgow demonstration was followed by a soirée which was attended by 3,000, and at which O'Connor was presented with a

diamond ring, from the female Chartists of Glasgow, by a sister of
James Moir. Then came 'a week of agitation such as I have never
experienced in the course of my life'. There were meetings and
soirées in Paisley, Larkhall and Strathaven, at which O'Connor
talked of the 'sophistry' of the corn law repealers; admonished the
physical force conduct of Douglas and Muntz; dealt with physical
force in 'a way satisfying even to cautious Scots'; praised the *Scottish Patriot,* which people ought to read in preference to his own
paper; and regretted that he had been unable to meet the Rev.
Patrick Brewster.[3]

This was not a pleasure long to be deferred. Brewster's absence
at the Paisley meeting had been due to his appearance before the
presbytery of Paisley on an indictment for preaching to the Glasgow
Chartists in April in St Ann's church, and he was now determined
to accompany O'Connor wherever he might go. During the last
three weeks of the tour, Brewster and O'Connor were almost constant companions and duettists in Dunfermline, Stirling, Perth,
Alloa, Montrose, Aberdeen, Glasgow and Paisley, where they
debated endlessly 'the best means of obtaining the Charter'.

The Rev. Patrick Brewster, who used to claim that he did not
read the *Northern Star,* had now become well acquainted with
O'Connor's letters and speeches, which had been published in the
Star during 1838. By these he endeavoured to show that O'Connor
had both directly and indirectly indicated the necessity for the possession of arms and for appeals to physical force. He had always
declared that he would be 'no laggard' and that he would be the
first in the ranks on the day of trial and danger. O'Connor had not
merely given his support to the strongest advocates, such as O'Brien,
who had declared the necessity of 'cutting off a great number of
the aristocracy' and middle classes, and applying 'the same bloody
measures' to the farmers, but he had stated that 'rather than submit
longer to the reign of tyranny, and lewd domination of the few'
he would lead the people to 'death or glory'. He further accused
O'Connor of having mixed up the Charter with the question of
repeal of the union with Ireland and with opposition to the repeal
of the corn laws. All the Chartist disasters, including 'the fatal
affair of Newport', were traceable to O'Connor and his leadership.
There could be no safety until all such doctrines as O'Connor had
adhered to were publicly and emphatically repudiated.

In reply, O'Connor would claim that even the Attorney-General had been unable to find guilt in his conduct. The extracts from speeches and letters which Brewster had produced did not prove that he had ever said more than that they were justified in repelling force with force. He had never advocated physical force—neither directly nor indirectly—and he praised the principles and conduct of Bronterre O'Brien. The Birmingham declaration and the Calton Hill resolutions had 'empowered the Government to pounce' upon their victims and send the best men in England to the dungeon or transportation. He himself had suffered hardships, and spent his time, health and money in the cause of the people. In 1839 alone, he had spent £9,000 and immense time and labour to obtain signatures for the National Petition.

Over the result of the meetings there was some controversy. At Dunfermline and Paisley both sides claimed the majority on a show of hands. At Paisley, O'Connor then climbed a tree, waved his hat and got the field to divide, but Brewster was reported to have a majority of 'at least five to three'. At Aberdeen, after a good initial reception, Brewster provoked an increasing storm of hissing and cheering, and a resolution that he was no Chartist was carried by '5,000 to 50'. At the final meeting in Glasgow, Brewster claimed to have gained majorities of almost twenty to one in Perth, Alloa and Montrose, but appeared willing to adopt a more conciliatory attitude than in the past. 'I do not condemn the men who hold a different opinion from myself,' he declared, and promptly followed this concession with an attack on O'Connor as 'another Robespierre' and 'a traitor to the cause', who was realising an income of more than £4,000 a year from his newspaper, for the benefit of which he conducted the agitation. The meeting ended with a vote of confidence in O'Connor, which also withdrew the confidence formerly placed in Brewster 'as an able advocate of the People's Charter'.

'Both speakers repudiated physical force,' reported the *Glasgow Chronicle*. 'The chief difference between them was that O'Connor wished to repair the ruins of Chartism as it at present exists ... Brewster wanted to pull it down and begin anew on a better foundation.'[4]

Only two months elapsed before Feargus the Lion returned to Scotland, and when the third annual Scottish Convention assembled in Glasgow on 3 January 1842 he presented his credentials as the representative of Rutherglen and Elderslie. The main item on the agenda was the question of the National Petition, which had been prepared by the National Charter Association, and of which several associations had voiced disapproval. As long ago as 23 August the Hawick Chartists had 'highly' disapproved of including the question of repeal of the union with Ireland in the proposed petition, and on 8 November the Glasgow Chartists had resolved, despite protests from Dr McDouall and the National Charter Association executive, to oppose the introduction of such questions as the Irish union and the English poor law.

Although O'Connor took little part in the debates, and appeared as benevolently delighted as usual with the proceedings and his Scottish colleagues, it emerged from his report several weeks later that he had found much at the Convention to displease him. He had, in fact, been a most unhappy man at Glasgow, where he had contended, almost single-handed, against 'the saints of the Glasgow Chartist Synod'. 'There were ten Glasgow preachers, all Whigs— not a drop of Chartist blood in their veins.' This was a comment dramatically different from the fulsome eulogies of the same men which he was elsewhere reported to have made at the conference. Not only had the Convention adopted a resolution of disapproval of the National Petition, proposed by the English executive council, because it embraced questions of detail such as the repeal of the Poor Law Amendment Act and of the Act of Union with Ireland. But Pattison, the most heinous sinner of the Synod, had even moved a resolution 'deprecating interference with meetings which had for their object the removal of what he termed "infamous monopolies" —a most rascally resolution—one calculated to hand us over bound neck and heels to the League.' O'Connor's wrath had obviously been kindled by the defeat by forty to ten of his amendment voting thanks to the working classes for the resistance they had made to oppression, by Pattison's resolution expressing satisfaction at the growing progress of Chartist principles amongst the middle classes.

The time is now arrived [declared O'Connor in the *Northern Star* on 29 January 1842] when every man must and shall speak out. I will no longer be the victim of private letter-writers ... grumblers in committees, stabbers in the dark and all such ... Of your Synod of Glasgow, I tell you that they are, one and all, humbugs—rank canting hypocrites, who would perpetuate grievances in order that they may have ready access to your feelings ... If you bled them all to death, you would not squeeze out a drop of democratic blood ... Scotchmen, should disunion be sown amongst you, and should you require my aid, send for me and you shall have a third visit this winter.

The promised third visit, however, did not prove necessary to 'clip the wings of the rotten leaders of Glasgow', whom he suspected of going over to the repealers. During the next six weeks the *Northern Star* waged open war on Glasgow, and published letters from Arbroath, Montrose, Forfar and Brechin repudiating the action of their representatives in opposing the National Convention. Disapproval of the Convention decision was also garnered from Leith, Lanark, Aberdeen, Elderslie, Kilmarnock and Coalsnaughton. On 5 February the *Northen Star* announced, somewhat prematurely, that Pattison had joined Brewster and 'gone over to the Corn Law Repealers, the enemy of the people'. Meanwhile, at anti-corn law lectures at the end of January, and at a repeal meeting on 16 February, Malcolm, Rodger and Jack were meeting with strong Chartist disapprobation for proposing resolutions in favour of 'full, free and fair representation' in opposition to Chartist amendments by Moir and Proudfoot. At the election of the directors of the Lanarkshire Universal Suffrage Association the following day, Pattison's name was removed from the list of nominees—for having joined the 'Corn Law Repealers'. O'Connor's victory seemed complete, with the Glasgow Chartists adopting the National Petition, of which they had previously so strongly disapproved.[5]

Feargus O'Connor was probably only partly aware of the significance of his intervention in Glasgow politics. It came at a time when relations between the middle and working classes of Glasgow and Paisley were becoming increasingly cordial. This was largely a consequence of the onset of a severe commercial depression in Paisley, Glasgow and the west of Scotland during the second half of 1841. Since July there had been reports of bankruptcies and growing unemployment. The Rev. Dr Burns, who was a member of the delegation sent to London in October to beg for assistance, claimed that out of eighty manufacturing houses in Paisley fifty had gone bankrupt in the previous three months. Not only did this produce a resurgence of the anti-corn law movement in the town which was a classical example of the repeal case, but it re-emphasised the economic interdependence of the middle and working classes at a time when the Chartists were having grave doubts regarding the wisdom of their obstructionist tactics as the best means of bringing the middle classes 'to their senses'. During the last part of the year there was some evidence of an increasing desire on both sides to settle their differences. Even James Moir was to be found at meetings of Glasgow electors, complaining of the 'misunderstanding' which had got abroad that the Chartists of Glasgow were against repeal of the corn laws. The reverse was the case, and the Chartists unanimously condemned those laws. In return, councillors Hastie and Whitehead declared the need for franchise extension, and for the union of the franchised with the unfranchised. Moreover, the emergence of Joseph Sturge as the leader of the Complete Suffrage movement encouraged hopes of a reform union, for while he enjoyed the support of a large section of the Anti-Corn Law League, he was also well respected by the Chartists as a noted philanthropist and honest man, and his visits to Glasgow and Edinburgh in January 1842 were arousing great expectations.[6]

'At a Convention of Anti-Corn Law delegates at Edinburgh, and a banquet at Glasgow,' wrote Joseph Sturge, 'ample opportunity was afforded of bringing the matter under the notice of a large number of the picked men of the middle classes.' Then in Glasgow on 15 January, and in Edinburgh on the 17th, enthusiastic meetings adopted the Sturge declaration and approved the formation of a 'cordial union of middle and working classes'. In both cities, provisional committees of influential citizens were appointed for the task of establishing Complete Suffrage Associations. These contained many of the best known middle class Radicals, such as councillors Turner, Bankier, Hamilton, Cross and Anderson of Glasgow, the Rev. Dr Ritchie and the Rev. William Marshall of Edinburgh, and John Dunlop of Brockloch, the temperance advocate.

These visits of O'Connor and Sturge to Glasgow in January 1842 marked one of the most important turning points in the history of Scottish Chartism. Within a few weeks there emerged a clear disruption within the ranks of the Glasgow Chartists between those who rejoiced in the leadership of O'Connor and those who, labouring under his stigma, were unwilling to seek any further reconciliation with that master of equivocation. For them the emergence of Joseph Sturge and Complete Suffragism was a welcome promise that Chartism might yet be able to throw off the tutelage of O'Connor. They saw no incompatibility between support for Sturge and their responsibilities to the older movement, from which they had no apparent intention of divorcing themselves. They were soon to find, however, that O'Connor's tactics were making certain that few of his admirers would follow their local leaders into the Sturge movement. When they were faced with violent attacks from O'Connor, the existence of the Sturge alternative both provided ammunition for the attacks and reduced their determination to fight back against the undermining of their local position. Despite the professions of Feargus O'Connor, at the Birmingham Complete Suffrage Conference of 18 February 1842, to be the friend of middle and working class unity, his followers in Scotland were already acting energetically on the lead indicated in the *Northern Star*. Complete Suffragism was promptly named 'The Plague'. Its supporters were 'Complete Suffrage Humbugs', who were regarded as identical in all respects with corn law repealers; Chartist leaders who showed sympathy with Complete Suffragism were met with cries of 'traitor', 'renegade' and 'turncoat'.

Between the two groups there were few sharp conflicts, largely because the main efforts of the Complete Suffrage committees were directed towards the mobilisation of support from middle class reformers, few public meetings were organised, and little apparent effort was made to enrol a large membership. Nevertheless, by the end of March an 'astonishing change' in the attitude of the middle classes towards suffrage extension was being reported, along with considerable progress in forming local associations. Complete Suffrage Associations were established in about twenty places, with fairly strong ones in Glasgow, Edinburgh, Aberdeen and Paisley. In most places well known Chartists provided much of the leadership. In Paisley, where the Association had more than 570 members by October, the principal office-bearers were Provost Henderson and the Rev. Patrick Brewster. In the Glasgow association there were about 1,000 members, with John Rodger as secretary and Malcolm McFarlane as vice-president. At its first meeting of members, James Hooey occupied the chair, while the main resolutions were moved by Robert Malcolm jun., William Thomson, Walter Currie, Charles McEwan, James Walker and William Pattison. Its sympathies were made clear by the list of honorary members, whom it elected at a meeting chaired by Pattison in June. This included William Lovett, John Collins, John Adam (editor of the *Aberdeen Herald*) and Arthur O'Neill (now pastor of the Birmingham Chartist church), in addition to Sturge, Francis Place, Richard Prentice, Sharman Crawford, Lawrence Heyworth and Edward Miall.

Apart from the Birmingham conference in April, and banquets in honour of Joseph Sturge and Sharman Crawford in Edinburgh and Glasgow in the autumn, only about thirty meetings in Scotland were reported in *The Nonconformist* in the first nine months of 1842. In September and October, Henry Vincent made a tour ranging from Glasgow to Aberdeen, giving lectures on Complete Suffragism, and in the Glasgow City Hall on 21 and 23 September he had audiences of more than 2,000.[7]

After the occasional conflict which had accompanied the formation of Complete Suffrage committees early in 1842, there appeared to be almost complete indifference on the part of the major sections of the Chartists towards Complete Suffragism. Amongst the working classes, the line of division remained between those who wished to have freedom to subscribe to corn law repeal in addition to the Charter, and those who thought that no honest Chartist could support any agitation other than for the Six Points. Tacit hostility was the prevailing mood of the O'Connorites, but after the Complete Suffrage conferences in Birmingham, in February and April, they seemed to be honouring a truce. When the moribund Lanarkshire Universal Suffrage Association was wound up in May, several of the directors of the Complete Suffrage Association were permitted to join the Glasgow Charter Association which took its place. While the *Northern Star* continued to claim that 'only a small portion' of Scottish Chartists 'looked to Complete Suffragism', there were occasional demands for a delegate conference of Scottish Chartists to decide upon their attitude to Complete Suffragism. The Chartist movement in Scotland, it was suggested, was being harmed because the lack of organisation was allowing 'the public mind' to run in three different channels. A portion of the people looked to Complete Suffragism, whilst amongst a considerable number the 'belief still lingered' that trades unions and strikes were 'a remedy for the evils of class legislation'. According to *The Scotsman*, which had little sympathy for Complete Suffragism, this new manifestation of the Chartist movement 'enlists the feelings of a prodigious mass of the working classes in towns. Whether wise or foolish, therefore ... its manifestations are too important to be passed over in silence.'

The attitude of the rump of the Scottish Chartist movement towards Complete Suffragism was still left undecided after the fourth Scottish Convention in October 1842. The Convention decided not to advise Chartist associations to send delegates to the conference to be held at Birmingham in December, but it was not willing to recommend hostility to the Complete Suffragists. In Glasgow, especially, the position was confused. When the Complete Suffrage Association decided, in October, to risk a bolder policy to encourage the spread of Complete Suffragism, a group of the Glasgow Charter Association, led by the Irish Catholic Con Murray, was determined to destroy these meetings. Meanwhile their president, James Moir, was to be found at middle class meetings advocating the objects and principles of the Complete Suffrage Association and insisting that no candidates should be supported in the municipal elections who refused to join that association.[8]

In November a deputation of the Glasgow Charter Association visited the directors of the Complete Suffrage Association to make arrangements for sending delegates to Birmingham. The Complete Suffragists, however, were willing to pay the expenses only of those pledged to the policy laid down by themselves. This was that delegates would be instructed to support all six points of the Charter and all motions which had the object of opposition to monopolies of the Church and the State. Delegates would be pledged to adopt only legal and constitutional means, but they would be allowed freedom in the choice of name for the new union. This was not acceptable to the Charter Association, and on 29 November they made a determined effort to pack the hall at which the Complete Suffragists were conducting their elections to the Birmingham conference. George Ross was elected chairman in place of Dr Eneas O'Donnell, the Complete Suffrage nominee, and after a three-hour debate the Complete Suffrage motion that the delegates should be pledged to the Six Points, but left free to support corn law repeal, was defeated. All six delegates elected were 'out and out' Chartists, and these were pledged by a resolution of Samuel Kydd, one of the young lions of the Charter Association, to abide by the Charter, 'name and all'.

Meanwhile, in Edinburgh, Robert Lowery, recently elected Chartist Organising Secretary for Scotland, was urging the Chartists to accept a proposal to have only half the Edinburgh delegation elected by Chartists. At the election meeting on 5 December in Dr Ritchie's church, Joseph Sturge, John Dunlop and the Rev. Dr Ritchie were elected by the enfranchised, while T. S. Duncombe, Henry Rankine and Robert Lowery were elected by the Chartists. Lowery was severely criticised for refusing to bind himself to the

Charter, 'name and all', and had to fight for his election. He ridiculed the idea of 'sticking to the past' as 'obstructive and detrimental to the political advancement of the people'. Union was now required amongst all reformers.[9]

Forty-two Scottish towns and large villages were represented at the Birmingham conference on 27 December 1842. Some of these were represented by Birmingham residents, but the majority were well known Scottish Chartists and Suffragists. The appointment of Birmingham men as representatives of poor Scottish associations had first been advocated by the Rev. Patrick Brewster, but this tactic boomeranged and the idea was chiefly taken up by O'Connorite groups. The Glasgow Suffragists managed to make up some of their lost nominations by getting Rodger appointed as delegate for Dunfermline, McEwen for Pollockshaws and Rutherglen, and Pattison for Rutherglen and Paisley.

Thomas Cooper, who must have been one of the few O'Connorites to hope for a happy ending to the conference, decided that there was no attempt to bring about a union.

We soon found that it was determined to keep poor Chartists 'at arm's length'. If Mr. Sturge, himself, or Edward Miall, or the Rev. Thomas Spencer, or the Rev. Patrick Brewster ... or any other leading member of the Complete Suffrage party present, had risen in that assembly, and spoken words of real kindness and hearty conciliation, I am persuaded that not even O'Connor himself, if he had desired it, could have prevented the great body of working-men delegates from uttering shouts of joy.

Many of the delegations, however, had been sent to Birmingham to wreck any scheme which involved less than the complete surrender of the middle class Suffragists to the People's Charter, 'name and all', so it is difficult to see what 'words of kindness' Mr Sturge or the Rev. Patrick Brewster (who distinguished himself by the length of his speech) could have spoken.

Cooper concluded that the Birmingham conference had 'ruined the prospects of Chartism; and the Complete Suffrage party never made any headway in the country'.

Such child's play [wrote the *Glasgow Argus*] is almost without parallel in the proceedings of any public body ... and the abuse hurled at each other, by men who were agreed on every point save a mere name, was equally instructive ... Mr. Heyworth said 'the fact was, the present conflict was "Who shall be your leaders?" ... ' The expectations of those who believed that good would arise from the Complete Suffrage movement have thus been completely frustrated.[10]

The immèdiate reaction of the Complete Suffragists, however, was not one of frustrated disappointment. In Edinburgh, Robert Lowery declared that it was impossible for the Complete Suffragists to damage the Chartist Associations, for these were already dead. John Dunlop thought it had been for the best that the division had taken place at Birmingham, and in Aberdeen, Dundee, Dunfermline, Edinburgh, Glasgow, Paisley, Rutherglen and Saltcoats the decisions of their delegates to act with the minority party at the conference were applauded.

There was no question, at that time, of abandoning the Complete Suffrage agitation, but apart from Glasgow and Edinburgh, Suffragist activity became desultory throughout 1843. Aberdeen and Dundee prepared fresh plans of organisation, but only Cupar could report regular activity. In April the decision of the Glasgow Complete Suffragists was the occasion for further abuse by O'Connor and his supporters of 'certain members of the late Central Committee for Scotland ... renegades who turn their back upon the Chartist movement ... Whigs to the backbone'. In November 'the Sturgeite faction', which had recently been reported by its Glasgow rivals as 'absolutely defunct', was busy making plans for suburban meetings and deciding to support the O'Connell agitation for repeal of the Irish union. George Julian Harney, on another Scottish tour in August 1843, found that

faction has cut the throat of Chartism in Edinburgh. Leaders have been the curse of the cause there as well as in Glasgow, and there, too, the traitors and deserters, still having the unblushing assurance to call themselves Chartists, are the worst enemies to the movement.[11]

NOTES

1. *Northern Star*, 28 July 1838; 12 and 19 January 1839; 16 January; 8 May 1841.
   True Scotsman, 12 and 19 January 1839.
2. *Scottish Patriot*, 10 April 1841.
   Northern Star, 22 and 29 May 1841.
3. *Northern Star*, 4 and 11 September; 16 and 23 October 1841.
   Scotch Reformers' Gazette, 16 October 1841.
   Glasgow Chronicle, 18 October 1841.
4. *Glasgow Chronicle*, 25 October; 3 and 5 November 1841.

Scotch Reformers' Gazette, 6 November 1841.
The Scotsman, 10 November 1841.
True Scotsman, 12 and 19 January 1839.
5. English *Chartist Circular*, No. 51.
Chartist Circular, 29 January 1842.
The Scotsman, 12 January 1842.
Northern Star, 4 September 1841; 15, 22 and 29 January; 5, 19 and 26 February 1842.
6. *Glasgow Chronicle*, 27 October 1841.
Scotch Reformers' Gazette, 30 October 1841.
7. *The Nonconformist*, vol. ii, pp. 55, 103, 452, 499, 638, 667, 671, 733.
Northern Star, 26 February; 12 and 26 March; 29 October 1842.
Memoirs of Joseph Sturge, p. 302.
8. *Northern Star*, 23 May; 1 and 29 October 1842.
Nonconformist, vol. ii, pp. 701–2.
9. *Northern Star*, 10 and 17 December 1842.
Nonconformist, 30 November; 7 December 1842.
10. T. Cooper, *Life of Thomas Cooper*, 1872, pp. 222, 228.
Glasgow Argus, 2 January 1843.
Nonconformist, vol. iii, pp. 36, 90.
11. *Northern Star*, 15 April; 2 September 1843.
Nonconformist, vol. iii, pp. 37, 55, 68, 122, 138–9, 218, 534, 599, 741, 806, 837.

CHAPTER FOURTEEN

The decline of Scottish organisation

One of the best indices of the real strength of Chartist organisation in Scotland was to be found in the fluctuating fortunes of the Chartist newspaper press. Both in the early days of the movement and in its latter years, its organisational strength lagged far behind its superficial strength. It seems clear that the heyday of the Scottish agitation coincided with the period in which the Chartist newspapers enjoyed a wide circulation—a period which was heralded by the publication of the *Scottish Patriot* in July 1839, and ended exactly three years later with the demise of the *Chartist Circular*.

In the initial stages of the movement, the Scottish Radicals had to depend largely on the *Birmingham Journal* and the *Northern Star*. However suitable Dr John Taylor's *Liberator* would have been for representing the views of the trade unions and the working class supporters of the People's Charter, it ceased publication in April 1838, burdened with financial difficulties, just a few weeks before it would have had an opportunity to build up its clientele and influence the new agitation. Although the *Scots Times* immediately espoused the cause of the Birmingham Radicals in May 1838, it was never more than lukewarm to Chartism. It was a mild reform newspaper, heavily dependent on advertising, with as much inclination to its Whig–Radical patrons as to the Chartists, and with only a modest circulation for several years before it ceased publication in April 1841.

The first of the Chartist weekly newspapers to be published in Scotland was the *Ayrshire Examiner*, which was started in Kilmarnock in July 1838. It shared a close identity in policy with Bailie Hugh Craig, who was its principal proprietor, and advocated an energetic 'moral force' campaign designed to arouse middle class reformers to join a national movement for universal suffrage under the leadership of Lord Durham. After Craig's withdrawal from the

Convention in July 1839, both he and the paper were denounced by the majority of his Chartist constituents, and it ceased publication in November 1839.[1]

The most important Chartist newspaper in the latter part of 1838 and throughout the first half of 1839 was *The True Scotsman*, a four-page folio weekly, with a format similar to that of *The Scotsman*. It was published in Edinburgh by John Fraser, and grew out of the *Edinburgh Monthly Democrat and Total Abstinence Advocate*, which Fraser had published since July 1838. With agents in forty Scottish towns, Manchester, Birmingham and London, the circulation soon exceeded 2,000 and rose to 2,700 in the spring of 1839, but it gradually fell off to about 750 a week a year later. Much of this decline was due to its loss of custom to *The Scottish Patriot*, which started in July 1839, and to which it displayed a strong aversion thereafter. In comparison to the *Scottish Patriot*, the *Northern Star* or the *Birmingham Journal*, the *True Scotsman* was a poor printing job and, especially in its early days, was an untidy and shapeless paper. But despite its defects there was an attractive warmth and humanity about the *True Scotsman*. Into its columns the somewhat moody Fraser infused a very personal atmosphere— in contrast to the highly impersonal, if more reliable, *Scottish Patriot*.

Great importance was attached to the building up in Scotland of a Chartist press. 'Public opinion,' declared William Thomson, editor of the *Chartist Circular*, was the 'power which will yet be effective in the struggle of humanity for universal brotherhood and charity.' This faith in public opinion and the force of reason was widely shared among the Scottish Chartists, and by the autumn of 1840 their efforts had achieved a considerable degree of success. At that time, when it could find no Chartist paper in London, the *Spectator* was able to report that

in Scotland alone, we find the *True Scotsman* (Edinburgh), the *Patriot* (Glasgow), the *Perth Chronicle*, and the *Dundee Chronicle*—fair average papers advocating 'the five points'. The *True Scotsman* has been some years in existence; the *Patriot* is, properly speaking, a revival of the *Liberator*, a newspaper which was carried on for several years, and which might have been flourishing still but for mismanagement in the business department; the *Perth Chronicle* is a well-conducted paper; of the *Dundee Chronicle* only one number has appeared since it passed into the hands of its new proprietory, but that is a creditable perform-ance.[1]

Another creditable performance was that of the *Chartist Circular,* which had maintained a circulation of more than 22,500 throughout its first year. In addition to these Chartist weeklies, there were at that time a number of Radical newspapers, not under the control of Chartists, but which could be found supporting the cause of universal suffrage. These included the *Glasgow Saturday Post and Renfrewshire Reformer,* the *Dumfries Times,* the *Aberdeen Herald,* the *Kelso Chronicle,* the *Stirling Observer* and the *John o'Groats Journal.* From time to time monthly papers, such as the *Monthly Liberator* (Glasgow), the *Aberdeen Patriot,* the *Scottish Vindicator* (Paisley), the *Northern Vindicator* (Aberdeen), the *Ayrshire Demo-crat* (Greenock) and the *Scottish Radical,* had also appeared, but most of these had only a brief existence.

By the spring of 1841 there were signs of distress amongst the Chartist press. The circulation and advertising revenue of the *True Scotsman* was the most seriously affected, the former having fallen steadily from 2,500 in the early months of 1839 to around 800 throughout most of 1840. With its circulation reduced in March 1841 to under 500, John Fraser announced that his health and financial resources dictated the cessation of publication. He could no longer cope with a situation in which, he claimed, no Chartist newspaper in Scotland was meeting its current expenses. The *Scottish Patriot* was also complaining of financial difficulties, and though it succeeded in maintaining its circulation at a steady 1,200 throughout 1841, which was only about 10 per cent lower than the 1840 figures, it also decided to cease publication at the end of the year. From the summer of 1841 the *Perthshire Chronicle* was also getting deeper into difficulties. Throughout its existence its circu-lation had been maintained at about 450 which fell to around 250 after July. After a nine-month struggle, it died in April 1842.

Even the *Chartist Circular* was struggling against financial difficulties, which were being met by William Thomson, its editor, drawing only half his salary in thirty-six weeks of 1841, and by growing indebtedness to George Ross. Although its circulation aver-aged 20,000 throughout 1841, it was suffering, like several other Chartist papers, from the growing indebtedness of its agents, who were finding it difficult to refuse credit to customers, who were being increasingly hit by the trade depression. On 18 September the *Chartist Circular* announced that it was gravely embarrassed 'by the culpable neglect or dishonesty' of men who would meet not merely 'disgraceful exposure' but 'legal prosecution'. Strenuous pursuit of the sanction of stopping supplies soon reduced the circulation without raising the inflow of payments. Against this background, the feud waged by Feargus O'Connor against Thomson and the other Glasgow 'saints' must have done considerable damage to the *Chartist Circular*, which ceased publication in July 1842, when its circulation had been reduced to 7,000. It must then have been running at a weekly loss of at least £15. The arrears of its agents amounted to £220, and from the names on the 'black list' of backsliding agents which it published in June it seems clear that many Chartist stalwarts who ran little newspaper businesses must themselves have been in severe difficulties. It also seems probable that many of them were giving a much higher priority to maintaining payments for their supplies of the *Northern Star*.

Meanwhile, in depressed Dundee, the Chartists who had bought the Radical-cum-corn law repeal-cum-Chartist paper with a circulation of around 700, in November 1840 for about £800 were finding it difficult to raise this money by the sale of shares at £1, and therewith repay the 'several devoted friends' who had advanced the money. After the Chartist takeover, circulation rose to over 1,000 for the first quarter of 1841, but dropped back to 700 in the second quarter. At this stage the directors engaged the 'talented, tried and consistent advocate of Civil and Religious Liberty, Mr. R. J. Richardson, to Edit their Paper'. After this appointment, circulation was maintained at around 850 until the spring of 1842, but there appears to have been a continued decline in advertising revenue. When R. J. Richardson was denounced by the Manchester Chartists and the *Northern Star* early in 1842, the Dundee Chartists made their peace with O'Connor by sacking Richardson, who was replaced by John Lamont, a Chartist poet who had worked on the staff of the *Scottish Patriot*. After this, however, there began a steady decline in circulation. By August it had fallen to around 600 and in a final attempt to effect a recovery, the *Dundee Chronicle* was transformed into the *Dundee Herald*, pledged to Voluntaryism in Church governance, to Radicalism, to the 'principles of the People's Charter in all their purity', and to the Complete Suffrage cause. In this new guise the paper continued, despite dwindling circulation, until September 1843—two months longer than the ghost of the

True Scotsman, which had haunted the scene, with a circulation of only around 350, since March 1842. At that time, presumably also in the hope of a strong Complete Suffragist movement developing, the *Scottish Patriot* also came back to life, but although it built up a circulation of 1,000 it was dead by June 1842—by which time the once formidable Scottish Chartist press had almost completely withered away under the stresses of internal dissention and commercial depression.[2]

Another fairly reliable index of the organisational strength of Scottish Chartism was to be found in the fund-raising efforts of Chartist associations for extra-local purposes. After the early months of 1840 these dwindled away, and one of the major contributory causes of the collapse of national organisation was the failure to obtain adequate funds for that purpose. The questions of corn law repeal, loyalty to Feargus O'Connor and Complete Suffragism splintered the movement only after it had been constantly weakened by lack of funds for national organisation.

So long as the attention of the Chartists was confined to running purely local associations, the money for their modest expenses was normally forthcoming, but the financing of all wider organisations tended to be left on a somewhat haphazard basis. Demands for financial support for the Central Committee were often made in the vaguest fashion. To some degree this was symptomatic of the fact that even in the best of times the bulk of the Chartist following seldom had enough for their own needs. While it had not been impossible to raise funds on an appropriate scale among factory workmen and even poverty-stricken weavers for the General Convention in 1839, this was much more difficult to achieve for an abstraction such as a central committee which would be devoted to educational propagandist work. Provided with a target figure, a specific spending purpose and a little oratory, the Chartists would empty their pockets, even in time of distress, but for most of them the Universal Suffrage Committee for Scotland seemed remote. In proportion to the distance of local associations from Glasgow, it was regarded as outside their responsibility, and to many districts the Central Committee remained a Glasgow organisation.

It was not that the leaders of the movement failed to realise the importance of sound finance. Many of them did, and systems of small weekly or monthly contributions to be shared between local and national organisations were constantly mooted and occasionally adopted. As the movement progressed there was a trend towards the adoption of more businesslike methods, but these usually came when the sources of income were already beginning to dry up, and too often they were operated under adverse conditions, with the onset of trade depression and unemployment, or with the spread of a sense of ineffectiveness. 'Pay if you can' was the ruling principle of officials who were determined to maintain a large following.

Moreover, although the General Convention was not regarded as a failure, its inability to achieve the immediately expected objectives had a blighting effect on later fund-raising for organisational purposes. Even in 1839–40, when there were many more Chartist associations in Scotland than had been in existence during the raising of the National Rent, and when organisation for all purposes was at a much more efficient level, it was impossible to approach the total of over £520 which had been subscribed for the National Rent and the salaries of Convention delegates during the winter and spring of 1838–39. It was even complained that the Convention and other conferences held in England had been the cause of ruining the funds of almost every locality in Scotland.

During the period of almost three years in which he was the General Treasurer for Scotland, George Ross spent only £235 14s, and even this modest rate of spending could not be afforded on the basis of contributions from local associations. These amounted to only £179 8s., of which only £54 was forthcoming during the last twenty-one months of the period. This compared poorly with £271 for the Frost defence fund, £191 for the national defence fund, and £178 for various funds for Lovett, Collins, Vincent, McDouall and the families of imprisoned Chartists which were all raised during the same period. By June of 1842, George Ross was owed £52 for his payments on behalf of the Central Committee, and even more serious was the growing indebtedness of the *Chartist Circular*, which now had assets of £28–£30 against liabilities of almost £210. This situation led to the cessation of the Circular a few weeks later, and with that the virtual end to any semblance of national organisation in Scotland.[3]

Amongst the most important of the factors which had contributed to this decline throughout 1842 were the internal divisions resulting from the vendettas of O'Connor and the National Charter Association against many of the most effective leaders of the Scottish movement, which separated the movement from alliance with the Complete Suffrage movement and caused it to lose much of its strength to the new movement. The disintegrating effects of the efforts of O'Connor, McDouall and the National Charter Association to impose their opinions regarding particular issues, such as Irish repeal and the new poor law, on the heterogeneous Scottish movement was pointed out by John Duncan, the pastor of the Dundee Chartist church. He had been chairman of the Scottish Convention in January 1842, and it was by his casting vote that the National Petition had been rejected. In a correspondence with McDouall, Duncan asserted that the strength of the Scottish movement lay in the tolerance allowed to its members on all questions apart from the fundamental principles of the Charter. On many matters their principles were not 'exactly the same', as McDouall was claiming, but were, in fact, very different. Within their ranks they numbered

Repealers and anti-Repealers, anti-Poor Law men and Malthusianism, O'Connorites, O'Brienites, Cobbettites, Churchmen, Dissenters, or no Church-at-all men and others...differing in their views of political economy, morals and religion, wide as the poles asunder.[4]

Probably equally important, however, was the deepening of commercial and industrial depression during the latter half of 1841 and throughout 1842. In July 1841, at a time when James Moir, the 'people's candidate' for Glasgow, was announcing the arrival of a 'new era' in politics, a new era was indeed being heralded by the onset of commercial panic in Glasgow and by a considerable deepening of the trade depression which had been chronic in Paisley since 1837. Idle hand-loom weavers looked towards the Chartists for leadership, while the Presbytery of Paisley debated whether they should be allowed one pennyworth or threepennyworth of relief per day.

Soon it was being reported that Glasgow was a 'mass of agitation', with 'political and misery meetings' occurring every day, and 'hundreds of plans of peace and violence' proposed, debated and rejected. Delegate meetings of the 'active leaders of the hand-loom weavers of Glasgow and corresponding villages in Lanark, Dumbarton and the Renfrewshires' were held in the Glasgow Chartist church to discuss the 'painful' nature of conditions, the 'grinding' nature of employers, and the necessity of acting in concert with the friends of the Charter. Chartists were asked to draw up memorials on the forlorn condition of the large assemblies of unemployed weavers on Glasgow Green, and Chartist deputations to the authorities to obtain work for the unemployed met with some success.

'Difficulties beset us; calamities threaten us,' declared the Edinburgh and Midlothian Universal Chartist Association in September 1841, in an address to the nation on 'the present critical condition' of the country. 'Commerce is crippled; trade is stagnant; manufactures are fast leaving us, and the great body of the working classes are enduring dreadful privations.' Robert Lowery was thereupon appointed Chartist lecturer for the county—which was then in a fairly flourishing condition as far as Chartism was concerned. In several other places, plans for reorganisation were adopted to seize the opportunity for more vigorous agitation, and these were fostered by the visit of Feargus O'Connor to Scotland in October.

Neither Chartist revivals, however, nor even visits by O'Connor could produce any amelioration of the condition of the working classes in several of the manufacturing and industrial areas from which the Chartists drew much of their strength. In Paisley destitution amongst the unemployed mounted from 4,200 to 5,600 during October, to 10,670 in November, and to 14,650 in January 1842. At a Renfrewshire county meeting in December 1841, the Rev. Patrick Brewster and the Rev. Mr Baird were rebuked by Lord Kelburne for using 'exciting language' when they declared that all property was sacred, but the property of the masses, labour, must also be protected—or every other kind of property would be rendered comparatively valueless. When human life was in danger, extreme necessity entitled them to take the first food they could find, without or against the consent of the proprietors.

Meanwhile Fox Maule, and later Sir James Graham, had been replying regularly from the Home Office to requests for aid from the provost of Paisley. They deeply regretted the destitution in Paisley, but the government could not, however, interfere, and trusted that seasonal work, improvement in trade, and private benevolence would assist the sufferers. When the distress mounted rapidly in the winter of 1841–42, Lord Normanby assured the provost that his (almost weekly) appeals were receiving his 'best consideration'. After April 1842, Sir James Graham also started to promise to give his 'best consideration' to the prevailing distress in Paisley. Relief in kind, 'bread, potatoes or oatmeal only in return for work', would now be permitted, since private charity was exhausted. The sheriff of Renfrewshire was exhorted to preserve public peace during the 'painful process by which alone habitual dependence on Charity can be checked', and able-bodied men brought to make exertions for finding means of subsistence for themselves.[5]

For some time, distress helped to increase the noise and numbers of the Chartist agitation, and the National Petition was signed by over 78,000 in Glasgow and Lanarkshire, almost 18,000 in Aberdeen and 16,000 in Dunfermline. Chartist orators continued to find the main cause of the distress in bad legislation, and to expound the Charter as the sole means of improvement.

It is a melancholy fact made more apparent by every day's experience [lamented the Chartists of Glasgow in June 1842] that our Unions have failed to protect the rights of labour, and that we are daily... sinking deeper and deeper into destitution and misery... We are still of opinion [that this state of affairs] arises wholly from class-made laws ... By these laws we are impoverished, degraded, and oppressed, and in this state we must continue to remain until unitedly we apply our strength to the thorough reformation of what is called the Commons' House of Parliament.

By July the degree of distress in Scotland was reported as 'unexampled'. Large meetings of unemployed on Glasgow Green demanded relief. The whole of the Lanarkshire coalfield was in a state of unrest, and there were fears of disturbances as a result of strike action in Dundee and Dunfermline, while a meal riot was reported from Dumfries. In the Vale of Leven, where the introduction of new block-printing machinery had aggravated the problem of unemployment, the unemployed resolved to take food where they could obtain it if relief were not provided.[6]

The Home Secretary, Lords Lieutenant, and sheriffs gave these matters their 'serious attention', and after the government had refused any aid except to Paisley, all necessary precautions were taken by alterations of the disposition of troops. Cavalry was transferred from Ireland to Scotland. The Yeomanry Cavalry was strengthened, and night patrols were instituted. Chelsea Pensioners were sworn in as special constables, and the permanent police forces were increased, especially in rural areas. In addition to these precautions, rewards of £100 were offered to starving populations in Lanarkshire and Fifeshire for information against depredators of potato fields and persons setting fire to factories. Sir James Graham welcomed the establishment of mounted patrols—to be paid for by private means—for the protection of private property in Lanarkshire, and explained to the Earl of Airlie his disapproval of allowing the discontented to march about in bodies of 300–500 men.[7]

Excitement was intensified in August by the reports of disturbances in England, and by the extensive strike of colliers and iron miners in Lanarkshire, Ayrshire and the Lothians. The part played by the Chartists amongst the strikers and unemployed is uncertain. Some minor Chartists were to be found at delegate meetings of coal and iron miners, urging strike action until the Charter was granted. At one of the largest of the meetings, at Airdrie, Thomas Roberts asserted that such a resolution had been adopted in Clackmannanshire, which he represented, and urged that the delegates should 'try to induce other trades, far and near, to strike until the Charter' was granted. In other parts of Lanarkshire there were meetings of miners 'friendly to democracy', but at Airdrie, Coatbridge and Holytown they were mainly interested in wages and local grievances, such as questions of 'lying-money' and a 'lying week in five'. Most of the Chartist leaders seemed to be alarmed at the dangerous nature of the situation, and endeavoured to prevent any outbreaks of violence. Few, if any, appeared to favour the use of strike action as a means of carrying the Charter, and strike action in existing conditions was generally deprecated, though the raising by strikers of the cry for the Charter was not unwelcome.

At a meeting on Calton Hill on 22 August, Robert Lowery declared that he was proud of the peaceful and orderly conduct of the people. He would not have 'counselled strike action in such a state of trade, but since those on the spot are better acquainted with condition' he applauded their determination to continue to strike for the enactment of the Charter. Two days previously, the Glasgow Chartists had held a meeting to memorialise the Queen 'to recall Parliament to enact measures to ensure the permanent tranquillity of the country'. This proved to be

the smallest out-door meeting ever held by the Chartists on Glasgow Green; and it is remarkable that notwithstanding the great excitement experienced at this moment all over the country, there was less enthusiasm and heartiness manifested in the cause than we ever saw exhibited on any previous occasion.

From this the *Glasgow Argus* concluded that there appeared to be 'no desire on the part of the Chartists in this neighbourhood to resort to extreme measures'.

The *Scotsman* observed that in the north,

> particularly at Dundee, great efforts have been made by the Chartists
> to get up a commotion. But the vast body of the working classes see the
> futility of any such movement. So far as the colliers are concerned, the
> strike appears really to have originated in a dispute about wages uncon-
> nected with any political object.

Attempts to create a general strike were reported to have been made
at Alloa, Montrose and other places, and 'delegates from Manchester
have been present in Glasgow endeavouring to create a sympathy
with the English "turn-outs".'[8]

Earlier in the month, the military had been called to Dunfermline
to prevent rioting as a result of a threatened reduction of weavers'
wages. On 14 August the Home Secretary complained to the Lord
Advocate of a 'want of zeal' on the part of the Radical provost
of Dunfermline on the night of the 9th, when factories were set on
fire. On the 13th a meeting of Fifeshire miners at Cannock agreed
that they would strike for 'nothing less than the People's Charter',
and that should their 'brethren now on strike make the People's
Charter their demand' they would 'at once join them in the glorious
struggle'. At the same time, moreover, they decided that 'strikes
among working men for rise of wages merely are not calculated to
be productive of permanent good to the labourer', and three days
later the same resolutions were adopted unanimously at a Coalsnaughton meeting. On this occasion the 'dense multitude' decided
to make 'one grand effort for the purpose of working out our
emancipation', and resolved 'to cease entirely from working, on or
before this day week, and never again to produce one pennyworth
of wealth till the People's Charter be law'. Similarly, in Dunfermline on 16 August a large meeting decided that class legislation was
the sole cause of their severe and long-continued sufferings.

> Therefore as a legal, peaceful and efficient means for putting an end
> to these intolerable evils, we now voluntarily resolve to abstain from
> all labour, except for the production of the indispensable necessities of
> life, for eight days from this date ... and as we confidently expect the
> producers of wealth generally to follow our example, in that case we
> pledge ourselves not to resume the production of wealth until the
> People's Charter becomes law.

This Dunfermline resolution was accompanied by a declaration of
'conviction that unless the people scrupulously abstain from all

violence and outrage' they could not succeed in wresting their rights from their oppressors, and abstention from all intoxicating drinks was 'most earnestly recommended'. This was followed by a run on the savings bank which compelled the directors to close.

The closest connection between the strikes and the Chartists was at Dundee, where the 'council and members of the Democratic Society . . . resolved to lose no time to add to the misery and distress already so prevalent'. At a public meeting on 16 August, John Duncan, 'a shoemaker . . . who is better known in town as the Chartist preacher, brother to the celebrated Abram Duncan, Chartist preacher in Arbroath', told his audience that they 'ought to rise with determination and power' and tell their oppressors that they would no longer be slaves, but also warned them that an outbreak would be the best thing the Whigs and Tories could get. The meeting decided to demand the restoration of wages to the 1839 level.

This was followed on 19 August, by a decision of 100 delegates from fifty-three different establishments, employing 1,500 workmen, to organise a strike. Most of them declared their willingness to strike, provided it were done on a national basis. Several wanted a 'rise of wages by every legitimate means' but without 'injuring persons or property'. Others were willing to protect themselves from starvation by taking food—if necessary against police interference. A 'considerable number' were willing to 'go the whole hog for the Charter'. On the next day a 'vast multitude' of 8,000–14,000 people decided at a meeting on Magdalen Green to strike for the People's Charter on the 22nd. The 'close connection of the mercantile and working class interests' was recognised in an appeal to employers to join hands with the working classes so that 'by a union of sympathy and action' they might 'build upon a lasting basis the peace and prosperity of our country'.

Despite the absence of any disturbance at these meetings, the Dundee magistrates, alarmed at the size of such assemblies, enrolled new constables, swore in special constables and issued a proclamation declaring their 'full determination to use all the means in their power to prevent and repress any breach of the peace'. In view of the resolution to strike work until the adoption of the People's Charter, they deemed it their duty to make known 'that all assemblages of persons having a direct tendency, under existing conditions, to endanger the public peace of the town, and all attempts to interfere with, or interrupt the peaceable and orderly in their usual avocations, are illegal'.

The strike for the Charter started rather inauspiciously, on 22 August, when half the workmen attending a meeting on the Green at 5 a.m. left at 6 a.m. to commence work, and deputations from Forfar and Kirriemuir failed to arrive. Later in the day, two to three thousand people attended a meeting which was addressed by the leading Chartists, Duncan, Hunter, Pryde and Anderson. John Duncan exhorted perseverance 'in the glorious struggle for liberty' which they had just commenced, but also strict preservation of order and property. It was resolved to appoint a deputation which would head a procession on the following day, and visit all public works to ask workmen to join the strike.

On 23 August about 4,000 people assembled on Magdalen Green to hear an address by Duncan on the need to reach a mutual understanding with the middle classes. As all the spinning mills and carpenters' yards and other public works were still functioning it was agreed to form a procession to parade the town. This called at the works along the Perth road, but was constantly split up by the police at road junctions on its way north to the spinning mills. The Riot Act was read by Lord Duncan at Quarry Mill, near his own property, but no collision took place between the crowd and the police; eventually, parts of the procession left Dundee and marched through Lochee. On the advice of John Mitchell, who reported on a mission to Forfar and Kirriemuir, it was agreed that a considerable number should march to Forfar to obtain reinforcements from there and from Kirremuir, and possibly also from Arbroath.

Meanwhile, in Forfar, there had been nightly meetings to hear the news from Manchester and the west of Scotland, and there was great excitement on Sunday 21 August, when an emissary from Dundee announced that 12,000 workmen in Dundee had agreed to strike until they received the 1839 level of wages. On the following night it was decided to support the Dundee strike. When it became known that a 'large body' of Dundee men were on the road to Forfar, a party of Forfar men set out to meet them. This 'large body' of about 400 men eventually arrived in Forfar at 3 a.m. on Wednesday 24, and was met by the sheriff, magistrates and special constables, but as they were not the formidable army which had been expected, and had obviously no intention of causing a riot, they were allowed to receive food and drink from the local inhabitants and hold a meeting in the market square. In the afternoon there was a procession throught the principal streets of Forfar, and then the men of Dundee marched home, accompanied for only a mile by their Forfar allies. Back in Dundee they found that some Chartists had already been arrested, and that warrants had been issued for the arrest of the leaders of the march to Forfar.

'Immediately after the suppression of the disturbance,' reported the *Dundee Advertiser* on 26 August, 'warrants were issued for the apprehension of the leaders in this foolish attempt at spreading commotion throughout Forfarshire.' Among those arrested were John Duncan, Alexander Stewart and Hugh Ross, who had acted as chairman at three of the meetings on Magdalen Green. 'No one knows for what offence John Duncan and the others were apprehended,' declared the *Dundee Herald*, which claimed that placards indicating that the Riot Act had been read were displayed an hour before it actually had been read. At no time, concluded the *Dundee Herald,* 'did the movements of the people betoken such disaster to the lives and property of the lièges as warranted the authorities in adopting the strong measures they did.'

Several of the arrested men were sentenced to terms of imprisonment after trial at Edinburgh, but the trial of John Duncan was constantly postponed, and he was never brought to trial. His sanity was affected by the strain and suspense caused by the postponement of his trial, and he died in an Edinburgh lunatic asylum in February 1845. Scottish Chartism had produced its second martyr, but the appeal for his widow and family produced little for their support.[9]

By the end of 1842, there had been little improvement in the condition of the working classes in most areas. The unemployed were 'reduced to the last extremity', while the Renfrewshire relief committee was sunk in debt, and the government refused further aid. Many of the Lanarkshire and Ayrshire collieries were still on strike, and when new hands were introduced from Glasgow there were disturbances in Midlothian in September, and in Ayrshire in October. The fear of the Chartists engineering outbreaks of violence amongst the unemployed, or further strikes for the Charter, however, had gone; and the Liberal press drew comfort from the reflection that

the late occurrences must have had a good effect in showing the working people how hopeless it is for them to attempt to carry their own objects in spite of the opposition of all other classes of society.

The *Scotsman* concluded that so long as the country could pay for soldiers and police

we may not have much to fear from this state of things, but every humane man must desire to see it remedied ... When we have separated Chartism and every other foul ingredient from the cauldron of discontent which has just boiled over, we shall find the residue made up of physical suffering, in its most aggravated and appalling forms.[10]

The damage done to Scottish Chartism as a result of the disorganised state of the movement throughout the summer of 1842, 'when there was no authorised or known source through which the opinions of the various localities could be gathered', caused the remaining activists in the movement to think once again about the question of reorganisation. The problem had been tackled at the Convention in January, and a plan had been adopted which was worked out by Abram Duncan, William Thomson, Robert Lowery, Henry Rankine of Edinburgh, and James McPherson of Aberdeen. This replaced the Central Committee for Scotland and the remaining county associations by six autonomous committees. These would direct the activities of districts centred on Glasgow, Dumfries, Dundee, Aberdeen, Edinburgh and Stirling (or Alloa). Each district committee would procure lecturers, disseminate tracts and form associations in every locality. At the national level, their activities would be co-ordinated through a corresponding or national secretary. This plan was put into operation in the west midland, south midland and eastern districts, thanks mainly to the efforts of Robert Lowery and Abram Duncan. But elsewhere it was only partially implemented, and it collapsed completely when the national secretary could no longer be afforded.

At the end of August, David Thompson of Alloa demanded the formation of a Scottish executive and the appointment of a further national secretary. A delegate conference should be held in Edinburgh to do this and to decide the policy of the Chartists towards the Complete Suffrage movement. The Edinburgh Chartists, who were also concerned at the anarchic state of the movement, considered that the January plan would have been efficient but for its dependence on the 'proper working' of the office of national secretary. This had not happened, despite the appointment of William

Thomson, and it was now 'vitally important' to implement this. They therefore took the responsibility of calling a delegate meeting in Edinburgh.

This call was obeyed by several of the remaining associations, and the Edinburgh conference took place on 3 and 4 October, with a 'fair' representation, according to the *Northern Star*. The conference decided to set up a national association on lines similar to the English National Charter Association, with a salaried secretary, a council of seven who would reside in Edinburgh, with sub-secretaries in each of the large towns who would correspond with the executive council and be entitled to sit on it. No more money would be spent on getting up meetings to memorialise the Queen. Instead they would support the publication of the *Scottish Chartist Pioneer*, which would be 'a record of the progress of the cause'. This would be edited by their secretary, Robert Lowery, who would receive a salary of a guinea a week until the association was properly established, when his salary would be raised to £1 10s.

Other funds were to be raised for the defence of the Dundee Chartists who were about to be tried, for the support of their families, and also to liquidate their collective debts to George Ross, who would once again superintend the accounts of the new association. Members would subscribe at least one penny per month to the national executive to pay the salary and expenses of the secretary and any lecturers engaged. On all occasions Chartists must take care, in calling public meetings, to do so according to the law, and when interfered with they should take proper evidence and take measures to prosecute the offending parties. Finally, the secretary should write urging alterations to the Sturge declaration, but the Chartist associations would not be advised to send delegates to the Universal Suffrage conference at Birmingham in December.[11]

Neither the agreement of the delegates at this Edinburgh conference, nor the appeals and lectures of the energetic Robert Lowery, succeeded in bringing the proposed association to life. The *Scottish Chartist Pioneer* was still-born, and most of the available funds in the hands of local associations were used, contrary to the advice of the conference, in financing delegations to the Birmingham conference. After this Sturge conference failed to improve the prospects for Chartism, nothing more was heard of plans for Scottish reorganisation for several years, and the year ended with a confession of the impossibility of maintaining any form of national organisation.

This complete collapse of national organisation, and the virtual disappearance of the Chartist press, were paralleled by the withering away of most of the local associations. During 1842 there had been an improvement in the number of associations reporting activity, compared with 1841, but by the beginning of 1843 there were probably less than forty local associations. These survived in varying degrees of disappointment and apathy, and only a handful of Chartist churches continued to display unshaken determination and confidence in the future.

NOTES

1. *Chartist Circular*, 27 June 1840; 18 September 1841.
   True Scotsman, 24 November 1838; 19 December 1840; 2 January 1841.
   Northern Star, 11 August 1838.
2. Returns of the Stamp Office.
   R. M. W. Cowan, *The Newspaper in Scotland*, 1946, pp. 160 et seq.
   W. Stewart, *The Glasgow Press in 1840*, 1920, pp. 20-4.
   Scottish Notes and Queries, September 1887; April 1890.
   Memoranda of the Chartist Agitation in Dundee, n.d., p. 20.
   True Scotsman, 20 October 1838; 16 February; 27 July 1839; 4 January 1840; 27 March 1841.
   Scottish Patriot, 7 and 21 September 1839; 2 and 9 January; 27 March 1841.
   Chartist Circular, 18 September 1841; 29 January; 12 February; 18 and 25 June; 9 July 1842.
   Scotsman, 12 January; 9 November 1842.
   Northern Star, 16 March 1839; 6 June; 29 October 1840; 5 and 26 June 1841; 26 February 1842; 30 September 1843.
3. *Chartist Circular*, 29 January; 18 and 25 June; 9 July 1842.
   Northern Star, 19 August 1843.
4. *Northern Star*, 15 January; 5 and 26 February 1842.
5. Home Office letter book 103.9 (Scotland), especially letters of 15 and 20 December 1841; 1, 9, 24, 31 January; 19 February; 29 April; 6 May 1842.
   Northern Star, 31 July; 14 and 28 August; 4 September 1841.
   Scotsman, 31 July; 24 November 1841.
   Glasgow Chronicle, 10 and 15 December 1841.
   Scotch Reformers' Gazette, 30 October 1841.
   Glasgow Argus, 15 January 1842.
6. *Hansard*, 1842, vol. lxii, col. 1375.
   English *Chartist Circular*, No. 72.
   Northern Star, 23 April; 9 July; 27 August 1842.
   Glasgow Argus, 11 and 18 June; 23 July 1842.

197

7. Home Office 103.9 (Scotland), especially letters of Sir James Graham to the Duke of Hamilton, Lord Belhaven, Sheriff Alison, Provost of Dundee, Earl of Airlie, Lord Advocate, 11, 12, 15, 22, 26 and 31 August 1842.

8. *Scotsman*, 17, 24 and 27 August 1842.
   Northern Star, 27 August 1842.
   Glasgow Argus, 27 August 1842.

9. Home Office 103.9 (Scotland), 12 and 14 August 1842.
   Scotsman, 24 and 27 August 1842.
   Northern Star, 29 July 1843; 30 November 1844; 22 February 1845.
   Memoranda of the Chartist Agitation, pp. 33–45, 59–65.

10. *Scotsman*, 27 August; 17 September; 1 and 5 October; 16 and 26 November; 3, 10 December 1842.
    Glasgow Argus, 10, 17 and 24 December 1842.

11. *Northern Star*, 23 and 30 April; 4 and 25 June; 17 September; 1 and 29 October; 5 and 11 November 1842.
    Chartist Circular, 29 January 1842.

CHAPTER FIFTEEN

The slumbering movement

When the Rev. William Hill, the recently sacked editor of the *Northern Star*, and Julian Harney, its future editor, visited Scotland in the summer of 1843, possibly in order to explore the prospects of setting up a Chartist paper, they were sadly disappointed to find the Scottish movement in a state of quiescence.

Chartism is shelved in Edinburgh [wrote Harney]. The body here have lost their Hall of meeting, and are consequently unable to hold meetings without the certainty of being involved in debt. Faction has cut the throat of Chartism in Edinburgh. Leaders have been the curse of the cause there as well as in Glasgow; and there, too, the traitors are the worst enemies to the movement, and are doing everything in their power to keep up discussion and create further disgust. In Glasgow, Chartism had been all but assassinated by the preaching prigs, and political knaves, who for a long time were looked up to as the leaders of the democratic cause in Glasgow. These fellows since their defection to the Complete Suffrage ranks, have acted as the worst enemies of Chartism...Not a meeting was held for many months but at which strife, bickering and denunciation was the order of the day, caused by the private slanders and open calumnies of these now justly detested traitors. Their defection, and the strife which preceded it, naturally caused the people to become disgusted with almost all public men and weary of all political agitation hence the present apathetic state of Glasgow.

Hill, however, refused to accept the complaint, which met him 'in almost every town', that the agitation was dead. He saw this absence of enthusiasm not as evidence of apathy but as proof that the people had 'ceased to be the creatures of passion; that they are less easily affected by sudden gusts of feeling, and more addicted to habits of thought'. This contention was borne out, in his opinion, by the fact that even where no regular Chartist activity took place, the Chartists refused to let any other faction appeal to the people:

If the enemy take the field, the people will turn out. If an anti-corn law meeting was to be held ... with but slight notice, and discussion allowed, they would muster strong and carry all before them. Any other party never thinks of it. Neither Tories nor Whigs, merely as such, would dare to hazard any appeal to the public voice.

It was pleasing to Hill to find that the puerile, though conspicuous and imposing, demonstrations, processions and pageantry had now given place to a less ostentatious determination. Except to hear 'a stranger who is much respected' or 'from whom they expect to learn something', the people no longer, in the

old cultivated Chartist districts, come out to hear lectures; just because they know all that the lecturers can tell them. They have heard the old story over and over again, till they are tired of it.

In Glasgow, Gorbals, Anderston, Hamilton, Aberdeen, Dundee and the Vale of Leven, Hill found that 'the strength and power of Chartism' now lay in the Christian Chartist churches and schools. In Dundee 'the Church has kept Chartism alive. It has long been the only prominent form in which it could be recognised'. In the Vale of Leven the Chartist church was 'the form in which Chartism appeared, while the school was the means of ensuring its continuance. The situation was similar in Glasgow, except that the party led by James Moir and John Colquhoun stood apart from the church, though they had 'more sense than to vituperate' against 'Church Chartists' or 'Temperance Chartists'. Harney also found 'the sacred fire of Chartism' being kept burning strongly in Gorbals, through the Chartist church and its school.

What Hill found distressing about Scottish Chartism in 1843 was that, in the absence of any effective national system of organisation, the various local organisations which had been identified with the agitation had been neglected. In many of the 'very best Chartist districts there is no Association—no Committee—no public body of any kind, although, individually, there are more Chartists than ever there were'. On the credit side, Hill found most gratifying in the Scottish Chartists 'the cool bearing and discretion of the people. They have little of the blind trustfulness of the Irish or of the hotheaded increasing enthusiasm which characterises many of the English; and hence though they have enough of dissension among "leaders" the people do not let the cause be damaged'.

Hill's analysis had been previously suggested by an Ayrshire correspondent of the *Northern Star*, and was supported by other correspondents. A Paisley Chartist claimed that while few meetings were being held and while there were no contributions, no lecturing and little or no organisation, 'a deep and firmly rooted conviction' had entered the soul that

no proposed remedy short of the Charter is in any degree worth one moment's consideration ... Chartism is in life, and waits only the call to awaken from a most refreshing slumber, which will be found to have invigorated, strengthened and given new energies to it.[1]

Nevertheless, however many individuals might continue to regard themselves as Chartists, there could be no disguising the disillusionment and loss of hope felt by the great mass of the Chartists. The period 1843–47 was enlivened by frequent tours by English Chartists, but only the 'national land scheme' of Feargus O'Connor had any marked success in rekindling Chartist hopes. Many of the old Chartist leaders continued to figure in local political affairs, but the period was marked chiefly by continued divisions amongst the Chartists, and the only Chartist organisations which remained strong were some of the Chartist churches. All attempts to reconstitute a broadly based union were stultified by the position of Feargus O'Connor in the esteem of his admirers, and by the absence of a Chartist press which could stand outside the antagonism between the *Northern Star* and the *Glasgow Saturday Post and Renfrewshire Reformer*.

The range of interests of the surviving active Chartists was wide. It varied from the production of dramatic 'representations' in Renfrewshire and Glasgow, for the repayment of the debt to George Ross, and in Ayrshire for the erection of a monument to Dr John Taylor, who had died of consumption in December 1842, to participation in public meetings for the promotion of public baths and Sunday trains. Performances of 'The Trial of Robert Emmett' were staged in Greenock, the Vale of Leven, Glasgow, Paisley and Johnstone by a company sponsored by the Greenock Universal Suffrage Association and their performances in Cooke's Circus, Glasgow, raised £70 for the liquidation of the debt to Ross. In the Vale of Leven the proceeds were devoted to financing a hall, and elsewhere to the liquidation of the debts of the Greenock association. This led the Glasgow Charter Association to accuse the Greenock Chartists of profiteering at the expense of the Ross fund. At the

Glasgow meetings for the establishment of public baths, Cullen, McFarlane, Pattison and Rodger were to be found playing prominent parts, along with Sheriff Alison, Professor Balfour and the Lord Provost. Matthew Cullen, Malcolm McFarlane, Andrew Harley and David Harrower were also in the forefront of the growing agitation for the Ten Hours Factory Bill, and Allan MacFadyen was the secretary of the Glasgow committee. Amongst the Irish repealers, Robert Malcolm jun., now sub-editor of the *Glasgow Saturday Post*, was emerging as a highly respected adviser and champion. In the 'Glasgow Repeal Reading Room on Teetotal Principles' he gave a series of lectures on the power of knowledge to improve the morality of the masses, and his appeal to Joseph Sturge to support him produced a declaration from Sturge on the establishment of 'Local Parliaments' for both Scotland and Ireland.[2]

The question of poor law reform in Scotland also attracted Chartist energy. At times of widespread unemployment, Chartists were also to be found organising meetings to direct public attention to the plight of the unemployed. In February 1843, when it was estimated that 7,529 people were unemployed in Glasgow and suburbs, and that 18,516 were in a state of helpless destitution, collections for their relief were taken in the Chartist churches, and James Moir advised the unemployed to assemble every day until the city authorities provided them with work. The conduct of parish authorities in their administration of poor relief enraged many Chartists, and the Rev. Patrick Brewster carried on a constant agitation against the relief activities of the Paisley authorities, and in particular against Provost John Henderson, editor of the *Glasgow Saturday Post and Renfrewshire Reformer*. This despite the fact that Henderson was a supporter of Dr W. P. Alison's proposals for poor law reform, and that Paisley dispensed more on poor relief, per head of population, than almost all other towns in Scotland.

In 1841 Brewster had formed a Society for the Protection of the Destitute Poor in Paisley, and in his efforts to do likewise elsewhere he had preached a sermon on the Scottish poor laws in the Glasgow Chartist Church. For this and similar sermons, Brewster had been suspended for a year from his ministerial functions by the General Assembly of the Church of Scotland in May 1842. Brewster denounced the 'boasted provision made for the poor in Scotland' as a 'murderous, unchristian and even illegal system', and maintained that it even starved the poor to death. His sentence was never carried out because of the disruption of the Church of Scotland at the following General Assembly. In December 1843, Brewster published a volume of the offending sermons, coupled with a vindication of his conduct in attacking the Radical provost of Paisley.

With a trade recovery in the summer of 1843, when most of the wage reductions imposed eighteen months before were restored, Chartist activity in relation to poor relief waned until 1845, when the Poor Law Commissioners were inquiring into the state of the poor. In December 1844, Robert Peddie and the Edinburgh Chartists held public meetings on the evidence which was being offered to the commissioners, and in Glasgow public meetings were held in June 1845 to promote the objects of the 'Association for the Protection of the Poor'. During 1845 and 1846 the *Northern Star* paid considerable attention to the questions of the Scottish poor laws, of Scottish landlords and of destitution in the Highlands—a subject which was of absorbing interest at that time to Dr Charles Marx. Towards the end of 1846 the Chartists were again to the fore in promoting public meetings of the unemployed.[3]

The most difficult of the issues which faced the Chartists in the period 1843–47 were the questions of their relationships with the Complete Suffragists on the one hand, and with the National Charter Association on the other. Closer relationship with either of these bodies precluded the possibility of co-operation with the other. The problem was particularly embarrassing for the Glasgow Charter Association, though the absence of any great strength in both these potential partners prevented the matter ever becoming too acute, and the issue was resolved mainly by personal choice.

Hopes were constantly expressed in the *Glasgow Saturday Post* for a coalition between the Chartists and the Anti-Corn Law League.

The great leading object of all parties is the same [it declared]. Everything that has been called for by Mr Attwood, by Mr Sturge, by Mr Cobden and their respective adherents, is necessary for the prosperity of the country; and therefore in place of driving at the different objects in detached masses, the whole strength of the reform interest should be made to bear on one question at a time ... individual views should be merged in the measure likely to be first successful and in the organisation which is the most complete and influential at the present time.

Since there were only two 'powerful agitations organised in England, the Anti-Corn Law League and the Complete Suffrage Association', the Chartists should come over to the Complete Suffrage movement. The prospects of such a *rapprochement* were somewhat enhanced by the favourable impressions created by Henry Vincent and Joseph Sturge during their tours in 1843 and 1844. Moir, Aucott, Gillespie and Lang, of the Charter Association, joined with Pattison, McFarlane and Rodger, of the Suffragists, in praising Vincent for his conduct as the Complete Suffrage candidate at the Kilmarnock election in May 1844. This followed several weeks of negotiations, in January and February, for the reconciliation of 'the old and new move parties'. These broke down at a conference on 9 February over the insistence of the Suffragists that the Chartists give up the leadership of Feargus O'Connor and systematic opposition to the Anti-Corn Law League. The most serious attempt at reconciliation was made in December 1844, when a meeting was called by Joseph Sturge to investigate the possibility of union between the leaders of the Complete Suffrage Association and the Chartist Association. At this meeting James Moir, of the Glasgow Charter Association, explained the threefold division which was crippling the efforts of the Glasgow Radicals. His recommendation that they should all combine was supported by James Lang and John Colquhoun, now of the Glasgow National Charter Association, but was opposed by Robert Malcolm jun., John Rodger and James Turner of the Complete Suffrage Association. If there was to be union, the Chartists must give up interrupting corn law meetings and voting Tory. Sturge outlined the proposed conduct of the Complete Suffrage party, and of Sharman Crawford in Parliament, but he could go no further than urge all parties to put forward Complete Suffrage candidates at all elections.[4]

Meanwhile, the more orthodox of the Chartists had been showing interest in the elaboration of O'Connor's land plan, and in the legality of the proposed scheme of national organisation. Although no Scottish representatives had been sent to the conference at Birmingham in September 1843, Colquhoun and Smith of the Glasgow Charter Association declared their intention of joining their English brethren if the plan of national organisation received the sanction of the certifying barrister. From Aberdeen John Smart wrote that 'we will now take up the new scheme with earnestness and determination', and the *Northern Star* declared that from all quarters north of the Tweed

we have letters of congratulation on the adoption of the 'New Plan'. We have long been talking of, and urging the union of the democrats of the two countries. That union will now undoubtedly be cemented. This alone is worth all the labour and expense of the late Conference.

In support of his plan for purchasing small allotments for the working classes, and of the reconstituted National Charter Association, Feargus O'Connor made a tour of Scotland in October and November 1843, accompanied by Thomas Duncombe, the Radical MP. At Glasgow, Edinburgh and Aberdeen there were banquets, soirées and processions in their honour. At Aberdeen a procession of the united trades, led by the United Bakers in 'full regalia', was held with great pomp and pageantry in honour of the 'Men of the People'. R. G. Gammage, who was also touring Scotland in the autumn of 1843, described the scene at Aberdeen, with the United Bakers clad in suits of rich pink muslin, splendid turbans, and headed by marshals in velvet, with broad swords of polished steel, mounted on richly caparisoned horses. There was a chaplain in 'full canonicals' and powdered wig, and another in sacerdotal robes, bearing a Bible on a red cushion suspended from his neck. The master had a rich train borne by 'five pages of beautiful appearance and richly dressed'.

In Edinburgh, on 23 October, O'Connor addressed the working classes on his new plan, while Duncombe was honoured by a soirée given by the Complete Suffrage leaders, John Dunlop, the Rev. James Robertson and the Rev. Dr Ritchie. Seven days later, at a Chartist banquet in Glasgow, O'Connor was greeted with both cheers and hissing when he took the occasion as appropriate for an attack on the middle classes, the shopocrats, the millocrats, the Liberal press and all its reporters. Whigs and Tories were abused with equal vigour, and he moved on to denounce the 'Complete Suffrage Humbug', the Anti-Corn Law League and its 'grasping, deceiving humbugs', whose only object was to maintain their own profits at the expense of the interests and wages of the working man. He proposed to carry the Charter by putting a stop to the proceedings of the House of Commons. This could be done with twenty men such as Duncombe—'whole-hog Chartists' who could speak for eight or nine hours at a time and move amendments to every motion for supplies. Seats could be purchased for the twenty in some English boroughs. Richard Cobden, John Bright and Colonel Perronet Thompson then came under O'Connor's lash, and he concluded with vituperation against the Church of Scotland.[5]

Wherever he went, O'Connor enrolled members for the National Charter Association. In Glasgow, where more than 500 enrolled, he insisted on leaving an additional 1,000 cards. Then in his report in the *Northern Star* he was able to claim that he had 'disposed of' 1,500 cards of membership in Glasgow. In Dumfries, where the Chartists claimed to be still 'the ruling faction', a 'well timed visit' by O'Connor added fresh zeal to the cause, and led to the merging of the seven year old Working Men's Association into the National Charter Association. In Paisley 'a few friends of the cause' decided to form a 'locality' of the National Charter Association, and at Long Govan the visit of O'Connor and Duncombe provided the inspiration for a brief revival.

Elsewhere, apart from Aberdeen, Alva and Lochee, little enthusiasm was shown for the National Charter Association, and O'Connor's tour was hardly an unqualified success. His claim that there were 1,500 members of the Association in Glasgow raised the eyebrows of the Chartist leaders, who were still debating whether to join the NCA. James Moir welcomed the new national organisation with a half-sovereign, but in a somewhat gloomy letter to O'Connor expressed his lack of faith in the national scheme; and the efforts of Colquhoun, Smith, Brown, Sherrington and Burrell to merge the Glasgow Charter Association with the NCA were frustrated by the opposition of Moir, Ross, Harley and 'Parson' Adams.

James Moir was convinced that Chartist strength was considerably less than the ever-optimistic estimates of O'Connor and the NCA executive. It was futile to dissipate the energies of their active adherents in support of the vague objects of the amorphous national organisation. The most profitable policy would now be to develop certain of the strongest Chartist districts into strongholds for parliamentary and municipal elections. He did not despair of the people doing their duty, but he could not help remarking on his grief and irritation at the 'dishonesty' of the Chartists in the performance of their past resolutions. In Glasgow, where they had had many

very multitudinous expressions of public opinion in favour of our principles...we have never had, in the whole city of Glasgow and suburbs, more than two thousand members in our Association; and I believe that we never had even that number for three months at one time.

This attitude pained and surprised O'Connor, who had long regarded Moir as the most trustworthy and faithful of his lieutenants.

Knowing Moir well [he wrote], I can only assume that he anticipates greater results from local than from national organisation—and this it is my duty to combat. Except as an element of national organisation, local organisation cannot be of any benefit ... It would be sycophantic in me to allow Mr Moir to suppose for one moment that the most popular man in the world could now diverge from the high road of Chartism into the bye-ways of local agitation.

The Glasgow heretic, however, remained impenitent despite this mild yet imperious reprimand. For the first time in his life, Moir spoke up strongly against O'Connor's attitude. He had not wished to criticise the National Charter Association for lacking strength, but the people for failing to provide support for it. He had even contributed to its funds, but it had proved hopeless to try to win strength for it in Scotland, where he was convinced it would never work. This conviction was due not to disaffection, but to annoyance at those who professed Chartism without supporting it financially either at national or local level. Despite O'Connor's excuses for the Chartists, it was not poverty that was the trouble. 'It is the want of will, and not the want of ability.' He doubted whether there were 300 persons in Glasgow taking an active interest in the advancement of Chartism. The lack of money in the exchequer of the National Charter Association in England was, for him, strong proof of the absence of union. Chartism might still be said to have a name, but it was nearly as dead as it could be.[6]

The vigour of Moir's criticism must have been quite a shock to O'Connor. Instead of being denounced and thrown to the lions with the other heretics, Moir was applauded as a 'reasoning politician', a 'zealous patriot' and an 'honest man'. Moir's policy of electoral organisation, however, was never taken very seriously, even in Glasgow. In October 1846 a 'Local Registration and Election Committee' was eventually established, consisting of Moir, Lang, Ross, Sherrington, Aucott, Brown, Colquhoun and twenty of their colleagues, and it was then reported from Glasgow that 'after four years of slumber, the friends of progress are once more called into action'. Prospects were declared to be

very cheering ... inasmuch as party differences appear to be buried in oblivion. The land movement, the prospect of an early dissolution of Parliament, and the election of town councillors under the new Police Bill ... have all contributed to secure this happy result. The preparations for the city elections are promising.

Earlier in the year Moir had been elected a General Commissioner of Police, but disappointment was in store for the high hopes which had been entertained of securing the election of Moir and Ross in the elections to the city council in December. Both were narrowly defeated, thanks to the Irish repealers failing to provide promised votes (despite Moir's support for repeal in recent years), but both were elected to the new parochial boards.[7]

James Moir's membership card for the Irish Universal Suffrage Association (reproduced half size)

The prospects for the election of a Chartist parliamentary candidate were never again so bright in Scotland as when Henry Vincent contested the Kilmarnock burghs in May 1844. So general was the enthusiasm for Vincent prior to the election, both among the electors and non-electors, that the Liberal Bouverie almost withdrew. In the event Vincent gained 98 votes for a programme which promised support for Sturge and the Complete Suffrage Union, abolition of the corn laws, Church disestablishment, and tax reduction. His supporters claimed that he had lost many more votes as a result of the success of Bouverie's agent in persuading Vincent's supporters in the scattered constituency that Vincent had withdrawn to avoid splitting the Liberal vote.

At the Greenock by-election in 1845, Chartist schoolmaster John McCrae won 'an enormous show of hands' on 15 April, but declared that the Chartists would not go to the poll, in order to reserve strength for the next general election. When that came, in July 1847, the Chartists made use of the hustings once again for propagating their faith. At Dumfries and Paisley, Andrew Wardrop and Robert Cochran made long speeches in proposing votes of thanks to the Returning Officers. At Greenock, Aberdeen and in the Fifeshire county election, Chartist candidates McCrae, McPherson and Gourlay went as far as the hustings, but only John McCrae, now pastor and teacher of the Dundee Chartist church, appeared determined to go to the poll. But even in his case the financial strength which had been 'reserved' from 1845 was deemed insufficient. During the 1847 elections in Scotland, only slight attention was paid to the tactics of the Chartists and Radicals, and they were much less feared by the Whigs and the Liberal press than had been the case in 1841.[8]

Even more distressing to the Glasgow adherents of the National Charter Association than the sceptism of James Moir was the message which Peter Murray McDouall brought to his fellow countrymen on his return from exile in France. While on a lecture tour in November and December 1844, McDouall disclosed his plans for establishing a Chartist newspaper in Glasgow. He had been delighted to find that at a time when no place in England could claim to have more than 200 members of the National Charter Association, Glasgow had over 800. Moreover, since he found that the interests and grievances of the English and Scottish peoples were different, and that assimilation was impossible, McDouall proposed the formation of a separate Scottish organisation, conducted purely by Scotsmen from its headquarters in Glasgow.

This attitude astounded the Glasgow Council of the Association, who had regarded McDouall as an accredited emissary of the NCA executive. McDouall's plan was particularly distasteful to Duncan Sherrington and James Smith, who had been mainly responsible for the splitting up of the Glasgow Charter Association in June 1844 in order to form a branch of the NCA. James Smith, the secretary, immediately wrote to Thomas Clark, of the executive, who had recently been in Glasgow and who had strongly recommended McDouall to Smith and his colleagues 'as calculated to render valuable assistance' in establishing localities of the National Charter Association.

I am indeed very sorry he is not the man I expected him to be; and I am afraid he will damn our future prospects. I do think the Executive is very much to blame in recommending a man holding such views, to the people of Scotland.

'We have set our faces against the system of private letter-writing formerly so prevalent and always so pregnant with evil consequences,' declared the NCA executive, who proceeded to try to exculpate themselves by publishing the private letter from Smith to Clark. Justice to all concerned required the publication of this letter, which came from 'so pure and good a source as leaves no doubt of its accuracy' and pointed out that

The Executive could not hold itself chargeable with any act of Dr McDouall, inasmuch as he was not appointed or even recommended as a lecturer by them . . . Dr McDouall is lecturing exclusively on his own account; and, as far as we know, is not lecturing for the Chartist cause.

This disclaimer by the NCA, its support for Smith's allegations, and its publication of 'private' correspondence in the *Northern Star* led to all-round recriminations. These moves were regarded by McDouall as an attempt to discredit him and ruin his chances of starting a newspaper in Glasgow. He declared that the members of the old executive of the Association, including himself, had striven hard to effect an Anglo-Scottish union but had failed. O'Connor had succeeded in his efforts to enrol Scotsmen in the National Charter Association—but only for a time. Then the best and most energetic of the working class and middle class men in the movement had worked 'day and night' to keep up the spirit, but they also had failed, and it remained to be seen whether Thomas Clark's recent attempt would bring any success.

The cause of failure [diagnosed McDouall] does not lie with the plan of organisation, or with the leaders. It rests with the people, who had sunk into a sleep of apathy, from which nothing seems capable of arousing them. I simply suggested that, as all had apparently failed in Scotland, the best plan would be to appeal to her nationality, to assemble her delegates and to give force to the organisation by the unanimous voice of a National Convention—nothing short of that, in my opinion, can effect it.

From Glasgow, on 30 December, James Smith wrote condemning the action of the executive. Not merely had they published a private letter in the *Northern Star*, but they had done so on the 28th, without publishing also a second letter from him to Thomas Clark, written on the 16th, in which he had modified his earlier

criticism of McDouall. This had followed a meeting on the previous day between himself, McDouall, Sherrington, Burrell and
Samuel Kydd, at which it was found that the difference in attitude,
even between McDouall and Kydd, was really only slight.

On 11 January 1845 the *Northern Star* tried to make amends by
publishing this and other correspondence expressing confidence in
both McDouall and Smith as 'honest Chartists'. This included
strong support from the Dundee Chartist Council for McDouall,
who would 'infuse life into the movement', along with condemnation of the 'inconsistent action' of the National Charter Association
executive in professing a desire to allay bickering while publishing
a document which must have the contrary effect. Meanwhile, after
a most successful lecture series in Aberdeen and Dundee, an irate
McDouall had returned to Glasgow to denounce Smith as 'a mean,
cowardly, sneaking spy' and to abuse the *Northern Star* and the
NCA for its encouragement of Smith and his friends.

This attack took place also on 11 January, when McDouall, after
a lecture on 'The rights of labour' and on 'The right of the people to
full, fair and complete suffrage', complained of the 'intolerant spirit
of overbearing despotism' shown by certain Chartists towards others
holding the same great principles but differing on other reforms.
In his attack on the *Northern Star* he was supported by James
Adams, Joseph Kerr and James Walker, who energetically denounced

the whole course of policy adopted by the *Star* and its supporters, not
only towards Dr McDouall, but towards every other talented Chartist
who was capable of displaying anything like ability and honesty in the
advancement of the movement.

The *Northern Star* now confessed itself 'at a loss for any justifiable
explanation of this cause . . . The *Star* did not interfere in the
dispute, nor take sides, and expressed no opinion on the question'.
Moreover the NCA executive must have

the right to set themselves right with the Chartist body as to the connection between them and a certain party whom they had more than
reason to believe was thwarting and undoing what they had deemed
essential for the good of the Chartist cause.[9]

To repair the damage done by the McDouall affair, the Association sent Philip McGrath, its president, on a Scottish tour at the
beginning of April 1845. McGrath lectured in Glasgow, Edin-

burgh, Kilmarnock and Hamilton on 'The benefits of trades unions' and on 'The probable results of a full and free representation of the people'. From Kilmarnock it was reported that he was 'the best Chartist lecturer that has been in this town', but elsewhere he failed to arouse any enthusiasm, and his tour was conveniently 'curtailed by the necessity to return to London' for the annual Convention on 21 April.

Although little interest had been taken in O'Connor's land plan during 1843 and 1844, something of the old Chartist faith was rekindled during the years 1845–47 by the Chartist Co-operative Land Society. This simple and specific object revived hope in the future for many, and provided a focus for fresh zeal in those areas where Chartism still had latent strength. For a time, however, the main interest lay in the criticism and ridicule which the scheme drew from Bronterre O'Brien, and the hostility between the O'Connorite and O'Brienite factions.

Hamilton rallied to O'Connor's defence against the attacks of McDouall, while Paisley assured him that his popularity

is too well-grounded in the affections of a grateful, though oppressed, people to suffer the least injury from the foul and unprovoked slanders sought to be heaped on his character by that precious trio of base calumniators, Ashton, Hill and O'Brien.

In Glasgow, the NCA group reflected with 'mixed feelings of regret and joy on the many attempts that interested men have made to injure the character of Mr. F. O'Connor':

We regret that men so base should have attached themselves to principles so holy . . . and we rejoice that Mr O'Connor, by a singleness of purpose seldom equalled, and by a devotion to principles never surpassed, has been fully able to establish his innocence in spite of the hideous calumnies circulated against him.

This outburst of admiration was the outcome of one of the efforts to calumniate this paragon of virtue when O'Brien was billed to lecture, in the Chartist church, Blackfriars Street, on 'O'Connor's villainy and treachery; his betrayal of Frost and others'. This unmasking of O'Connor's 'treachery' on 22 April was carried out by James Adams, Joseph Kerr and James Walker, as O'Brien failed to appear. The meeting was disrupted and the O'Connorites manhandled Walker and other denunciators of O'Connor.[10]

The land scheme was introduced to many of the Scottish Chartists by Philip McGrath when he again toured Scotland during October and November 1845. Several of his lectures were still on trades unions, machinery, and the corn laws, but most were now devoted to exposition of the great possibilities offered by peasant smallholdings. Such was the productive power of the land that Britain's 67 million acres of cultivable land could comfortably support a population of 134 million people. McGrath agreed with the 'great principle of Nationalising the Land'. Until the people had the land as their inheritance, and the Charter to protect it, the tendency of their condition in the social scale would be downwards.

In the promotion of Scottish branches of the Society, McGrath met with some success, and local societies were established or strengthened in Glasgow, Greenock, Hamilton, Linlithgow, Newmilns, the Vale of Leven, Alva, Arbroath, Campsie and Dundee. Then, for the first time since 1842, a Scottish delegate was sent to a Chartist conference in England. At the Land Conference in Manchester in December 1845, almost all the Scottish branches were represented by Duncan Sherrington, an aged Glasgow Chartist, who was elected chairman of the conference. In his opening address Sherrington stressed the value of legal protection, which would be afforded by registration either as a friendly society or as a joint stock company, and proposed that the advance of £15 to each allottee should stand as a lien, with 5 per cent added per annum, until all members were established on the land. This would be reserved rent which should always revert to the Society in one form or another. He thought it would be impracticable to fix rent except by the scale of the cost of the acreage.

Considerably more branches of the Land Society were formed during 1846, and further impetus was given to this movement by a lengthy tour, in September, October and November, by Christopher Doyle. By the end of 1846 about twenty-six branches had been formed in Scotland. About thirty lectures by Doyle dealt with the extent of cultivable land in Great Britain, and its productive capacity when laid out in small allotments and cultivated on the small farm principles set forth by O'Connor. The only effectual remedy to counteract 'the baneful effect of land and machinery' was provided by the principles of the Chartist Land Society. During his tour, in addition to his efforts for the Land Society, Doyle succeeded in enlisting the support of more than fifty leading Chartists in thirteen

Scottish towns for Julian Harney's 'Democratic Committee for Poland's Regeneration'.

After the annual conference of the Land Society, at Birmingham in December 1846, Robert Burrell visited O'Connorville and was lost in wonder and astonishment

while I gazed upon what I may be allowed to designate a paradise. I cannot find words or language sufficiently to express the pleasurable impressions which thrilled through my frame, when the grand, the sublime spectacle burst upon my sight.

Nevertheless, despite such ecstatic testimony from men like Burrell of Greenock and Sherrington of Glasgow, the provision of support for the scheme was only slight in Scotland in comparison with the response in England. The number of Scottish shareholders was not numerous, and the rate of inflow of subscriptions never became substantial. During the last five months of 1846 only Glasgow, Edinburgh and Alva contributed more than £20 each, and the total subscribed by twenty-six Scottish branches was only £265. Even in the summer, when the land scheme was at its peak and the number of Scottish branches had risen to thirty-four, their subscriptions seldom exceeded 5 per cent of the total for Great Britain.[11]

NOTES

1. *Northern Star*, 2 and 9 September 1843.
2. *Northern Star*, 1, 22 and 29 April; 13 May; 17 June; 9 September; 27 November 1843.
   Glasgow Saturday Post, 26 October; 23 and 30 November; 28 December 1844; 11 and 18 January 1845; 12 December 1846.
   Glasgow Examiner, 6 and 20 July 1844.
   Ayr Advertiser, 8 December 1842.
3. *Glasgow Chronicle*, 24 and 27 February 1843.
   Glasgow Argus, 6 and 20 May 1841.
   Glasgow Saturday Post, 19 and 26 August; 2 and 9 September; 23 December 1843; 26 December 1846.
   Northern Star, 4 January; 15 March; 24 May; 7 and 21 June; 5 and 12 July; 9 August; 20 September; 18 October 1845.
   P. Brewster, *Seven Chartist and Military Sermons*, 1843.
4. *Glasgow Saturday Post*, 2 September; 23 November 1843; 4 June; 30 November; 7 December 1844.
   Glasgow Examiner, 1 and 8 June 1844.
   Glasgow Argus, 9 December 1844.
   Glasgow Chronicle, 24 February 1843.
   Northern Star, 17 February 1844.

5. *Northern Star*, 15 July; 5 August; 9, 16 and 23 September; 2 December 1843.
   Glasgow Saturday Post, 28 October; 4 November 1843.
   R. G. Gammage, *History of the Chartist Movement*, 1894.
6. *Northern Star*, 30 September; 4 and 18 November; 2 and 9 December 1843; 15 and 29 June; 13 July 1844.
7. *Northern Star*, 13 July 1844; 17 October; 26 December 1846.
   Glasgow Saturday Post, 26 December 1846.
8. *Glasgow Saturday Post*, 25 April; 1 and 4 June 1844.
   Glasgow Examiner, 25 April; 8 June 1844.
   Northern Star, 5 and 19 April; 27 December 1845; 17, 24 and 31 July 1847.
   Scotsman, 21 July; 4 August 1847.
   North British Daily Mail, 30 July 1847.
9. *Northern Star*, 23 November; 7 and 28 December 1844; 4, 11, 18 and 25 January; 1 February 1845.
   Glasgow Saturday Post, 18 January 1845.
10. *Northern Star*, 1 and 8 March; 12, 19 and 26 April 1845; 31 May 1845.
11. *Northern Star*, 25 October; 1 and 15 November; 6 and 13 December 1845; 26 September; 10, 17, 24 and 31 October; 7, 14 and 28 November; 26 December 1846; 2 October 1847.

CHAPTER SIXTEEN

1848 : a brief reawakening

The year 1848 saw little more of a Chartist revival in Scotland than that which had been confidently predicted in October 1846 but which failed to materialise. Nevertheless, largely as a result of the excitement aroused by the European revolutions of February 1848, Chartism, even in Scotland, succeeded in creating considerable trepidation in middle class breasts. Indeed, for several months, with stagnant Chartist associations suddenly coming back to life, it did appear as if the long-heralded reawakening of Chartism was about to take place.

Lecture tours by Samuel Kydd at the end of 1847, by Peter Murray McDouall early in 1848, and by Ernest Jones in April rekindled some sparks of the old enthusiasm, and these were fanned by the *North British Weekly Express*—'The Only Democratic Newspaper published in Scotland'—which was edited by the Rev. William Hill, formerly editor of the *Northern Star*. This paper became the property of the leading Chartists of Edinburgh at the end of 1847, and reflected a determination on their part to make Edinburgh Chartism a force to be reckoned with. In addition to advocacy of the Charter and the 'Rights of Labour' it was also dedicated to 'Repeal of the Union'.

Unemployment and short-time working, which were alarmingly widespread at the end of 1847 in Glasgow and Paisley, deepened in the early months of 1848; destitution spread throughout Lanarkshire and the depressed industrial areas. Hunger demonstrations by the unemployed, especially the unrelieved able-bodied unemployed, developed into food riots in Glasgow, Edinburgh and several other towns. For a short time, especially in April, it appeared that a substantial movement directed by the Chartists might emerge from the prevailing distress.

In some parts of the country the 'brotherly feeling' between Chartists and Irish repealers which had been manifested at several demonstrations in 1847 developed in fraternal unions. In Edinburgh in March there were meetings to form a National Guard, and wild speeches there and elsewhere on the possession of firearms and on the formation of a Chartist National Guard in Edinburgh, Dundee and Aberdeen encouraged fears that Chartism was becoming militant. But while there was dilatoriness on the part of the authorities in providing adequate relief, and possibly some incapacity in the handling of police forces in March, there was more froth than substance to Chartist threats, and serious apprehension of insurrection was never justified. After July 1848, Scottish Chartism was as quiescent again as it had been after August 1842.

The gloomy background against which this Chartist drama was to be played was perceptively noted, at the turn of the year, in an editorial in the *Glasgow Examiner*:

The new year is ushered in, not amidst mirth and gladness, but with gloom and fearful foreboding...We are prostrated...The year 1847 will be an epoch in our history...[Some] will view it as the year in which the inhabitants of the wealthiest and most powerful nation which has ever existed, were on the borders of starvation. Her people crying for bread, and, to satisfy her urgent entreaties and perishing wants, the produce of many kingdoms were landed upon her shores. The fearful visitations of pestilence and want, which conspired to assail that most miserable of all countries, Ireland, where anarchy reigns uncontrolled ...shall be remembered...We have had a series of unexampled bankruptcies, the severity and rapid succession of which have humbled our pride and broken our spirits. This commercial hurricane has swept over our land, and left traces of its ravages in every quarter...Mills, closed or working short-time, were found everywhere; reduced wages were paid to our operatives, and mechanics were thrown out of employment under the gloomiest apprehensions.

At the end of 1847 in Paisley, 3,000–4,000 were receiving relief, in addition to 850 on casual pauper relief. Many unemployed were being 'sent home' to Ireland. No new webs were being given out to hand-loom weavers, who were entirely dependent on public charity. The growing severity of this depression was stressed in Parliament by Lord George Bentinck in May 1848. Nothing in the commercial history of Scotland approached the sequestrations during the first nineteen weeks of the year. Only 1842, with 222 sequestrations in a comparable period, came near that. Of fifty-seven mills in Paisley and Glasgow, eighteen had stopped altogether and seven were working short-time. Three Paisley manufacturers had given notice of intention to turn 1,000 families out of their houses, and 3,000 other families had also received notice that they would be turned out. Ruin assailed 'mill-owner, operative, planter, broker, and domestic servant'. Already by February there were 13,000–15,000 unemployed in Glasgow. This included large numbers of engineers, machine makers, iron founders, shoemakers and tailors, but did not include workers in power loom factories, who had gone on strike when faced with wage reductions of 17–28 per cent.[1]

Serious disturbances took place in Glasgow on 6 March, when a gathering of several hundred unemployed on Glasgow Green decided to show its dissatisfaction with the magistrates and the relief committee by marching into the city. Soup kitchens had been promised by Bailie Stewart, the acting chief magistrate, but these were not immediately forthcoming, and while the police returned from the Green and assembled at the Central Police Office a mob attacked provision stores and a gun shop in Glasgow's main street, the Trongate, and in London Street. The police who had been in attendance at meetings on the Green had not expected any trouble to materialise. There had been no exceptional incitement in the language of the leaders, and the crowd had dispersed in all directions at the end of the meeting. While the police and magistrates were recovering from their surprise on hearing of shopbreaking and rioting, a mob was allowed to run riot virtually unchecked through the streets of Glasgow between 3 and 5 p.m. Eventually the Riot Act was read and military forces were called in to patrol the city, but further rioting occurred on the following day at Bridgeton, where the pensioners fired on a crowd which was pelting them with stones. Six people were shot, including a special constable.

Disgraceful and formidable riots were reported by the *Scotsman* on 8 March to have taken place at Glasgow,

and some less serious ... ones in our own city last night. In Glasgow the disturbance ... was not put down till the mob had been fired on, and at least one life lost; in Edinburgh, peace was restored with less trouble and without great injury to person. In both cases the object of the riot was only mischief and plunder; and it is a mistake unjust in itself ... to call the disturbances 'Chartist Riots'. They had nothing political about them, and it is unfair to attach their disgrace to any political party, however rash and violent.

The rioting fever was not confined to Glasgow and Edinburgh, but the principal other riots—at Kilmarnock and Ayr—were attributed to 'ill-disposed boys', 'thoughtless youths' and 'Irish navvies' who set old oil hogsheads on fire. From Leith it was rumoured that the Chartists were to hold a meeting and 300 university students marched down from Edinburgh 'to keep the peace'. A riot was confidently expected, but the students returned disappointed. At Greenock, the provost gracefully declined to occupy the chair at a meeting which was to petition for the Charter. He knew that the Chartist committee was well intentioned, but there was a danger that the present excitement would be 'taken advantage of, by scoundrels attending from a distance'.

Meanwhile, the Glasgow readers of London newspapers had been finding that it had been 'Chartist mobs' which had created these serious disturbances. Armed madmen had been shouting 'Down with the Queen!' while others had torn up the railway lines on the Paisley and Airdrie railways. It was also discovered now that policemen had been shot. 'No doubt people at a distance are bamboozled over reports of events in Glasgow', reflected the *Glasgow Saturday Post*, which declared of these more flamboyant details, that, after running

all the way to London on the electric wire, and [coming] back again by train in good round print, the most important of them will be entirely new to our fellow citizens ... The circumstances must tend mightily to impress them with the importance and value of telegraphic communications.

The *Glasgow Saturday Post* alleged that the Glasgow police had left the city in the hands of a 'small band of rioteers' for at least two hours on 6 March.

Every person who saw the riot gives the same account. Gentlemen ... assure us that even at its worst in Exchange Square and Buchanan Street ... a dozen to twenty active men could easily have mastered the whole depredators. One shopowner single-handed seized one of the ringleaders and by expostulating with the crowd caused them to abandon the assault on his premises. A single female did likewise in the same neighbourhood. If the police force is incapable of controlling 50 to 100 disorderly rioters, principally boys, it should be dismissed ...

Public meetings were held in Glasgow and Gorbals to consider the conduct of the police, and Captain Pearce, the superintendent of police, resigned. At an 'Inquiry into the Conduct of Efficiency of the Police', in May, Superintendent Pearce gave evidence that from the quiet way in which the Glasgow crowds had conducted themselves on the three previous days, and after the apparent satisfaction of the crowd on 6 March with his announcement that meal tickets would be prepared while they waited on the Green, he had 'never expected anything like plunder' to take place. Nothing had transpired at the 'French revolution meeting' on 29 February, nor at the meetings during the week following, which led him to suppose that a breach of the peace would take place, provided food were distributed and the promise of work given. There appeared to have been a complete lack of pre-arranged plans to deal with emergencies of this kind, despite the fears of Lieutenant Stirling that the people would not wait beyond 6 March for relief. Only Assistant Superintendent Cameron realised that quick action was required that afternoon. Then much time was spent in consultations between the superintendent and the magistrates. The instructions of the magistrates were not immediately carried out, and when the police eventually did march out, they marched in the wrong direction and got caught up with a great crowd at the Exchange, where they waited for another hour.[2]

These disturbances had followed several meetings of unemployed in Glasgow, Paisley and elsewhere during February and the early days of March, at which relief work had been demanded. At one of these, 2,000 unemployed had declared their willingness to work on any terms. At most of the meetings in praise of the French revolutionaries, and at some of the meetings of unemployed, Chartists had played a leading part, but the press of Glasgow and Edinburgh was not as ready as Glasgow's chief magistrate, whose parliamentary duties kept him at Westminster, to assert that the riots were Chartist-inspired. Certainly it is doubtful whether the Rev. Patrick Brewster, in whom the unemployed of Paisley had found an energetic champion, or even Dr McDouall, who had addressed a large meeting of unemployed on Glasgow Green on 3 March, had any intention of inflaming general discontent into Chartist insurrection. Most of the blame for these events was placed on the procrastination of the city magistrates, who had allowed the unemployed to starve for several weeks, permitted the police to absolve themselves from their duties, and relied upon 'ill-disciplined veterans and pensioners', who fired into a crowd.

'The disclosure of another week,' declared the *Glasgow Examiner* on 18 March, had amply confirmed

all we asserted, regarding the character of the rioters ... The leaders in these riots are better known in the cells of the Police Office and prison than in the workshop or factory. The slightest effort on the part of the police would have prevented the Monday disturbances, and the least foresight on the part of the superintendent would have anticipated and prevented the fatal occurrences of Tuesday ... On mature consideration we can make nothing of the riots but that they are a disgrace to our police system, and a proof of the necessity of a resident Lord Provost.

As a result of the Glasgow riots, sixty-four persons were arrested. Forty-one of these were under 25 years of age, twenty-three were labourers and twenty-six were Roman Catholics. Twenty of them were convicted, and on 9 May, in sentencing George Smith to eighteen years' transportation for mobbing, rioting and theft, Lord Medwyn spoke with authority for the feelings of injured respectability of his society:

The sentences ... though lenient ... will be a sufficient warning to the operative classes in this great city, whenever there occurs any depression in trade, and a consequent failure of employment, and the distress which accompanies such a state of things, that they should not listen to the bad advice of designing men, preaching to them about their rights. Let them trust to the benevolence of those in this Christian country who are ever ready to grant relief to real want, which they should receive thankfully and gratefully, patiently enduring what is so inevitable, till the state of trade again admits of their full employment.[3]

It was in an atmosphere tense with resentment, apprehension, confusion and even exuberance that the various reports of disorder in many parts of Scotland were heard, and in which the People's Charter was reintroduced as the focal point of agitation. In Airdrie, where there was discontent with the wages of colliers, 'nothing was talked of but the Charter, or concerning the question of the suffrage'. At Paisley, public meetings which met to pass addresses to the heroes of the French revolution also passed resolutions in favour of the People's Charter, and heard accounts from Adams and Harley of Glasgow, explaining the non-Chartist origin of the Glasgow riot. During the second half of March, cheers for the French revolution mingled with cheers for the adoption of the National

Petition at Crieff, Kilbarchan, Pollockshaws and Dumfries. Large, enthusiastic meetings in Aberdeen, Dundee, Paisley, Glasgow and Edinburgh adopted the National Petition and elected delegates to the forthcoming Chartist National Convention. From Aberdeen it was reported that the Northern Charter Union had been reorganised, and that since the revolution in France, the civic authorities had affected great alarm whenever Chartist meetings were held, and 800 men had been sworn in as special constables. In contrast to this, the Glasgow Chartists were permitted to hold a crowded meeting in the City Hall on 24 March without the presence of any policemen. A 'union' of Irish repealers and Glasgow Chartists took place in the Lyceum Rooms on 27 March, when cheers were given for repeal, the People's Charter, John Mitchel, John O'Connell, Smith O'Brien, Feargus O'Connor and James Adams. At this meeting John Daly, a repealer, refused to be called to order, and declared that prayers and petitions were the weapons of slaves and cowards. Arms were the weapons used by the brave and the free. They could assist their fellow countrymen by keeping an army in Scotland. The chairman tried, without much success, to interpret this speech into constitutional language. At Ayr and Dalry, also, meetings for the adoption of the National Petition concluded with cheers for Mitchel and the United Irishmen. Once again considerable energy was being expended in obtaining signatures for the National Petition.[4]

In their reports to the National Convention which met in London on 4 April, the Scottish delegates painted neither a very bright picture of their prospects nor yet a very dull one. James Shirron of Aberdeen confessed that, although they had obtained 10,000 signatures in Aberdeen and always had a good turn-out at big occasions, they were not well organised. Dr Hunter of Edinburgh also confessed that Edinburgh was not as democratic as he could wish, but James Cumming, the other Edinburgh delegate, thought that the Chartists there were not poverty-stricken Chartists but Chartists from principle. James Adams of Glasgow declared that he had brought 100,000 signatures to the National Petition, and that another 30,000 had been forwarded. His report was by far the most optimistic of the Scottish reports. The middle classes had begun to fraternise with the Chartists, and in the Trongate, Glasgow's principal street, the Chartists had a large hall, with a large notice saying 'Democratic Hall', where meetings were held almost every evening. Poverty and discontent were widespread, but the Chartists had had no connection with the recent riots. There was now the best of feeling between Irish and Chartists, and discontent was so strong that they could, at least, keep all their soldiers to themselves. He was, however, opposed to any precipitate action, which was calculated only to injure their cause:

Regardless of unpopularity, he would condemn the manner in which a great many gentlemen in that Convention expressed their opinions as to what should be the proper policy for the Convention to pursue. He was sent there by a very large constituency to procure the enactment of the Charter, but he had not been sent there to compromise the cause, nor . . . for the purpose of committing suicide. The most judicious, wise, and indeed courageous course, was to act temperately and moderately, and to keep out of view, for the good of the cause, any ideas they might entertain of the future policy it might be necessary to pursue.

The general tenor of the speeches of the Scottish delegates was decidedly in favour of such moderation. James Graham of Dundee was ready to support the People's Charter 'by every means', and he was convinced that the people of Dundee would resent any coercion of the Irish, but Dr Hunter thought the Charter could be made law by moral force and by moral force only. Robert Cochran, of Paisley, had been instructed by his constituents merely to wait upon members of Parliament and to reason with them.

The pattern of events in Scotland in April 1848 was similar to that of June 1839. Ernest Jones, Dr Hunter and James Adams paraded Scotland as missionaries of the National Convention, addressing large meetings or demonstrations at Aberdeen, Alexandria, Barrhead, Beith, Dundee, Dunfermline, Edinburgh, Glasgow, Greenock, Hamilton, Leith and Paisley. Chartism was certainly more alive now than it had been since 1842, and arrangements were made for the appointment of delegates to a National Assembly, whose aims, methods and powers were even less clearly defined than those of the General Convention in July 1839.

Considerable excitement was aroused over the preparations of the Convention for the meeting on Kennington Common on 10 April, but attention from its outcome was diverted to the Bill for the security of the Crown introduced in the House of Commons by Sir George Grey on 7 April 1848. In Edinburgh, on the 10th, 'not fewer than 10,000 persons' gathered on Calton Hill to hear John Grant declare that 'the time was now come when it was the duty of every man, for his own individual safety, to arm himself'. If they did not depend upon themselves, they would run the risk of being butchered. In the past few days 'the base, bloody and tyrannical Whig Government' had introduced a measure 'by means of which no man who spoke at a public meeting was sure but that he might be liable to be put into a dungeon'. Now the government had stopped the working of the electric telegraph, and they could not know what was happening in London. Henry Rankine thought that this was not the time for speeches. The time was come for action. While he knew that a revolution would not be for the benefit of any class, let them show their hard task-masters that they were determined to be slaves no longer, but that if perish they must, they were prepared to die by the sword rather than by hunger. The meeting then heard Robert Hamilton urge the necessity of everyone purchasing a musket or pike, but it closed with the adoption of a memorial, proposed by Robert Cranston, calling upon the town council to support resolutions in favour of universal suffrage, and with the appointment of a deputation to the town council.

On the following evening, the Edinburgh Chartists and repealers met in the Waterloo Rooms to condemn Sir George Grey's sedition Bill and the decision of the government to prosecute Smith O'Brien, Mitchel and Meagher. Despite a caution from the chairman, Robert Hamilton violently declaimed that he 'intended to talk sedition'. He had preached moral force for the last fourteen years and he was now tired of it. 'Just let every one of them make the same stand as he did and the government would find that the jails would not be sufficient to hold them all'. He was convinced that the government had not sufficient force to put down the working classes, and although he did not wish 'to butcher the aristocracy' he must say that they well deserved it. Mr Scott, on behalf of the repealers, disclaimed such physical force sentiments. Thomas Blackie then moved support of the Six Points, and Robert Cranston moved thanks to Bailie Stott and those town councillors who had supported the resolutions in favour of universal suffrage, proposed in the council that day.

Meanwhile, in Glasgow there was consternation amongst the Chartists over the arrest on 11 April of their printers, David Harrower and William S. Brown, who were due to start publication on the 15th of the *Weekly Democratic Circular*. Their arrest followed the publication of a poster entitled THREATENED REVOLUTION IN LONDON which had been extensively posted in Glasgow on the 10th. On the day after the arrest, a packed Chartist meeting with over 6,000 present, was held in the City Hall to express indignation at the 'unconstitutional infringement of liberties' involved in the proposed sedition Bill, which might prevent the exercise of the right of meeting to discuss grievances and to petition for their removal. Samuel Bennet, the chairman, claimed that no Chartist in Glasgow had ever been convicted of violating the peace, and the reporter of the *Glasgow Herald* decided that, after listening to speeches by James Moir and the two printers (who had been released on acceptance of bail from Moir and Ross) 'the speeches throughout the evening were of a much less exciting character than those recently spoken at public meetings by the same gentlemen'.

Two days later, on Good Friday, Ernest Jones opened his Scottish tour with an 'eloquent speech' in the City Hall. The venerable Duncan Sherrington was in the chair, but nothing more exciting happened than the election of James Adams, Andrew Harley and Con Murray (of Dublin) as the delegates to the National Assembly. Then followed a fortnight of large meetings and demonstrations throughout the country to hear Jones and pass resolutions against the Ministry. At Aberdeen, on 17 April, 10,000 listened to Jones announce that a memorial to the Queen, in favour of the Charter, would be signed by the working classes, and that if this resource should fail, monster meetings would be held, with a view to appealing to armed force as a last resort. Next day, at Dundee, Jones's speech was 'frequently interrupted by storms of applause both from the people within the hall, and from the immense throng surrounding the windows outside'. There was 'almost unanimous response' when Jones asked if they were determined to back the National Assembly in working out 'any measure it may desire, sufficient to secure our rights'. John McCrae, the pastor of the Chartist church, moved a resolution of disapproval of the conduct of those who were 'trying to destroy the honourable position' of Feargus O'Connor, and was shortly afterwards appointed delegate to the Assembly in place of James Graham. The latter had fallen from favour for reporting that he was not 'sanguine of immediate success', having discovered the feeling of London to be decidedly against the Chartits. There had been false statements by the Chartists regarding the National Petition, and he could see no use for a permanent National Assembly.

THE CHARTIST MOVEMENT IN SCOTLAND

Edinburgh was reached by the Convention delegation on 19 April. 'The great merit of the Charter,' explained Ernest Jones at the meeting in the Waterloo Rooms, was that it was

a bread and cheese question—a roast beef and plum pudding question; for if they only had it, it would give food, clothing and shelter to every man in the country. [They were] not merely political reformers but social reformers. [In Scotland, where feudal despotisms had been succeeded] by the vast monied interest ... there would now be a third great change—a struggle against capital. That struggle would not consist in the destruction of property or of capital, but in the rescuing of industry from its unconditional despotism.

The great value of political power was that it would enable them "to procure social amelioration—it would give bread to the poor, protection to industry and justice to all." This meeting followed a much larger one on Calton Hill, two days earlier, which the Chartists claimed to have been attended by 25,000–30,000.

In the west of Scotland, Jones and Adams addressed meetings in Glasgow, Paisley and Greenock on 20, 21 and 22 April. At Paisley, Jones claimed to have been met by 30,000 men with 100 banners and twelve bands of music, and at Greenock, after an open-air meeting, a procession was formed to escort the deputies on their way to the Vale of Leven. Despite the imposition of a ban on processions by the provost, the Chartists persisted in their intention, and the special constabulary, supported by a detachment of infantry from Glasgow, was called out. The procession was halted at various streets, and attempts to break through resulted in serious injury to several Chartist hotheads.

The most auspicious of the demonstrations, however, were those held in Glasgow and Edinburgh on 17 April without the presence of Ernest Jones. In Glasgow the Chartists succeeded in mustering a very large gathering—estimated by them at 100,000—on Glasgow Green. This figure was inflated to 200,000 in Harley's report to the National Assembly two weeks later, and was deflated to 25,000 by the Scotsman. The sober Glasgow Herald calculated that owing to the beautiful weather and to curiosity, 40,000 people were present on the Green before the commencement of the proceedings. Processions through the streets had been forbidden by the sheriff and magistrates, but about 5,000 Chartists, marching six abreast, headed by the Chief Superintendent of Police and 'a Chartist leader on a grey horse', entered the Green in procession, with bands playing and banners flying. Placards exhorting PEACE, LAW, ORDER were displayed by the promoters of the meeting, along with their banner, which read LIBERTY, EQUALITY, FRATERNITY on one side and THE CHARTER AND REPEAL on the other.

James Moir was called to the chair, and 'speeches of the usual nature by the usual parties' followed. Daniel Paul moved for the continuance of agitation for the Charter. Robert Wingate of Barrhead appealed for repeal of the union with Ireland, and condemnation was recorded of the new security Bill. James Adams defended the National Convention from charges of cowardice regarding the meeting on Kennington Common, and a vote of confidence was passed in the Convention. Captain Miller of the police, who had officiated at almost every large Chartist demonstration in Glasgow since 1838, and who had been recalled from Liverpool to Glasgow after the March riots, was once again thanked for his courtesy. According to the *Glasgow Herald*, the 'best order and feeling was shown throughout the proceedings'.

Earlier in the day the same paper had declared that

we have no apprehensions whatever of the public peace being disturbed ... So far as bona-fide Chartists and Repealers are concerned, we never had the slightest doubt that the meeting today would go off very quietly ... But those who promote, and figure at, these demonstrations, might do worse than retire into private life—if only for a season, until the excitement on France dies down and commercial confidence is restored, or until the French, now armed with the Six Points, realise a political and social millenium.

James Moir, also, had doubts about the utility of the demonstration. As it came to an end, he told those of his vast audience who could hear what was said from the platform, that after it was over the number of persons attached to the principles of the Charter would be just as much a matter of dispute as it had been before. 'Instead of wasting their time assembling in this manner', they should enrol themselves as members of one or other of the two associations that were being formed that week to obtain the Charter. If 100,000 appended their names and subscribed one penny each, this would enable the executive committee to put a legal gentleman at their head, to conduct their affairs in the best manner, without it being felt a burden.[5]

When Ernest Jones reported to the National Assembly on 2 May, he claimed to have 'stated the result of his tour without colouring'—

indeed, he should think himself 'criminal' were he to deceive them. Nevertheless, the determination and preparations of the Scottish Chartists began to assume formidable dimensions. Glasgow was apparently pledged to support the National Assembly whatever its decisions, and Dundee was 'ready to support the Assembly to the utmost'. At Edinburgh there had been strong feelings and talk of forming a National Guard, while at Aberdeen a National Guard of nearly 1,000 men had been formed. This force was determined to support the National Assembly should it declare itself a parliament. He had addressed immense and enthusiastic meetings and he had received pledges from Alexandria, Hamilton and elsewhere of full support for the Assembly.

Much of the speeches of the Scottish delegates—particularly those of Robert Cochran and Andrew Harley—was taken up with the social distress suffered in Scotland during the winter, which was still being acutely felt, but corroboration for Jones's report was forthcoming from several of the Scottish delegates. Swinton McLean declared that in Alva, where many of the people had been involuntarily unemployed and living on turnips for the last fifteen months, 800 men had practised rifle shooting and were excellent marksmen. Alex. B. Henry, of Aberdeen, had been given instructions to get the Charter—by moral means if possible, but to get the Charter. 'If the people waited much longer, they would be in their graves.' John McCrae, whose constituents in Dundee had found themselves without bread at all instead of receiving the big loaf promised as a result of free trade, announced that the working classes of Dundee had agreed that 'moral force was all a humbug' and had resolved to form a National Guard. Henry Rankine indicated that things had gone a stage further in Edinburgh, where it had been agreed at a public meeting to form a National Guard of 1,600. This would be used for the suppression of 'domestic anarchy and foreign invasion', and it would be 'sub-divided in regular military order, headed by captains, lieutenants, etc.'

When the National Assembly moved on to more serious business, such as the form of national organisation which was to be established, it was startled, on 5 May, to find Scottish objections to the title and method of financing the National Charter Association developing into a full-blooded attack on the absent Feargus O'Connor, M.P. It must be a very dignified Association, declared Harley amidst uproar, that had only 5,000 members on its books. In Scotland they had tried to get up a national movement, but they had failed because the belief that it would be under the control of 'a certain individual, who had done all the damage he could to the movement'. By this he meant O'Connor and he hoped that O'Connor would appear before the Assembly to hear what some members had to say of him. Some of the men in the old Association had disgraced themselves. Therefore the name of their organisation should be changed to show that they were 'going on a different tack'. Henry Rankine, who thought that each locality should form a Chartist association with complete management of its own affairs, also believed O'Connor to be a barrier to the power of the democratic party throughout the country. James Adams, and James Shirron of Aberdeen, who had been elected secretary of the Assembly, moved that the association be called the 'Democratic Confederation of Great Britain and Ireland for obtaining the immediate enactment of the People's Charter'. So long as they called themselves the Charter Association, it would be called 'O'Connor's Association'. Shirron felt 'bound to state from his own knowledge the fatal consequences arising from that [National Charter] Association'. Men had been sent to Scotland who had damned the cause by their intemperance, and he could not endure that such an association should be permitted to state that it was conducted with dignity. His main complaint, however, lay not against the executive but with O'Connor, who had been guilty of mistakes of judgment. Nevertheless, for the sake of unity he would be willing, if necessary, to co-operate with O'Connor again. This was not good enough for Robert Cochran, of Paisley. The Chartist movement had been allowed to slumber for the last two years, until the executive had been awakened by the recent revolutions abroad. It was absolutely essential that a new movement should be commenced under men other than O'Connor, Brewster or O'Brien.

The publication of these attacks, and O'Connor's letter in his own defence in the *Northern Star*, provoked the familiar reaction from his admirers in Scotland. Letters and votes of confidence were immediately received from Alva, Crieff, Falkirk, Kirkcaldy, Tillicoultry and Wigtown. Parkhead assured O'Connor that its 'confidence in you, as our honest bailiff, is unshaken'. Dundee sent an address to O'Connor—'the working man's best friend', while Kirkcaldy expressed its 'utmost confidence in our father'. Denny Chartist Association expressed its 'unbounded confidence in our leader, and our closer attachment to him for his conduct on, and his advice since, the memorable 10th of April'. The Leith Charter Association added its 'confidence in our father and teacher, and in the *Northern Star*, our guide'. From Blairgowrie the branch of the Land Company deplored 'the base and scandalous attacks' upon O'Connor, and in Paisley a meeting of the local trades and districts regretted the manifestations of suspicion. It was astounded by the wish of some of the delegates to the National Assembly to change the name of the National Charter Association, and expressed its full confidence in O'Connor.

Perhaps O'Connor's most important success was gained in Glasgow, at a meeting in the Democratic Hall on 8 May.

It was with feelings of extreme sorrow and regret [wrote William Dogherty, chairman of the committee appointed by the delegates of the Public and Associated Trades of Glasgow] that we read your letter in the *Northern Star* of the 6th inst ... We declare that we never authorised our representative to sow the seeds of dissensions by attacking the character of individuals ... We beg to assure you, that so far from representing the Chartists of Glasgow, or meeting with their approbation, his conduct in this respect has called forth public indignation, so much so that he has been requested to resign his seat as a representative of Glasgow in the National Assembly.

This was followed by a letter to the executive committee, in which Dogherty appealed that 'all ammunition shall be cast away from our movement for ever'. Let the pilots 'sink all acrimony, all foolish ideas of superiority, all unmanly strife for popularity and leadership'.

This appeal resulted in a resolution proposed by McDouall, on behalf of the executive committee, which repudiated 'all personalities' and declared that the Assembly had entertained no question affecting the character of O'Connor. Their earnest desire was for perfect unanimity and a firm course of action. In this spirit Adams, Rankine, Cochran, Cumming, Shirron, Henry and Harley were appointed commissioners for six weeks, while McCrae, the loyal O'Connorite, was elected to the executive. Then, in obedience to the instructions of his constituents, Andrew Harley resigned.[6]

It was in Edinburgh that Chartist activities throughout the period April–June assumed the most formidable dimensions, and the authorities soon began to take serious note of what was taking place at Chartist meetings. At one of these, in the Adam Square Hall on 28 April, policemen in plain clothes were observed taking notes.

On this occasion 120 persons enrolled for the formation of a National Guard, after a scheme to establish a National Guard of 1,600 men in Edinburgh had been outlined by Donald Mackay, an old soldier who appears to have had sufficient resources to move about the country instigating such projects. There were to be four divisions of 400 men each, with sub-divisions of 100 and sections of 25. The first and third divisions would be armed with lances, while the second and fourth would have muskets. The qualifications for eligibility would be pledges to protect the lives and properties of the Queen's loyal subjects, and to arm for the defence of their country against foreign invasion and domestic anarchy. These proposals were met with 'great laughter', and there was strong opposition from Peter Anderson, who warned that this would drive all peaceable, intelligent and trustworthy persons from the Chartist Association. The Charter would succeed only if their appeal were to reason. For all their boasts, Bussey, Dr Taylor, Dr McDouall, Bronterre O'Brien and O'Connor had not led them to death and glory, and thirty soldiers had defeated 3,000 Welsh rioters. The absence of the most prominent of the Edinburgh leaders seemed to indicate disapproval of the purpose of the meeting, but Henry Rankine and John Grant acquiesced in supporting the National Guard proposal.

A further fit of excitement seized many parts of the country in June. On 14 June the *Scotsman* reported:

Last Monday, being Whit-Monday, and in England a sort of holiday, was pitched upon by the Chartist leaders for great 'demonstrations' all over the country. The activity of the authorities, aided by the determination of the people themselves of all classes, everywhere effectually prevented disorder, and awed the anarchists. The only result has been to add multitudes more to those who have been brought to regard the Chartist agitation as the curse and enemy of all men who wish to live in industry, peace and freedom.

In Edinburgh, great precautions had been taken by the magistrates to preserve the peace on the 12th, and to prevent the Chartists of Leith and Edinburgh marching through the city to Bruntsfield Links. More than 200 police, 750 special constables and sizeable contingents of pensioners and the 33rd Foot regiment were stationed throughout the city. The Lord Provost and the superintendent of police succeeded in dissuading an Edinburgh assembly from forming a procession, but a march was made up Leith Walk by about 300

Chartists with a band playing and banners flying. This procession was attacked by police and special constables, who routed the Chartists and destroyed the big bass drum.

The meeting on Bruntsfield Links was attended by 10,000–12,000 people, who heard a 'mild and guarded' speech from the chairman, John Grant, and several violent ones, including one from a blind man, John Cockburn. Robert Hamilton, by now noted for the vehemence of his appeals to physical force, made yet another clarion call to his colleagues to get guns and bayonets. Similar speeches were made at a meeting in the Waterloo Rooms, on the 19th, when the conduct of the authorities on the 12th was condemned and handbills were distributed, calling on the people to organise and enrol in the National Guard, and follow the example of France.

Elsewhere there was much less excitement on 12 June. In Dundee, where, on the prompting of old soldier, Donald Mackay, a brigadier and a secretary had been appointed on 16 May for the 'Dundee military division' of the National Guard, a demonstration in Magdalen Yard Court was content to voice its disapproval of Lord John Russell's statement that the lower and middle classes did not want any extension of the suffrage. In Aberdeen the outstanding feature was another furious attack on Feargus O'Connor by Alex. B. Henry, who reported on the National Assembly and was accorded a unanimous vote of thanks for his conduct. O'Connor, in putting down the Assembly, had done for the government what it could not have done for itself. Henry felt he must confess, however, that he had not contradicted the statement of Ernest Jones that there were in Aberdeen 6,000 Chartists, 'armed to the teeth and waiting for the fray', as this might have done some good. He himself had told the men of London that the Chartists of Aberdeen were 'up to the mark and procuring arms', but he was ashamed to find that they had made him a liar, as he now found only one person who had done so.

This led to recriminations between the *Northern Star* and the Aberdeen Chartists as to who had been misleading whom. The *Northern Star* rebuked those who had misled Ernest Jones; and John Smart, the Aberdeen secretary, replied that Ernest Jones had been told of their intention to form a National Guard of 3,000, and that for this purpose 600 had enrolled—not '6,000 Chartists armed to the teeth and waiting for the fray'.

Meanwhile 'the same old story' had been told once again in

Glasgow, where the demonstration on the Green, on 10 June, was described as the 'most signal failure which has occurred in Glasgow for the last twenty years'. On an exceedingly beautiful day, not more than 6,000–7,000 were reported to have been present—only as many as would be 'called forth on any occasion by a boat-race, or a cricket match'. At the time scheduled for the meeting, four detachments of police, amounting to more than 400 men, outnumbered the Chartists at the hustings. Despite a good 'deal of speechification' the only thing approaching strong language was emitted by

Parson Adams, who stated that, for his own personal convenience, recreation and amusement, he had joined a society recently instituted in Glasgow for the practice of target shooting, and that the club intended to purchase their muskets at the wholesale price.[7]

While these attempts to fan the flickering embers of Chartism were being made by its more violently inclined exponents, a somewhat unexpected development in the background had been the demonstration of greater willingness on the part of the middle class reformers to reunite with the working class Radicals and Chartists. Since April the new movements for suffrage extension sponsored by Hume, Cobden, Bright and the parliamentary Radicals had been meeting with some initial success. What had been considered extremism on the part of the Chartists twelve months previously now became moderation among the middle classes of Scotland. Commercial depression and the events in France, resulting in a chamber of middle-class deputies elected by universal suffrage, swept away many of the objections to universal suffrage. In meetings in many parts of the country the middle-class Radicals evinced an almost unaccountably sudden desire to embrace the five or six points of the Charter, which startled even the Chartists.

In Glasgow, Paisley, Edinburgh, Dundee, Dunfermline, Falkirk, Greenock and several places in Fifeshire, 'influential meetings of electors' agreed to petition Parliament in support of Joseph Hume's motion for extension of the suffrage, to repudiate Lord John Russell's allegation that the middle classes were not interested in further reform, and to attribute the sufferings of the people to 'the present system of taxation and the prodigality of the Government'. At several of these meetings the most prominent Chartists of former days, such as James Moir, George Ross, Matthew Cullen, William Pattison, Malcolm McFarlane, Robert Malcolm jun. and Thomas

Gillespie, were to be found collaborating wholeheartedly with chief magistrates, who were constantly engaged in the preparation of measures to repress the exuberance of the new leaders. In Glasgow, Edinburgh and elsewhere, electoral associations, or 'People's Leagues', were formed, with working class participation, often having equal numbers of Chartists and Complete Suffragists for their office-bearers, to agitate for full, fair and free representation, and to put forward candidates at parliamentary and municipal elections. Town councils were invited to follow Glasgow city council's example, on 22 June, and petition for Joseph Hume's motion.

The Radical press was in some haste to announce that 'the immediate danger from Chartism' was past, and that the 'moral weight of Chartism' was

quenched and extinguished, not so much from the want of success in the numerical demonstrations ... as from their union with the Irish repealers and the disaffected of all castes. Chartism as it at present stands, is repudiated by those who ... would be glad ... to see great changes carried out in a legal and constitutional way.

The burden of taxation had now become the root of all evils, and the 'reasonableness of further reform' was deemed evident.

That a change in the suffrage is now demanded [declared the *Glasgow Examiner*] the various meetings of the middle classes throughout the country significantly prove. Our legislators may make themselves merry at the monster petition and its Pugnoses and Longnoses—they may laugh at the simplicity of a Cuffey, and despise the threats of a Jones. They may marshal the citizens to prevent processions and issue laws to restrain treasonable demagogues. They dare not, however, despise the movement now going on amongst the middle and industrial classes combined.[8]

The strength of the new Radical movement, however, was as superficial and fleeting as that of the parallel Chartist movement. Even by June, the *Scotsman* could note that Hume and his friends were unable to point to

any clear evidence of anything like general assent, far less enthusiasm, in the public mind regarding their scheme. A considerable number of meetings have been held, and a large number of petitions got up, but not nearly sufficient in numbers or importance to be taken as representing a national demand.

Only in Glasgow, where the new Electoral Association could claim a membership of 12,000, and where most of the influential working class leaders had been won over to its support, had there been any substantial measure of success. Even in Glasgow the initial impetus was soon lost, and apart from playing a part in placing James Moir at the top, and Lord Provost Alexander Hastie, MP, at the bottom of the poll in the municipal elections in November, its activity in the second half of 1848 was comparatively slight.

The second half of 1848 was in many ways a complete anti-climax to the first half of the year. In December the Glasgow Electoral Association held a 'reform banquet' to 'unite the scattered elements of democracy' but otherwise showed few signs of life. Nor did tours by John McCrae, now the secretary of the penniless National Chartist executive, nor even by Feargus O'Connor rekindle much Chartist enthusiasm. O'Connor lectured in Dundee, Aberdeen and Glasgow, and as usual he 'carried all before him'. His meetings attracted attention chiefly on account of the interventions of James Adams in Glasgow and James Shirron in Aberdeen, who both received short shrift from their erstwhile constituents when they attempted to expose 'the vile imposter whose unprincipled hypocrisy' had destroyed the National Assembly. At Glasgow, O'Connor, who was 'extremely humorous', succeeded in pacifying 'Parson' Adams by promising that he should be allowed to expound his grievances in the *Northern Star*. Shirron, however, remained completely unrelenting and died very shortly after.

It is with much regret that we have to announce the death of Mr James Shirron, a young and enthusiastic Chartist [wrote the *Aberdeen Herald*]. We shall not forget Mr Shirron's appearance on the evening of Mr O'Connor's visit to this city...He had lost the buoyant vivacity which usually characterised his demeanour and addresses. The tone of his voice betrayed determination and anguish... anguish to see those, who knew better, toadying at the feet of a man whose words and deeds have been so much at variance with each other... When he heard his plain statement of facts hissed by the same parties who had so often, on former occasions, applauded to the echo the sentiments which from the same platform... he had addressed them... this was too much for poor Shirron he sunk to his seat with a look of melan choly anguish which... he strove in vain to conceal. From that night, his spirits and his health sunk rapidly—he fell into fever—was subsequently attacked by erysipelas and died in the Infirmary on Sabbath last, a victim to his own honesty and to the fickleness of the multitude.

According to the *Inverness Courier*, he 'was 27 years of age, and died, it may be said, of a broken heart.'[9]

During the latter part of the year there was also a sequel to the Edinburgh Chartist demonstration on Bruntsfield Links on 12 June. At the time of the demonstration it had been rumoured that some of the most violent speakers would be arrested, but it was not until six weeks later that the authorities took such action. The office of the *North British Express*, which was also used as the Edinburgh Chartists' committee room, was raided; books and correspondence were removed; and on 26 July editor Henry Rankine and printer Archibald Walker were arrested along with, more surprisingly, Robert Cranston and James Cumming. This was followed with the arrest, on 31 July, of John Grant, Robert Hamilton and the west of Scotland agents of the *Express*, James Smith of Glasgow, and Robert Burrell and Andrew Neilson of Greenock. These arrests and the 'tyrannical invasion of the office of the *North British Express* evoked protest meetings in Greenock, Glasgow and Edinburgh. Sympathy for the leaders, who had been imprisoned on charges of sedition, was expressed, and the 'reign of terror' was strongly denounced.

The most important of these meetings was a demonstration held on Calton Hill on 31 July, at the end of which the main part of a 'very numerous assembly' formed a procession and marched to the part of Calton Hill opposite the gaol. Cheers were raised for the imprisoned patriots, and some of the crowd then proceeded to the County Hall, where they met police interference. Some windows were broken, but large bodies of police, special constables, pensioners and Yeomanry had been stationed at strategic points, and the 'danger of riot was soon dissipated'.

Only four of the arrested Chartists were brought to trial: Cumming, Rankine, Grant and Hamilton. Their trials took place in Edinburgh, in November, before the High Court of Justiciary. A number of important legal technicalities added considerable interest to the proceedings, but apart from information on the attitude of the Edinburgh Chartist committee towards the formation of the National Guard, and some rather dubious details regarding the strength of the various arms clubs in Edinburgh, there were no important disclosures of information about the activities of the Chartists beyond what had already been reported in the newspapers. Evidence confirming the press reports of the use of violent language at the meetings in the Adam Square Hall on 28 April, on Brunts-field Links on 12 June, at the Waterloo Rooms on 19 June and on Calton Hill on 24 July was given by police officers and newspaper reporters, whose reports were mutually corroborative. Other evidence gave the impression that Grant and Rankine had been very much more guarded in their deeds than in their public utterances. Also that they had adopted a rather equivocal attitude, in committee and in public, regarding the National Guard project. According to Walter Pringle, Peter Anderson, and Alexander Elder, the responsibility for the initiative and development of the scheme had been entirely that of 'Brigadier-General' McKay and his colleague John Gray, who had also shouldered the financial responsibility connected with the meetings and with the printing of handbills and placards. The committee, and in particular Rankine, who had always been known to the witnesses as a moral force Chartist, had opposed the National Guard project but had allowed a meeting to take place on 28 April to consider the matter publicly, as otherwise McKay was determined to carry out the work secretly.

In the trial of Grant, Rankine and Hamilton, the counsels for the defence stressed the narrow distinction between constitutional agitation and sedition. There were eminent members of the Bench who had taken part in the 1832 demonstrations, which would have provided a broader basis for sedition than all that had been said or done on Bruntsfield Links or Calton Hill by all the Chartists of Edinburgh. Rankine's counsel maintained that while Rankine's language on the Links had been 'inflated and extravagant', it had contained the assertion of a truly constitutional doctrine held by Fox in 1795, and by Earl Grey in 1832—the doctrine of resistance to illegal attack. While Rankine could not be 'sent from the bar with prudence stamped on all his actions', he had not transgressed the law.

In his summing-up in this trial, the Lord Justice-Clerk considered that the charge of conspiracy to effect, by force, an alteration of the laws of the realm could scarcely be proved against Grant or Rankine, or even against Hamilton. On the charge of the use of seditious language 'intended and calculated to excite popular disaffection, commotion, and violence, and resistance to lawful authority', the most important evidence against Hamilton and Rankine was the speeches made on Bruntsfield Links on 12 June. The non-interruption of speakers, however, on the part of Grant was 'hardly sufficient to bring home the charge to him'.

The jury then found 'the charge of conspiracy against the three panels as libelled not proven', and also unanimously found Grant 'not guilty of sedition as libelled'. This result must have been a pleasant surprise to Grant, who had fled to France and who had been reluctantly persuaded by his cautioners—who had stood bail of £150 on his behalf—to return and face trial.

The jury, however, found Hamilton 'guilty of using language calculated to excite disaffection and resistance to lawful authority' and, by a majority of one, Rankine was found 'guilty of using similar language'. On the suggestion of the Lord Justice-Clerk, this verdict was altered to read: 'That the jury unanimously find Robert Hamilton guilty of sedition, in so far as that he used language calculated to excite popular disaffection and resistance to lawful authority: and by a majority of one find Henry Rankine guilty of sedition in the same terms'.

Thereupon the defence counsel maintained that this verdict was equivalent to one of not guilty, as the jury had deliberately omitted the word 'intended' from the averment. On the Bench, this objection was upheld by Lord Cockburn, who maintained that there could be no crime without guilt in the mind of the criminal, and that he knew 'nothing in law that had been more unequivocally laid down by the authorities than that the guilt of sedition was not contracted where the intention ... was innocent'. In the present case the verdict was not according to, but to the exclusion of, everything charged. The verdict contained a verdict of sedition with a limitation that made it no sedition. The other members of the Bench, however, considered that the verdict was a conviction which required a sentence. The sedition had been proven, though in a much less aggravated light. The Lord Justice-Clerk declared that he had 'somehow collected the impression from the whole demeanour of the prisoners during the trial that they would not again act rashly ... and recklessly use such language as they had done on the occasions libelled', and sentenced both to four months' imprisonment.

The most interesting item of evidence was produced in the case of James Cumming, the elderly shoemaker, who was tried separately from his fellow Chartists. This was a letter, written by Cumming on 22 July, listing the Edinburgh arms societies and describing the tide of feeling in Edinburgh. Instead of being delivered by the postal authorities to James Smith, the secretary of the Glasgow Chartists, it found its way into the hands of the law, at a time when the authorities were deciding whether to take action against the Edinburgh leaders and the *North British Express*.

According to Cumming's letter, the club membership was: 'Muir Club', 200; 'Mitchell Club', 56; 'Baird and Hardie Club', 20; 'Gerald Club', 26; 'Burns Club', 25; 'Washington Club', 25; 'O'Connor Club', 12. Besides these there were 500 enrolled in the National Guard and an unascertained number in the 'Emmet Club'. The National Guard had given an order for forty muskets with bayonets, 'but a great many have provided themselves with arms; those ordered are for those who pay in weekly contributions for that purpose'. Some of the clubs had purchased 'a few muskets at £1 each' and these had been shown at the meetings. When the National Guard had been supplied with the arms ordered, it might safely be said that there would be 100 armed. The pervading feeling was 'decidedly warlike' and the general topic of conversation was 'arming and streetfighting'. The Irish papers, particularly the *Felon*, were read with avidity and hailed with rapture and enthusiasm. During the twenty years in which he had been connected with the reform movement, there had never been such a 'strong feeling of resistance to the Government', though it was difficult to know 'whether they would fight or not'. An Edinburgh mob would generally fly if attacked, but having arms might 'inspire confidence'.

There was no definite indication in the letter that Cumming had been a member of any of these societies, but he was charged with having distributed, or causing to be distributed, a placard calling a meeting of the National Guard on 28 June 1848 to which 'the various clubs' were respectfully invited. The libel affirmed that

in consequence of openly reading this placard, a number of persons assembled for the purpose of being enrolled as a National Guard; that the prisoner took the chair at this meeting, which was to form an illegal and disloyal body to compel by force of violence an alteration of the laws and constitution of the realm, by procuring and using guns and pikes, in order to levy war; and that an individual, whose name is unknown, did at this meeting, and in the hearing of the prisoner, and with his sanction as chairman propose to undertake to furnish or to supply guns and bayonets to those who desired them.

This was the first case to be tried in Scotland under the recent statute for the 'security of the Crown and the suppression of seditious designs and practices', and several objections were raised to the competence and sufficiency of the indictment. In repelling the objection that the act alleged amounted to high treason under the Act of 36 George III, while the indictment had not specified any overt acts showing the existence of treasonable intent, the Lord Advocate contended that since the recent statute, what had been the common law of Scotland before the Act of 36 George III, which had excluded it on this point, again became applicable. This led to a debate on whether the offences of sedition and conspiracy could be tried at common law. The defence counsel contended that what was charged was not only a statutory offence but an offence subsisting by and in the statute, and therefore not competent, or rather having no existence whatever, by the common law of Scotland. This view was upheld by the Lord Justice-Clerk, who did not think it possible to try the sedition and conspiracy charged under the common law, as they amounted to a statutory offence. Moreover, the fourth section of the recent statute declared that no person should be prosecuted for any felony by virtue of the Act unless the information was given within six days and the warrant issued within ten days afterwards. Because of this provision, he did not think it competent to do the same thing at common law, although the information was not given within six days and the warrant not issued within ten days. This view was repelled by the majority of the Bench, and Cumming then pleaded 'not guilty' to the indictment, but the case was adjourned until after the trial of Grant, Rankine and Hamilton. A week later, the Lord Advocate intimated that he would desert the diet against the prisoner, and James Cumming was discharged.

In retrospect, Lord Cockburn thought that the language used at 12 June meeting, especially by Robert Hamilton, was 'not only plainly seditious, but it was by far the most seditious that had ever been charged against any Scotch prisoner'. When he asked Lord Campbell, who was a member of the Cabinet, for his opinion on the validity of the verdict, Lord Campbell gave his private opinion that the verdict ought to have been considered as one of acquittal. 'He thought that on principle it was just the English abortive verdict of "guilty of publishing only".' In his *Journal*, Cockburn reviewed the events of 1848, concluding:

Besides the chronic sedition that adheres naturally to the practice of the constitution, considerable masses of the people were this year under a violent attack of the acute complaint...chiefly brought on by continental contagion. What the French call a Republic had been recently set up in their country; every throne in Europe had been shaken or overturned by popular convulsion; Ireland was in rebellion; there was great mercantile distress in Britain...and these various excitements brought out those called Chartists, not only into seditious oratory, but into displays of treasonable organisation. These circumstances crowded the English courts with political prisoners, but as only four individuals were prosecuted in Scotland, it at least cannot be said that there was any eagerness in resorting to the terrors of the law...It formerly constituted sedition, and proved it, that the prisoner had advocated universal suffrage and annual parliaments. But the doctrine of the public prosecutor now is—'With respect to these political doctrines of the Chartists, let me explicitly avow that they are well entitled to hold these opinions, to express and promulgate these opinions, and to associate in order to maintain and advance them by all legitimate means— by addresses to the Crown, petitions to Parliament, public meetings orderly conducted, argument, intreaty and remonstrance. They are entitled by all constitutional means to carry out their political object...' The prosecution, though to a great extent it failed, was useful. It implied and proclaimed that to form, or to attempt to form, a national guard, or any military organisation was criminal. The proceedings were conducted both by the prosecutor and the Court most liberally towards the prisoners, and the mildness of the sentence deprived them of all sympathy.[10]

NOTES

1. *Northern Star*, 4, 11 and 25 December 1847; 27 May 1848.
   Glasgow Examiner, 1 January 1848.
   Glasgow Saturday Post, 5 and 19 February 1848.
2. *Scotsman*, 8 and 11 March 1848.
   Glasgow Saturday Post, 11 and 25 March 1848.
   Glasgow Examiner, 6, 13 and 27 May; 10 June 1848.
   Northern Star, 11 March 1848.
3. *Glasgow Saturday Post*, 4 March 1848.
   Scotsman, 15 March 1848.
   Glasgow Examiner, 18 March; 13 May 1848.
4. *Glasgow Saturday Post*, 11 and 25 March; 1 April 1848.
   Northern Star, 18 and 25 March 1848.
   Glasgow Examiner, 1 April 1848.
5. *Northern Star*, 8 and 29 April; 6 May 1848.
   Scotsman, 12, 19 and 22 April 1848.
   Glasgow Examiner, 15, 22 and 29 April 1848.
   Glasgow Herald, 17 and 21 April 1848.
   Glasgow Saturday Post, 15 April 1848.

6. *Northern Star*, 6, 13, 20 and 27 May 1848.
7. *Scotsman*, 29 April; 6 May; 14 and 21 June 1848.
   Aberdeen Herald, 10 June 1848.
   Northern Star, 15 July; 5 August 1848.
   Glasgow Herald, 13 June 1848.
   Glasgow Examiner, 17 June 1848.
   Memoranda of the Chartist Agitation in Dundee, pp. 75–6.
8. *Glasgow Examiner*, 6 and 27 May; 10, 17 and 24 June; 15 and 22 July
   1848.
   Glasgow Saturday Post, 8 and 15 April 1848.
   Scotsman, 12 April; 17 June 1848.
   Glasgow Herald, 5 May 1848.
9. *Scotsman*, 24 June; 8 and 25 November 1848.
   Glasgow Examiner, 12 August; 23 September; 28 October; 9 December
   1848.
   Northern Star, 15 and 22 July 1848.
   Inverness Courier, 23 November 1848.
10. *Scotsman*, 14 June; 2 August; 8, 15 and 29 November 1848.
   Glasgow Examiner, 5 and 12 August; 4 and 18 November 1848.
   Northern Star, 5 August 1848.
   H. Cockburn, *Sedition Trials*, 1888, vol. ii, pp. 226–43.
   Journal of Henry Cockburn, 1874, vol. ii, pp. 235–7.

CHAPTER SEVENTEEN

The end of Chartist organisation

However fitful and narrowly based the Chartist agitation may have been in 1848, it was nevertheless made clear on several occasions during the next two decades that the force of Chartism was not yet completely spent. Every town, village and hamlet had its local 'Cicero or Demosthenes, to shake the pillars of the earth and set free the world from the shackles of corruption'. Nor was there any political principle for which the people had greater respect than universal suffrage. 'It was a delusion,' suggested the *Glasgow Examiner* as late as October 1858, 'to suppose that the old party "spirits" were departed—they were only dormant, and would manifest themselves as soon as opportunity occurred.' If there had been little partisanship of Chartist principles in the intervening years, it did not mean that these principles were less widely held among the working classes.

Yet the years immediately following 1848 saw a further marked decline in Chartist organisation. By 1852 virtually nothing remained of the once formidable network of Chartist associations. Even the few local organisations which struggled on until then to preserve their identity were poorly supported, and often lacked the assistance of many of their former leaders. Most of these men still embraced Chartists principles, but many had begun to devote their major energies towards social reformist or local government activities. In 1851, which saw the last faint revival of Chartism, there were only nine or ten Chartist associations in existence in Scotland, and thereafter there appears to have been a total eclipse of Chartist organisation, except for one or two Chartist churches.

One of the most remarkable features of this period was the confidence and warm affection with which Feargus O'Connor continued to be regarded by his large following. Even when branches of the Land Society could see no hope of receiving funds to liquidate debts for room rent, secretary's salary and expenses, loyalty to the father of the movement demanded constant procrastination over the decision to close down. Even when it was agreed, as at Aberdeen in July 1849, that it was 'not honourable in Mr O'Connor' to enter into arrangements for a new land scheme until a settlement had been achieved for the members of the existing one, a motion to suspend the branch was defeated, and the Chartist secretary, John Smart, wrote that the Aberdonians exonerated O'Connor from the failure of his scheme. The paid-up members of the land scheme realised that it was the people who were to blame—not O'Connor, whom they held in the highest esteem, and who would always be welcomed there with joy by many thousands.

Similar letters were forthcoming from many parts of the country. Brechin regretted that O'Connor was being made 'a scapegoat for others' black deeds'. Calton Charter Association deprecated O'Connor's decision to retire from public life, and urged reconsideration of that decision. The Markinch branch of the Land Society expressed its 'deepest grief and sorrow' at the repeated determination of O'Connor to retire. In Duncan Sherrington, the aged secretary of the Glasgow district of Land Society branches, O'Connor had his staunchest supporter. Ever since chairing the conference at which the scheme had been adopted in 1845, Sherrington constantly expressed his faith in its soundness if it were 'honestly tried', and strove to uphold O'Connor's reputation in Glasgow against a succession of discontented detractors of the land scheme. In February 1850, he furiously denounced the evidence given before the Court of Exchequer by Alexander Clelland, an allottee at Snig's End, who claimed to have been better off in Glasgow as a hand-loom weaver. Whereas Clelland now claimed to have been receiving wages of 10s–21s a week, he used to complain that he could not average 8s. In August 1851 Sherrington was still as active as ever in O'Connor's defence, 'proving' that a lecture given by James Beattie, one of the ejected allottees of Charterville, was a 'tissue of falsehoods as regards the condition of the allottees'. Beattie, who was claiming that the scheme had been nothing but a 'snare and a delusion', had let his land, refused to pay rent, spent his entire time stirring up discontent amongst the allottees, and had never grown enough to feed a pig. As usual, the debate resulted in a vote of 'the fullest confidence' in O'Connor.[1]

Cheers for the Charter were again heard frequently at public meetings during the second half of 1849, when large public meetings were held in Glasgow, Edinburgh, Paisley, Aberdeen, Kirkcaldy and Hamilton to sympathise with the 'republics' of Rome, Baden and Hungary. At these meetings, organised or sponsored by the Chartists, the base conduct of France, Austria and Russia in their aggressive military interventions was censured, and resolutions were adopted in favour of the Charter and the National Petition.

At Paisley, the interventions of the Rev. Patrick Brewster in such meetings were greeted with great applause, while the Chartists of Edinburgh, Glasgow and Kirkcaldy found a new champion in the Rev. Alexander Duncanson, pastor of the Congregational church, Falkirk, whose outlook was typical of many Chartists of this period. To Duncanson it was clear that 'every man in whose bosom existed the love of God and man' must have as his aim the fusion of the whole family of man into one common brotherhood. Towards this end, every movement for the 'amelioration of the condition of the human family' deserved the support of the Chartists. The peace movement was an essential element in Chartism, as was temperance and personal reform. Capital punishment must be ended, and those engaged in the anti-slavery movement should be encouraged not to spend all their energies across the Atlantic, but wherever man could not find a fair equivalent for his labour. The enactment of the Six Points, therefore, would be the prelude to a great programme of social reform.[2]

The preservation of some lingering coherence in the Scottish movement was due, however, less to the teachings of Scottish clergymen and demonstrations of sympathy for foreign liberals, than to the periodic visits from the most famous of the Chartist leaders who remained active. Until 1852 the latent strength of Chartism in Scotland warranted lecture tours by Samuel Kydd, Feargus O'Connor, Julian Harney, Bronterre O'Brien, G. W. M. Reynolds, Ernest Jones, George Jacob Holyoake and Thomas Cooper. Invariably, their meetings were well attended and their speeches enthusiastically appreciated. Nevertheless, after hall expenses and lecture fees or expenses had been paid, little remained over for the funds of the movement, and regular organisation was seldom effected as a result of such tours.

An exception to this was George Julian Harney, who spent the autumn of 1849 in Ayrshire recuperating from throat trouble, and several months in the summer and autumn of 1851 touring Scotland. Although he was much less active than on his earliest Scottish tours, in 1840 and 1841, Harney was still imbued with a pioneering spirit for establishing or reforming local associations. Unlike most of his colleagues, he seemed more concerned with convincing potential local leaders of the necessity for continued local organisation than with paying fleeting visits wherever an enthusiastic audience could be expected. In 1851 he visited Aberdeen, Montrose, the Vale of Leven, Alexandria, Dumbarton, Hamilton, Troon, Wishaw and Kilbarchan, where he made very long speeches on the causes of the Hungarian struggle for national independence and on the coming struggles in Continental politics. But much of his time was spent in forming provisional committees for the establishment of Chartist associations and canvassing support for the Fraternal Democrats. In Edinburgh, where his *Democratic Review* and *Red Republican* had had good circulations, a soirée was given in his honour by the Edinburgh Democratic Tract Society.[3]

In contrast, Thomas Cooper, who also spent several weeks in Scotland in the summer of 1851, was less of a Chartist missionary than a freelance lecturer on Robert Burns and other 'poets of the people', whose terms were £2 per 'oration' or 30s for each oration delivered on successive nights. Cooper was delighted with Scotland, where he gave 35–40 orations during his brief visit. He was greatly impressed with the 'sublime warning' given by Ailsa Craig and the peaks of Arran to the sea traveller about to enter 'the land of the mountain and the flood—the land of romantic beauty'. Despite the fact that no one ever praised Glasgow, Cooper found its squares and the western part of the city more stately than anything in England, outside London. He was entranced by the majesty of Edinburgh, but found the Scottish Sabbath and the strength of teetotalism rather too sour and depressing. Pilgrimages were made to the birthplace of Burns, Tannahill and William Thom, and to Thomas de Quincey at Lasswade. Above all, Cooper was delighted with the Scots. It had been disappointing to find a neglect of Chartist organisation in many places, but he had found himself 'at home' from the first moment when addressing Scottish audiences.

I freely declare that I would choose to address some such audiences as I have addressed in Scotland, sooner than any English audience I could name . . . and I would sooner lecture to an Edinburgh audience than any other audience in the world.[4]

Another visitor of some importance in 1851 was George Jacob Holyoake, whose arrival in Dundee was marked by a hostile article in the *Dundee Courier* of 14 May. The *Courier* had 'thought Chartism defunct' but found that it had overlooked the fact that there were 'too many interested in keeping it alive'. A flock of hungry patriots was being fed, and 'many venal unattached agitators had received employment by means of the Chartist movement'. It was not surprising, therefore, that an effort should be made 'to perpetuate such a profitable concern'. Holyoake was infuriated by the taunt 'hungry patriot', and proceeded to lecture on the character of Chartist leaders and the moral tendency of their principles. But his main concern in Dundee, Paisley and Glasgow was with the objectives of communism and co-operation.

Communism, at least as in Britain [he explained], sought to raise men morally as well as physically. It went on the theory that all men are improvable ... One of the great means would be the abolition of the competitive system, and the establishment of co-operation in its stead, whereby every man would enjoy the fruit of his own industry.[5]

Feargus O'Connor, who since May 1848 had been declaring that the Chartist movement was dead and not merely slumbering, travelled to Aberdeen in October 1849 to test the possibility of a revival in conjunction with the Parliamentary and Financial Reform Association. The prospects for this new alliance, he decided, were distinctly promising, despite the fact that Aberdeen and Edinburgh were 'the two most priest-ridden towns in Scotland, or perhaps in the world'. A further Scottish tour was undertaken by O'Connor in June 1850, despite all his threats to retire, and in Glasgow, Edinburgh, and Paisley he urged 'the adoption of measures to resuscitate the agitation for the Charter'. The only apparent results were votes of confidence in O'Connor, following attacks by his old antagonists, Robert Cochran of Paisley and James Adams of Glasgow. The meeting in Glasgow was one of the most riotous ever held by the Glasgow Chartists. Uproar lasting about two hours took place in the crowded City Hall, which was capable of holding 6,000 people, when 'Parson' Adams attacked O'Connor in the same fashion as he had done in 1848. The chairman, Daniel Paul, became hoarse, and respected George Ross was called to the chair. He had always succeeded in restoring order in similar emergencies in the past, but he could not persuade Adams to stand down, nor the crowd to listen to him. The meeting was dissolved under police supervision, while O'Connor addressed the rump of the assemblage on the suppression of free speech in France.[6]

When Bronterre O'Brien visited Scotland in February 1850 he was elected president of the Scottish National Reform League, although its branches had not yet been formed. These were to be in Glasgow, Edinburgh and other towns, as part of the National Reform League movement, advocating the Charter, gradual nationalisation of the land, mines and fisheries, and the establishment of a currency system 'based on real consumable wealth'. O'Brien now expounded the belief that the Chartist movement had failed because the people had looked on Chartism as an end, and because thorough discussion of social rights had not been permitted. Although he saw signs of better times, he found the condition of the working classes in Glasgow worse than when he was last there. Free trade had brought only cruelty to tradesmen and starving workers, who saw the shops filled with French and German goods. No branches of the National Reform League, however, appear to have been formed as a result of this visit.

Aberdeen invariably appeared to show the greatest warmth for important Chartist visitors. On 5 February 1850, G. W. M. Reynolds was honoured at a soirée, at which the Aberdeen Chartists resolved to join the reorganised National Charter Association, and in September a festival was held to celebrate the visit of Ernest Jones, newly released from prison. Jones appears to have become the most popular of Chartist orators, and in September and October 1850 he addressed crowded and enthusiastic Chartist meetings in Cumnock, Dundee, Edinburgh, Glasgow, Hawick, Kilmarnock, Kirkcaldy and Tillicoultry. According to Gammage, Ernest Jones made a similar tour in 1852, but this does not appear to have attracted any attention from the newspapers.[7]

Partly as a result of such tours, there was during these years a closer connection between the Scottish Chartist associations and the National Charter Association than had existed prior to 1848. Nine or ten associations now contributed to the National Association's funds, and Dundee, Edinburgh, Glasgow and Paisley were amongst its most substantial financial supporters. In 1851 Glasgow alone had over 20 per cent of the total membership reported to the Association by its 'localities'.

At the National Convention in 1851, Scotland was better represented than at any other Chartist conference after the National Assembly of 1848. Aberdeen, however, objected to conferences being held always in London, and suggested that some should take place in Scotland. Edinburgh was represented by its secretary, Walter Pringle, and by Thornton Hunt; Glasgow, by Daniel Paul; Dundee by a rehabilitated James Graham; and Paisley and Falkirk by the Rev. Alexander Duncanson. The Scottish delegates were especially concerned to allay the divisions between the Chartist leaders, and Duncanson wanted to go further and have conciliation with every class of reformer. He refused to accept the contention that an extension of the franchise as proposed by the Parliamentary Reformers could hinder their own efforts to attain the Charter. This policy was strongly opposed by Graham, as the middle classes had been the bitterest enemies of the Chartists.

A different sort of approach was advocated by Walter Pringle, who expounded the belief of the Edinburgh Democratic Tract Society that there existed a 'vast substratum in society which is beyond the reach of our public meetings, lectures, and even newspapers'. Tracts were the only agents that could be successfully employed, and it should be the aim of the Chartists to establish Democratic Printing Societies in all large towns, so that there could be an interchange of productions and 'a constant stream of tracts'.

As in 1841 and 1842, there were Scottish objections to the proposal to get up another national petition, on the grounds that in the existing dismembered and disorganised state of Chartism this could only expose their weakness. Instead they should agitate the country and organise a series of simultaneous local petitions. The Rev. A. Duncanson succeeded in getting only one of his resolutions adopted, and this censured Feargus O'Connor for his 'uncalled-for, unjust and anti-democratic sentiments' regarding foreigners. Although he was a personal friend of O'Connor, he felt the need to remark on the want of care and the precipitancy of language which had often placed O'Connor in a false position, and had injured the cause of democracy.

'What a progress three years have shown,' declared *The Leader* somewhat optimistically. 'The new attitude of Chartism commands, on the whole, respect; and those who stood aloof ... have no further justification for inactivity and isolation.' No enthusiasm, however, was shown for the new social reformist programme or the new approach to the Six Points. Only in Glasgow did the Convention manage to infuse any fresh life into the dying body of Chartism. There, under the joint leadership of James Adams and Charles Don, the rival factions agreed to cast aside their 'petty squabbles', and a joint committee was formed, whose policy would be 'measures, not men'.[8]

No revival followed the 1851 convention—nor, indeed, had there been any real promise, so far as Scotland was concerned, after 1848 of the resurgence of a strong Radical agitation, except through the Parliamentary and Financial Reform Association. In most of the larger Scottish towns, the Parliamentary Reformers, helped by the agitation in sympathy with the continental liberals during the summer of 1849, had received the support of many of the most influential spokesmen of the middle and working classes. Their meetings in the autumn of 1849 had been well attended, mainly by working class men, and, with the adoption of a conciliatory policy by Feargus O'Connor, the prospects of a strong alliance of reformers of all classes became decidedly promising.

During the last three months of 1849, Scotland figured prominently in the programme of this new reform alliance. The campaign was opened on 15 October with the 'largest and most enthusiastic meeting held in Aberdeen for a long time'. Feargus O'Connor, who was accompanied by his fellow members of Parliament, Sir Joshua Walmsley and George Thompson, was the star attraction. Considerable interest was aroused in Edinburgh, Aberdeen, Paisley and several smaller towns, and a programme was announced of meetings to be held in November in Newcastle, Berwick, Edinburgh, Glasgow, Dundee and Aberdeen, at some of which Joseph Hume would be present. Nevertheless, despite O'Connor's blessing, the widespread acceptance of the new movement was by no means assured. In Dundee the Chartists showed hostility, and 'the apparent apathy manifested by Glasgow to the progress of various important and urgent measures of reform' continued to be 'a matter of surprise everywhere'. By the end of October the only attempt made there had ended in failure. This was, however, redeemed by two highly successful meetings in November.

Joseph Hume failed to keep his promise to appear at any of the Scottish meetings, but the success of the meetings attended by Walmsley and Thompson at Edinburgh, Glasgow, Perth and Greenock exceeded expectations. In Edinburgh on 19 November the meeting was sponsored by the Lord Provost and many members of the city council, besides the Rev. Dr Ritchie, the editor of *The Scotsman*, and several working class leaders. At the Glasgow meeting on 26 November, most of the past and present Chartist leaders were to be found on the platform. Matthew Cullen, who acted as spokesman for the operatives of Glasgow, moved the appointment of a committee to carry out the objectives of the new association, namely a large extension of the suffrage, shorter parliaments and the adjustment of representation to population. As a result, an enormous committee of about eighty persons was appointed. Amongst them were ex-Lord Provost Hastie, MP, several councillors, Turner of Thrushgrove and many of the best known middle class reformers, James Moir, George Ross, Matthew Cullen, Duncan Sherrington, Malcolm McFarlane, most of the well known Chartists and nine or ten workmen as the representatives of public works and factories. At Greenock, on the 30th, the Chartists, led by Robert Burrell, demanded the inclusion of payment of members in the objects of the association, but decided to support the resolutions, since they were glad that 'a large and influential party were willing to go so far for political justice'.

The initial success of these meetings produced some rather extravagant claims for the strength of the movement.

The hearty response with which the principles of the London Association has met [declared the *Glasgow Saturday Post*] places it in a degree of prominence and invests it with a power which was not attained for a long period in all the previous agitations of this century, remarkable as they have been owing to the unprecedented unanimity which already prevails amongst the industrial classes of society.[9]

It was, however, more than two years later before the reform movement again achieved any prominence in Scotland.

Lord John Russell's promise last session to introduce a new Reform Bill this session [wrote Lord Cockburn in his *Journal* on 30 January 1852] seemed for some months to have scarcely struck the public ear, but since the time for redeeming this pledge has begun to draw near, the Reform mind has been stirred in some large towns. A public meeting on the subject was held here on the 27th instant, but though held at an hour in the evening that enabled handicraftsmen to attend, it was a very poor affair. No great crowd—not one man of reputation or influence present—poor talk—and except in a desire for some change, no definite process or scheme—a contrast to the old Edinburgh meetings ... The only parliamentary reformers who think themselves consistent are the crazy Chartists who, in spite of the example of America and France, rave about supplanting the British constitution by a senseless but instant Republic, in which they are all to be great men.

In Glasgow the impetus to the cause of parliamentary reform still came from the working classes, and at the time of the introduction of Lord John Russell's Reform Bill they decided to hold a public meeting to demand 'a more comprehensive reform Bill than Lord John's peddling measure'. A meeting of delegates was held, and the middle classes were sounded for union on a common programme. Eventually, in April, a public meeting was held which was graced by the Lord Provost, three MPs and an impressive array of bailies and councillors. Walter Buchanan explained that those who held the principles of the People's Charter had abandoned, for a time, these claims, and that it had been decided that those of the London Parliamentary Reform Association were best calculated to effect a compromise. This basis had been adopted for their movement, and already more than 1,000 working men had become members of the Association. Moir, Cullen and Pattison (who became the secretary) moved the principal resolutions, which were, to constitute the Glasgow Parliamentary Reform Association, to secure city candidates who would support the measures of the association, and the appointment of a suitable committee.

By 1852 the Scottish Chartist movement had been superseded by, or absorbed into, the Parliamentary Reform Association. This association, concluded the *Star of Freedom*,

is a large body. It has too that recommendation which is of such great importance ... it is respectable. Its leaders are men of wealth and station who have the opportunity of speaking their opinions before assembled legislators. The funds which are applied to promote its objects ... are considerable. Some hundreds of meetings have been held throughout the country, at which the crack orators of the party have spoken. Addresses have been issued, and newspaper advocates have not been wanting. With a good cause straightforwardly and consistently expounded, such materials could hardly fail to command success. Yet the Parliamentary Association has done as little ... as any other political body. Much noise and little work has been the order of the day. They have sounded the trumpet, but have not fought the battle.

The cause of parliamentary reform now seemed to be moving somewhat slowly, in circular fashion, back to the position it had reached in 1834. Many of the former Chartist leaders wished to participate in movements associating Radical reformers of all classes. Co-operation and conciliation amongst leading reformers of all classes was becoming once more possible over a wide range of liberal and humanitarian objectives, even if their supporters might again be numbered in small cliques rather than in multitudes. To some considerable degree the pattern of behaviour of Scottish reformers was reverting to what it had been in the evolutionary period of the 1830's. In September 1852, James Turner of Thrushgrove was again to be found presiding over a meeting of the Glasgow Reform Association, which adopted a programme of household suffrage, triennial parliaments, and vote by ballot. The only important differences between this and similar meetings in 1833–36 were an accompanying demand for equal electoral districts and the fact that the 'overflowing' meeting was composed mainly of the working classes.[10]

NOTES

1. *Northern Star*, 21 and 28 July; 4 and 18 August; 10 November 1849; 16 February; 2 and 30 March 1850.
   Glasgow Examiner, 26 January 1850; 30 October 1858.
2. *Northern Star*, 5 May; 2 and 30 June; 7 and 28 July; 11 August; 1 September; 13 October 1849.
   Glasgow Saturday Post, 6 October 1849.
3. *Northern Star*, 19 July; 11 October; 29 November 1851.
   The Leader, 26 July 1851.
   Reynolds' Weekly Newspaper, 22 June 1851.
4. *Northern Star*, 23 and 30 August 1851.
   Autobiography of Thomas Cooper, 1874, pp. 326, 384–5.
5. *Northern Star*, 7 June; 30 August 1851.
   Glasgow Sentinel, 3 and 24 May 1851.
   The Leader, 1851, p. 519.
6. *Northern Star*, 20 October; 10 November 1849.
   Glasgow Examiner, 8 June 1850.
   Gammage, pp. 380–1.
7. *Northern Star*, 9 February; 2 March 1850.
   Glasgow Saturday Post, 16 February 1850.
   Glasgow Examiner, 12 October 1850.
   Gammage, pp. 380 1.
8. *Northern Star*, 15 and 22 March; 5, 12 and 19 April; 17 May; 5 July; 18 October 1851; 10 January; 14 February 1852.
   Glasgow Sentinel, 3 May 1851.
   The Leader, 1851, p. 352.
   English Republic, 1851, pp. 352–3.

9. *Northern Star*, 29 September; 13, 20 and 27 October; 24 November; 1 and 8 December 1849.
   Glasgow Saturday Post, 27 October; 17 November; 1 December 1849.
   Glasgow Examiner, 24 October 1849.
10. *Glasgow Examiner*, 24 April; 2 October 1852.
   Star of Freedom, 18 September 1852.
   Journal of Henry Cockburn, 1874, vol. ii, p. 270.

CHAPTER EIGHTEEN

The Chartist aftermath

During the decade following 1850, emigration and colonisation drew many thousands of working class people away from Scotland, while for those who remained some benefit was derived from the conditions of fuller employment and the improved economic climate which accompanied the expansion of heavy industry on Clydeside. For many, the improvement in conditions of living was remarkable —at least in comparison with their experience during recent years of industrial depression. Nevertheless, there were still important sections of the population living at starvation level. For several years during the early 1850's there was renewed agitation regarding the refusal of poor relief to the able-bodied and their families, and, especially in years of slackness in the iron trade, many people considered that there was no question of greater importance to the working classes than the promotion of schemes for the assisted emigration of 'surplus operatives'.

The plight of the hand-loom weavers once again attracted attention. The weavers complained that the promises of some of the leading firms in the trade to advance the scale of wages were never carried out; they were classified as able-bodied poor and denied relief. Appeals were made on their behalf to the manufacturers and the government for regulation of the trade and other measures, such as emigration assistance and the use of public funds to support the manufacture, by weavers, of kelp. Despite a growing awareness of grave defects in industrial and social life, the outlook of the press during the 1850's was decidedly hopeful, and often optimistic:

Free Trade and Australia are operating most beneficially on the material prosperity of our working classes [declared the *Glasgow Examiner* in July 1853]. The downward and depressing movement has now been arrested, but it has been through much suffering and severe discipline. The Corn Laws were only repealed because a black cloud was visible on the horizon—the potato rot in Ireland inundated our shores with Celts flying from impending starvation, and the great mortality prevalent throughout Great Britain and Ireland decimated the population ... [Now] the value of labour has been advanced and all our working classes are receiving an enhanced rate of remuneration, and in many cases their hours of labour have also been diminished ... The greater part of recent legislation has had for its design the relief of the masses, by removing or mitigating the pressure which has crushed them so fiercely in past times ... and a slow and painful, but successful effort is being made, year after year, to equalise taxation, and compel all persons to be burdened according to their capabilities. Those who are reaping the benefit of this procedure are the working classes of the empire ... Better education, better dwellings, better recreations, and better sanitary arrangements are all pursued after, with some measure of success.[1]

In the political climate there was the feeling, not born entirely of despair, that the fortunes of the nation could be left yet awhile in the hands of Parliament, the land-owners, the mill owners and the shopkeepers. There was alive, however, the conviction that neither industrialism nor disgusting conditions of urban life should be allowed to demoralise completely the unfortunate sections of the nation. Perhaps above all, there was a revived awareness that much of the potential improvement of the standards of life and labour for the working classes lay in their own positive measures of combination and co-operation.

During a period of almost fifteen years the Chartist agitation had passed across the social and political face of Scotland. It found the mass of the Scottish people in political apathy, and it left them, still unenfranchised, in apparent political apathy. In the various social reformist movements, however, the participation of well known Chartists, which had been observable after the collapse of 1842, continued for a generation. Scottish Chartism had drawn its leaders from the existing social and political movements, and when the tide of Chartism ebbed after 1842, and more completely after 1851, these leaders were largely returned to their other agitations— often with enhanced reputations, and with close connections with the leaders of allied movements.

As in the 1840's, the Rev. Patrick Brewster, John Fraser, Malcolm McFarlane and Robert Cranston continued to play an active part in the temperance movement. Brewster was still president of the Paisley Total Abstinence Society, while John Fraser, with the assistance of his musically talented daughters, gave concerts to promote the principles of the temperance movement. McFarlane, who was prominent in a variety of agitations, including those for the abolition of capital punishment, the Glasgow Working Men's Association for the Protection of the Sabbath, co-operation and trade unionism, was a prominent member of the Scottish Temperance League. In Edinburgh, in 1848, Robert Cranston started a chain of 'temperance hotels' with the Waverley, which was followed during a long life by others in Glasgow and London.[2]

Amongst the trade unionists were to be found Allan McFadyen, W. C. Pattison and Matthew Cullen. McFadyen, once the secretary of the Glasgow Universal Suffrage Association, continued to hold the office of secretary of the Ten Hours Bill Committee of the Glasgow Trades for many years after 1843. In 1849 and 1850, McFadyen and his committee were alarmed by the prospect of an extension of the Ten Hours Act to eleven hours, and organised protests by the workmen of Glasgow and neighbourhood. Pattison was the secretary of the Scottish Steam Engine Machine Makers, whose branches were absorbed into the Amalgamated Society of Engineers in 1851. He also ran a printing business, which produced the *Practical Mechanic and Engineer's Magazine*. This had developed out of his plan in 1840 to form a Chartist joint stock printing and publishing company, which became the 'National Printing and Publishing Company of Scotland'. Duncan Robertson, who had been the most energetic disseminator of Chartist principles amongst the coal and ironstone miners of Lanarkshire and Renfrewshire, was another of several leading Chartists who remained active in this field. Another was Matthew Cullen, who was active in most of the social reformist movements of the period, including the Glasgow Emancipation Society and the Glasgow Poor Law Reform Association, which sought the establishment of a general system of taxation for the support of the poor in place of the system of separate assessments for each parish.[3]

In the upsurge of co-operation which took place about 1850, and more strongly around 1860, the links with Chartism appeared to be especially close. In a few cases, flourishing co-operative societies of the 1850's were survivals of the Chartist co-operative stores, while there were several cases of Chartist leaders becoming prominent advocates of co-operation. Amongst them were Andrew Wardrop of Dumfries, Henry Dove of Hawick, and William Sanderson of

Galashiels. Dove, who had been one of the most zealous of the Hawick Chartists, a supporter of O'Connor's land scheme and an admirer of Ernest Jones, gave his name to the Hawick Chartist Provision Store when, at the instigation of the Excise authorities in 1852, its title was changed to Henry Dove and Company. William Sanderson, who had founded the flourishing Galashiels Provision Store Company in 1842 with the assistance of his Chartist followers, was considered 'the founder of the present plan of co-operative stores'—the 'equitable system', whereby all purchasers shared in the profits of the society, whether they were members or not. Amongst other Chartist leaders giving support to the co-operative movement was the ubiquitous Matthew Cullen, who would normally speak of the importance of such movements in fostering the 'independent self-respect of the working classes' by supplying them not merely with food, but with 'comfortable raiment to allow them to appear in their respective religious congregations'.[4]

Even at the height of the Chartist agitation, municipal politics had never been entirely neglected by the Chartists. There had usually been a few ultra-Radicals, or Chartist sympathisers, on the town councils of Glasgow, Aberdeen, Perth, Edinburgh, Paisley and Dunfermline, while in Newmilns in 1839 and 1840 the Chartists became so strong that they held a majority after the elections of November 1840. Prior to the Chartist agitation, Bailie Hugh Craig, James Moir, William Carnegie and several others who became Chartist leaders had been active in local politics. It was hardly surprising that when the agitation declined many of them should again devote their energies to the affairs of local government. Several, such as Ross, Pattison and Moir, were elected police commissioners, and they and others became members of the recently created parochial boards. A few, such as James Moir, Robert Cranston, Robert Cochran and James McPherson (of Aberdeen), became town councillors. Moir and Cranston, at least, became highly respectable bailies, while Cochran became Provost of Paisley in 1885.

James Moir, who became president of the Scottish National Reform League at the end of 1867, and a Justice of the Peace in 1875, had possibly the most outstanding career in this field, in which he remained for more than thirty years after 1848, when he was first elected to the Glasgow city council. Throughout this part of his life, his main preoccupation remained that of improving the amenities of Glasgow for his fellow citizens. To this end, he sought the in-

10. The Trongate, Glasgow

11. The old Waverley Hotel, Princes Street, Edinburgh, in 1876

12. (*left*) James Moir in 1877. 13. (*above*) *Robert Cranston* (*a*) as a young man and (*b*) in later life. 14. (*right*) Robert Cochran in 1888.

crease of hospital accommodation for fever patients, the improvement of prison conditions and of the slum areas of central Glasgow, the preservation of Glasgow Green, better access for the public to parks, and the erection of urinals in George Square and other public places. For his constant struggle for popular rights he was often enthusiastically applauded by the public, though sometimes ridiculed by his fellow liberals and Radicals. When he died in 1880, he left a handsome bequest and his own library to the Mitchell Library.[5]

Comparatively little attention was paid to the Scottish Rights movement, and none of the former Chartists appears to have figured prominently in the National Association for the Vindication of Scottish Rights. This was probably not due to any great extent to the fact that the National Association was dominated by noblemen and Conservatives, for its aims gained sympathetic attention in the Radical newspapers. It had been shown most clearly, declared the *Glasgow Examiner* in November 1853,

that the Treaty of Union, which provides that equal privileges shall be extended to both countries, has been infringed, and that there is an abundance of facts to show that Scottish affairs receive little or no attention from the English Government ... There are proofs of a decided inclination to trifle, if not to treat with contempt, Scotland and her affairs.

The main grievance was the centralisation of administration in London, but there was growing resentment on many other issues, such as the need for a Secretary of State for Scotland, an equitable share of public spending, and removal of the disproportion in parliamentary representation between the two countries. On the basis of population the *Glasgow Examiner* calculated that Scotland should have nineteen more representatives, while on the criterion of revenue derived from England, Scotland and Ireland, its calculation was that Scotland needed twenty-five more representatives to redress the balance.[6]

Questions of foreign affairs—especially the liberation of Louis Kossuth, the Eastern Question, slavery in the United States and the struggle for Italian independence—aroused considerable popular interest and Radical activity during this period. Meetings were held in 1850 to protest against the enactment of the Fugitive Slave Bill, and in 1852 for the working men of Glasgow to make a presentation to Mrs Harriet Beecher Stowe. At these, Malcolm McFarlane and Matthew Cullen denounced slavery as subversive of reason, justice and religion, and called upon the United States to grant immediate emancipation to the three million slaves she held in bondage. In 1854 and 1858 enthusiastic meetings were addressed by Louis Kossuth, for whose liberation the Liberals and Radicals had combined in 1851 to demand intervention by the British government. In November 1853 he returned to Glasgow, where he claimed to have 'commenced his public labours', and was gratified to find alive that enthusiasm which had been lacking on previous occasions, when he had expounded his views on the oppressions of Russia and on the sinister designs of the Czar to involve Britain in a war with France. Councillor Moir, who was in the chair, denounced the policy of the Russian emperor and urged Her Majesty's government to aid the cause of the oppressed. In this he was supported by James Proudfoot, George Ross and Robert Buchanan, former Owenite missionary and now editor of the *Glasgow Sentinel*, who declared that the present invasion of Turkey was part of traditional Russian policy to dominate the rest of Europe and extinguish national independence and political freedom. Throughout the 1850's, funds were continually being organised for the cause of European freedom by the Rev. Charles Clarke and John McAdam, with substantial contributions being made to the London Committee for Italian Independence. In 1857 there was a series of large public meetings for this purpose in Glasgow, Edinburgh, Paisley, Hawick and other towns. For several years interest in this cause was maintained by the brothers John and William McAdam of Glasgow, who also did much in the 1860's to stimulate interest in Polish independence. This reached its climax in 1863 with the Polish revolution, and the visit to Glasgow of Lord Palmerston. Contrary 'to all predictions', Palmerston was received with 'wild enthusiasm' at a workmen's soirée in the City Hall, with the Lord Provost presiding and with Matthew Cullen acting once again as the spokesman of the working classes.[7]

Though the links which had connected the Chartist agitation with the Radical agitations since 1816 were seldom in evidence in the 1850's, there was still a strong undercurrent of Radicalism among the Scottish working classes which continued at least until the passing of the second Reform Bill in 1867. The talk of organisation for parliamentary reform, which had virtually ceased in 1852, was again heard in 1857, when the *Radical Reformer* declared:

The question of a renewed movement for their rights on the part of the people is receiving considerable attention in various parts of the country ... Already there has been too much delay. We have afforded our opponents too much ground to charge us with indifference to the success of the principles we profess. The people it is said are contented; they ask for no organic changes in the constitution; they have no interest in the question of the extension of the Suffrage, and still less in that of the Ballot. Nor, we regret to say, can these charges be altogether denied ... [but] the indifference and supineness of the people are more apparent than real; and an emergency will call forth their dormant energies and talents. Let an earnest and enlightened movement be but set fairly afoot in any part of the country, and the people will again arouse themselves to demand their rights ... while we cease not to demand all that we are entitled to, let us support with earnestness the statesman who is willing to advance furthest in our direction.

Whatever excitement there was in 1857, however, quickly disappeared after the general election, for which the Scottish Chartists were able to muster only a solitary candidate, C. F. Wordsworth at Paisley.

With the promise of Lord Palmerston to introduce some measure of reform in the new session of Parliament, there was again talk of reform in the early months of 1858, but the *Glasgow Examiner* feared that there would be

but little pressure from without to compel a proper measure. The country is at present politically dead. Political parties are defunct, and isolated reformers have but little influence ... There is abundance of orators ready to make speeches, but audiences cannot be found. Food is cheap, and till lately, employment was abundant.

In February the 'Friends of Parliamentary Reform' in Glasgow, who included Councillor Moir, James Adams, John McAdam, Robert Buchanan and the Rev. Mr Crosskey, met to consider a revival of reform agitation. The desirability of manhood suffrage and of union between the middle and working classes was again discussed, and a committee was appointed to watch over proceedings in Parliament. But it was decided that they should not commit themselves beyond the policy adopted at the last great public reform meeting in Glasgow in 1852, namely household suffrage, vote by ballot, triennial parliaments and a more equal distribution of electoral districts. It was also decided not to arrange any public meeting, nor make any declaration of policy, until Palmerston had produced his measure. A month later there was some talk of another reform Bill, manufactured by Lord Derby and Benjamin Disraeli. Then, in April, there were complaints from *The Workman* about the levity of the House of Commons and Mr Thomas Duncombe towards parliamentary reform, when the Duncombe motion for the production of the promised Bill was both intended, and treated, as a joke.[8]

By the end of 1858 there had once again been a transformation of the political scene, largely as a result of the success of John Bright's campaign, during the autumn, in re-stirring the embers of Radicalism.

It was a delusion [commented the *Glasgow Examiner* on 30 October] to suppose that the old party 'spirits' were departed—they were only dormant, and would manifest themselves as soon as opportunity occurred. [That the country was] now fairly in for another fierce and determined Reform agitation is now certain. All classes, from the Janus-faced Premier to the reddest republican, seem to have arrived at the conclusion that there must be a change ... Veterans of former times are reopening their batteries, and are anxiously leading a fresh generation into the field. The meeting in the Lower Trades Hall on Tuesday evening was largely composed of the old Chartist elements, and to some degree pervaded with the old Chartist spirit ... Manhood suffrage, or in other words, universal suffrage was all but universally recognised as the basis of any bill that would meet with hearty support from the working classes.

This Glasgow meeting in support of John Bright's pressure for reform had been called by Councillors Moir and McAdam, and was 'principally attended by delegates from the various trades'. When 'the majority of those who spoke ... most noteworthy among whom was Parson Adams, expressed a disposition to demand manhood suffrage', James Moir took the opportunity to tell the Chartist remnants that, with some exceptions, they were 'unprincipled scoundrels' and that he wished to have nothing more to do with them.

In December, John Bright reached Scotland, where he addressed large and enthusiastic audiences in Edinburgh and Glasgow, and held conferences with the 'Advanced Liberals' and representatives of the working classes. The platform parties contained all the familiar names, with the addition of lord provosts, MP's, numerous bailies and councillors, and delegates from neighbouring towns. Foremost amongst the Paisley delegation at the Glasgow meeting was the Rev. Patrick Brewster, who died three months later. The Glasgow Reform Association was again brought to life, and began to enrol members and send delegates to workmen in several public works. But despite the enthusiastic and apparently widespread support which Bright received during his visit to Scotland, the agitation was not long sustained, and it was not until three years later that there was any further talk of reform.

Foremost amongst the factors favouring a revival of reform agitation towards the end of 1861 was the existence of commercial distress, and in Glasgow it was the United Trades Council which was the prime mover. The Trades Council had a programme of conciliation courts, Saturday half-holidays, assisted emigration and a free library, museum and art gallery service for the public. In November 1861 it published an address which asserted that the trade societies were the best existing machinery for effecting reform. While they were aware of the reluctance of trades unions to interfere in politics, the trades had been baffled in their attempts to establish councils of conciliation and arbitration. The inequality of the law between master and servant could be rectified only by the possession of political power. The trade societies should therefore memorialise the government to fulfil its pledge of electoral reform. After that, a monster petition should be got up for presentation to Parliament in favour of a comprehensive measure of reform.

With the blessing of John Bright, information from the London Council of the United Trades on its preparations to promote parliamentary reform, and the promise of the Edinburgh Trades Council to do what it could, the Glasgow Trades Council decided to establish a regular organisation for further reform agitation. When the Glasgow Parliamentary Reform Association met again on 15 February 1862, under the presidency of Matthew Cullen, George Newton and Matthew Lawrence, the future secretary and president of the Trades Council were appointed to represent the Glasgow Reform Association at the National Reform Conference in London. This took place on 20 and 21 May, and Newton declared that although the men of Glasgow were well known as advocates of manhood suffrage, they would be willing to accept a £16 borough and a £10 county franchise as practical politics. Lawrence reiterated that manhood suffrage remained their objective, but they had already fought long enough for abstract principles and they must now fight for the practical.

Yet once again the agitation petered out. Newton was disgusted with the lack of response from the working classes, and even more with their 'toadyism' to Lord Palmerston; in March 1863 he declared that in view of the present attitude of the working classes, the Trades Council would be prevented from taking any active steps in the cause of reform for many years.[9]

Thereafter the progress of the Radical cause continued to be desultory. In May 1865, Glasgow and Paisley were again represented at the National Reform Conference, but the Scottish National Reform League, with a programme of residential manhood suffrage (including lodgers as well as householders) and vote by ballot, and in which James Moir, Robert Cranston and Robert Cochran played prominent parts, was not formed until the autumn of 1866. By that time the John Bright reform campaign was sweeping across the country almost as the Birmingham Radicals had done twenty-eight years previously. The links between Chartism and the latest agitation were to be found not merely in the physical appearance of the mass demonstrations which were held, but also in the numerous Chartists and ex-Chartists who still thronged the platforms. The tendency, however, was to avoid mention of the 1838–39 demonstrations and to make comparisons with those of 1831–32.

After the immense demonstrations in Birmingham at the end of August, and at Manchester in September, great expectations were once again held of Glasgow and the west of Scotland.

The Reform Campaign, which was inaugurated at Birmingham a few weeks ago, is advancing steadily northwards [announced the *Glasgow Sentinel* on 13 October], and on Tuesday Glasgow and the West of Scotland will show to their countrymen that they are the worthy representatives of those who rendered such valuable assistance to the cause of Reform thirty-five years ago ... All the towns in the Western counties are to send deputations to swell the assemblage. Greenock, Paisley, Rothesay, Dumbarton, Port-Glasgow, Hamilton and a number of other places will all be represented ... In Glasgow the 16th will be observed as a general holiday, and the different trades will thus be enabled to take their places in the procession which will be formed on the Green.

In the weeks prior to the Glasgow demonstration several preparatory meetings were held to form branches of the Scottish Reform League, and to aid the reform demonstration. Amongst these was one at Johnstone on 9 October, where John Fraser of Newfield House was called to the chair, and at which 'Mr. Moir and Mr. Cochran delivered very effective addresses, and were warmly applauded'. On their motion, pledges were taken to form a local branch, based on manhood suffrage and the ballot, and to support the demonstration.

On 16 October 40,000 people marched in a procession six miles long, and 150,000–200,000 people on Glasgow Green was considered to be a safe estimate.

The gathering on Tuesday was the largest political meeting which ever took place in Scotland [declared the *Glasgow Sentinel*], and were the people indifferent to their just rights they would never have sacrificed a day's wages and put themselves to all the inconvenience of assembling.

John Bright was accompanied by Edmund Beales, George Potter and Ernest Jones. Most of the leading Liberals, Radicals and trade union leaders of the west of Scotland seemed to be assembled on six platforms on the Green. George Newton moved the vote of thanks to John Bright and all other true friends of reform in Parliament. Amongst the platform chairmen were James Moir, George Ross and Councillor Robert Cochran, while those who were called upon to move the principal resolutions included Matthew Cullen and John Fraser, 'who had been concerned in the cause of reform before 1820'. Fraser declared that he was there

to maintain the cause of the people, the universal liberty of mankind ... [before] a magnificent meeting gathered together by the spirit of patriotism, by the spirit of morality, of sobriety, of intelligence, in order to show their attachment to the right of men to the franchise.

Following the Glasgow demonstration, much was done by the Scottish National Reform League to carry out John Bright's injunction to 'organise reform associations in every town', and to 'be prepared, if need be, with funds'. Ernest Jones and Edmund Beales remained in Scotland for some time after the Glasgow affair, and assisted Moir and Cochran at demonstrations in Dumbarton and Kilmarnock. Until the end of the year, reform demonstrations were still being held in Scottish towns, at which many of the familiar figures of an earlier generation were again to be seen. The old cry for the 'securing of a full, fair, and free representation of the people in Parliament, by means of manhood suffrage, a redistribution of seats, and vote by ballot' was still to be the popular demand.[10]

Thereafter the old Chartists and ex-Chartists lived on as local worthies, whose participation in Radical-flavoured social and political movements was appreciated, and whose deaths were marked by respectful newspaper obituaries. There was at least one 'Old Chartist Festival'—in Dundee, in the 1870's—to reminisce with nostalgic pleasure on what these veterans felt to have been an honourable and worthwhile campaign, which had probably not been fought in vain. For the activists of the movement, who had sacrificed their time, energy, family relationships and occasionally even personal security, there had been constant challenge and drama, and the excitement of living in the public eye. For many, Chartism had meant a grounding in political and social affairs, while for the rank and file of the movement it had held out hope that the future would be less bleak than the present. For them it also had meant excitement and a sense of participating in something important. There was satisfaction in hearing that others cared about the condition of the working classes, and that justice and morality stood on their side. Even for the mass of the people, who only came out for the demonstrations, there was in Chartism an excuse for a holiday, and the colour and entertainment of processions with their banners and bands of music.[10]

How far Chartism was responsible for any improvement in the physical, as opposed to the mental and moral, condition of the Scottish people is, however, beyond exact assessment. Improved conditions of trade and employment, new social legislation, and some benefits from free trade, all contributed to the raising of standards of living, though much of the population continued to live at the level of starvation and misery. Chartism was merely the most important of a number of social movements which aimed at fostering habits of reason, self-respect and sobriety amongst the working classes, and which eventually succeeded in raising the question of the condition of the people of Great Britain as the most important of public matters.

Perhaps the chief part which the Chartist agitation had played in the life of the people of Scotland was that during a period of rapid social and industrial transformation, which was punctuated with years of the most acute commercial and industrial distress, and which ended with the emergence of a highly industrialised and largely urbanised nation, it provided a vehicle for the expression of the pent-up grievances and aspirations of the people. These were expressed in accordance with the soundest principles of popular action evolved in earlier agitations. What was best in the old Radical tradition was preserved in the Scottish Chartist movement, while in many of its aspects—its emphasis on local organisation, its development of a Chartist press, the maintenance of close relations with the trades unions, and the largely ethical and educational impulse given to the agitation through the Chartist churches, schools, co-operatives and temperance associations—it was the means of training considerable numbers of working class men to adopt a high sense of social responsibility and duty. The process of the political education of the people was developed and speeded up by the Chartists, who made sure that the Scottish people became well steeped in democratic principles. It was this conviction of the eventual triumph of the democratic faith, and the social benefits of a democratic way of life, that kept hope in the future alive in the hearts of large sections of the people throughout the 1840's. For many working class men with latent talent and aspirations it afforded educational opportunities and a local politicians' ladder. It provided opportunities for experiments in organisation and group communication which helped to establish a pattern of local democratic behaviour that remained strong through many generations.

NOTES

1. *Glasgow Examiner,* 7 February; 17 April; 5 June 1852; 30 July 1853; 18 September 1858.
   Journal of Henry Cockburn, vol. ii, p. 232.
2. *Glasgow Saturday Post,* 23 December 1848; 14 July 1849; 5 January 1850. *Glasgow Examiner,* 17 November 1849; 20 April 1850; 4 January 1862.
   L. C. Wright, *Scottish Chartism,* 1953, pp. 210–11.
3. *Glasgow Saturday Post,* 16 June 1849; 19 January 1850.
   Glasgow Examiner, 17 November 1849; 17 April 1852.
   Northern Star, 21 September 1844; 10 March 1849.
   W. H. Marwick, *The Working Class Movement in the Nineteenth Century,* 1938.
4. *Northern Star,* 29 September 1849; 18 January 1851; 10 January 1852.
   Glasgow Sentinel, 20 December 1862.
   Jubilee *History* of the Hawick Co-operative Society, 1889, pp. 31–32, 39.
5. *Glasgow Examiner,* 3 January; 2 and 9 June 1849; 21 December 1850; 18 January 1851; 17 April; 20 November 1852; 18 September; 23 and 30 October; 6 November 1858.
   Glasgow Saturday Post, 27 October 1849.
   Glasgow Sentinel, 18 October; 1 November 1862; 14 March; 4 April 1863.
   The Workman, 24 April 1858.

Glasgow Herald, 4 September 1860.
The Bailie, 13 November 1872.
Scrapbook of James Moir.

6. *Glasgow Examiner,* 5 November 1853; 30 October 1858.
   Journal of Henry Cockburn, vol. ii, p. 291.

7. *Glasgow Examiner,* 30 November 1850; 20 November 1852; 26 November 1853; 8 July 1854; 20 November 1858; 5 January 1861.
   Glasgow Sentinel, 14 June 1851; 16 May 1857; 4 and 11 April 1863.

8. *Glasgow Sentinel,* 28 February; 4 April 1857.
   The Radical Reformer, 18 April 1857.
   Glasgow Examiner, 9 January; 6 February; 6 March 1858.
   The Workman, 24 April 1858.

9. *Glasgow Examiner,* 30 October; 13 November; 11, 18 and 25 December 1858; 23 November 1861.
   Glasgow Sentinel, 16 January; 9, 23 and 30 November; 7 and 14 December 1861; 17 February; 21 March 1863.
   * *Report of the National Reform Conference,* 1862.

10. *Glasgow Sentinel,* 1 September; 13, 20 and 27 October; 3 November; 29 December 1866.
    Report of the National Reform Conference, 1865.
    Wright, pp. 209–12.

Appendix 1

(a) Indicators of activity

Year	Local Organisations in existence	Chartist churches	Chartist co-operatives	Chartist newspapers	Branches of Land Society	Localities of NCA
1838	78	–	–	3	–	–
1839	169	4	9	4	–	–
1840	127	20+	20	5	–	–
1841	68	23+	6	5	–	–
1842	98	17	5	3	–	9
1843	39	12	5	2	–	4
1844	18+	8	5	–	–	6
1845	15+	6	5	–	14	6
1846	19+	4	4	–	26	5
1847	5+	4	4	1	34	2
1848	20+	2	4	1	5+	2+
1849	9+	2	4	1	6+	6
1850	7+	2	4	–	1+	0+
1851	10+	2	4	–	3	12

Year	Localities represented at conferences	Extra-local financial effort	Large demonstrations	Regular social meetings
1838	15	23	13	–
1839	69+	48	19	6
1840	56	23	16	5
1841	22	5	4	2+
1842	65+	6	5	2
1843	–	3	2	2

(*b*) Quarterly sales of stamps to Chartist newspapers

Year	Ayrshire Examiner	True Scotsman	Scottish Patriot	Perthshire Chronicle	Dundee Chronicle (and Herald)	Northern Star
1838						
c	12,000	–	–	(6,960)	(8,000)	136,400
d	9,000	35,500		(4,000)	(6,000)	155,000
1839						
a	7,000	30,000	–	(6,000)	(8,000)	425,000
b	6,000	27,150	3,000	(4,000)	(8,000)	545,000
c	4,800	22,000	30,500	5,000	(9,760)	563,000
d	2,800	18,200	13,500	4,800	(8,000)	316,000
1840						
a	–	13,800	17,500	6,000	9,125	286,000
b	–	10,000	18,500	6,000	7,000	169,000
c	–	9,900	16,000	4,000	9,000	249,000
d	–	9,800	17,000	6,000	9,070	272,000
1841						
a		6,700	13,375	6,000	13,500	191,000
b		–	15,250	5,000	9,500	165,000
c		–	15,000	3,000	11,000	154,000
d		–	15,500	4,000	11,000	196,000
1842						
a		1,500	–	3,000	10,500	148,000
b		6,000	–	500	8,800	159,000
c		5,000	–	–	8,020	168,000
d		4,550	–	–	7,175	175,500
1843						
a		4,500			6,075	107,500
b		1,500			5,175	104,000
c		–			3,750	126,000
d		–			–	117,000

(*c*) Advertisement duty paid

	£ s d	£ s d	£ s d	£ s d	£ s d	£ s d
1838	11 12 6	7 4 0	–	63 6 0	132 14 0	114 13 6
1839	23 0 6	27 1 6	8 15 6	57 12 6	164 12 6	91 10 0
1840	–	39 9 0	30 3 0	58 12 6	117 19 6	44 18 6
1841	–	8 0 6	36 10 6	51 0 0	59 3 6	52 11 6
1842		5 9 6	4 7 0	13 11 6	40 8 6	57 0 0
1843		3 3 0	–	–	26 12 6	

(*d*) Scottish contributions to various Chartist funds (excluding funds for local and county organisation, Land Society, etc.)

	£	s	d
National Rent (1838–39)	522	16	4
Stephens defence fund (1839)	7	2	0
National Defence Fund (1839–40)	190	18	6
Collins, Lovett and Vincent fund (1839–40)	60	13	3
Frost defence fund (1839–40)	270	19	9
Frost appeals (1841, 1846)	19	13	0
McDouall appeal (1840)	26	17	0
General Defence Fund (1840–41)	25	3	4
Wives and families of imprisoned Chartists fund (1839–41)	38	0	6
George Ross appeal (1840)	52	18	3
John Fraser (hustings) appeal (1840–41)	28	0	0
Universal Suffrage Central Committee for Scotland (1839–1842)	179	8	4
Other miscellaneous funds (1841–45)	110	4	8

(*e*) Contributions of National Rent and National Petition Signatures

		£	s	
Ayrshire	Hugh Craig (and John McCrae)	168	10	17,000
Dumfries and the borders	Abram Duncan	27	10	3,350
Dunfermline, Kirkcaldy, Alloa, Stirling and Clackmannan	Alex. Halley	56	10	23,000
Edinburgh and Midlothian	W. S. V. Sankey	14	10	16,000
Forfarshire and Aberdeenshire	W. G. Burns	45	0	18,600
Glasgow and Lanarkshire	James Moir	102	10	78,000
Perthshire and East Fifeshire	Pattrick Matthew	38	10	45,000
Renfrewshire, Dumbartonshire, Alva and Tillicoultry	Dr John Taylor	70	0	10,800

Appendix 2

(*a*) Members of the Universal Suffrage Central Committee for Scotland

1839–40
David Allan†
Robert Currie
Walter Currie
Matthew Cullen*†
John Duncan
Michael Gilfillan
Thomas Gillespie*†
John McGavenny†
James Moir†
Arthur O'Neill
James Proudfoot*
William C. Pattison*†
John Rodger*†
George Ross*†
William Thomson

1840–42
William Allan
Walter Currie†
Matthew Cullen†
John Gairdner†
Michael Gilfillan
John Howie†
Malcolm McFarlane
John McGavenny
James Moir
Arthur O'Neill
James Proudfoot†
William C. Pattison†
John Rodger
George Ross†
William Thomson†
Charles McEwan
John Strathern

Office-bearers

1839–40
Presidents: James Moir, Matthew Cullen.
Treasurer: George Ross.
Secretary: William Thomson.
Editor: William Thomson.

1840–42
President: James Proudfoot.
Vice-President: Matthew Cullen.
Treasurer: George Ross.
Secretary: William Thomson.
Editor: William Thomson.

* Director of the Glasgow Universal Suffrage Association.
† Member of the executive committee of the Universal Suffrage Central Committee for Scotland.

(*b*) Miscellaneous Chartist organisations (1838–42)

(i) *County organisations*

Ayrshire Universal Suffrage Association
Border Union of Chartists
Border Union of Teetotal Chartists
Edinburgh and Midlothian Universal Suffrage Association
Fifeshire and Kinross Chartist Union
Forfarshire Chartist Association
Lanarkshire Universal Suffrage Association
Northern Charter Union (Aberdeenshire and Kincardineshire)
North Midland Chartist Union
Perthshire Radical Reformers' Association
Stirlingshire and District Chartist Union
West Midland Chartist Union

(ii) *City associations*

Glasgow
    Universal Suffrage Association
    Universal Suffrage Electors' Association
    Democratic Club
    Charter Association
    Complete Suffrage Association

Edinburgh
    Radical Association
    Universal Suffrage Association
    Political Union
    Charter Association
    Complete Suffrage Association
    Democratic Tract Society

Dundee
    Political Union
    Working Men's Association
    Trades Democratic Universal Suffrage Association
    Youths Democratic Universal Suffrage Association

(iii) *Female Chartist associations*

Aberdeen, Alva, Bridgeton, Calton and Mile End, Dunfermline, East
Woodside, Forfar, Glasgow, Gorbals, Hawick, Kilmarnock, Kirriemuir,
Montrose, Mount Pleasant, Partick, Perth, Sinclairtown, Strathaven,
Stirling, Tillicoultry.

(iv) *Christian Chartist churches*

Alloa, Anderston, Arbroath, Bridgeton, Campsie, Cupar, Darvel, Dundee, Eaglesham, Glasgow (2), Greenock, Gorbals, Hamilton, Inverleven, Johnstone, Kilbarchan, Kilmarnock, Lanark, Leith, Linlithgow, Newburgh, Newmilns, Partick, Paisley, Pollockshaws, Shettleston, St. Ninians, Vale of Leven.

(v) *Chartist co-operative societies*

Aberdeen, Alexandria, Alloa, Bonhill, Calton and Mile End, Dalkeith, Darvel, Edinburgh, Galashiels, Galston, Gorbals, Greenock, Hawick, Inverleven, Leith, Lochee, Newmilns, Mauchline, Musselburgh, North Quarter, Partick, Tradeston.

Bibliography

The sources which have been the most useful have been indicated in the references given at the end of each chapter. It will be obvious that the newspapers of the period have been very heavily relied on. The standards of reporting in Chartist times compare well with those of the present day, and with official reports of Chartist events. Inevitably there was an element of exaggeration and bias which needs to be discounted, and it is necessary to check the accounts given in rival Chartist newspapers against each other, as well as against reports in local non-Chartist papers. A serious problem here is the incompleteness of files of Chartist papers, including the most important ones, the *True Scotsman* and the *Scottish Patriot*. An extremely valuable guide to the Scottish press is R. M. W. Cowan's *The Newspaper in Scotland, 1815–60* (Glasgow, 1946).

The treatment of the agitation in Scotland in the official records is so slight that it adds little to the picture derived from newspaper sources. Likewise, its treatment in most of the standard works on both Chartism and Scottish history has been scanty and unsatisfactory. This has mainly been due to the fact that too little was known about Scottish Chartist developments, and much of what was 'known' was mistaken or misleading. Most reliable in setting the Scottish background to Chartism have been several studies by W. H. Marwick, and L. J. Saunders, *Scottish Democracy, 1815–40* (Edinburgh, 1950). The outstanding book for providing a fairly comprehensive picture of the Chartist movement is Asa Briggs (ed.) *Chartist Studies* (London, 1959). L. C. Wright's *Scottish Chartism* (Edinburgh, 1953) places the Scottish agitation into the framework of the national movement and against its peculiar native background. It draws attention to the strong social reformist features of Chartist organisation and policy in Scotland, and although it contains much inaccurate detail its conclusions are mainly sensible and perceptive. The most relevant of the other books on Chartism are D. Read and E. Glasgow, *Feargus O'Connor* (London, 1961) and A. R. Schoyen, *The Chartist Challenge* (London, 1958). F. C. Mather's *Public Order in the Age of the Chartists* (Manchester, 1959) is the most important study of this critical aspect of the period. The books by Schoyen, Mather and Wright have excellent bibliographies.

I. OFFICIAL AND MANUSCRIPT SOURCES

Home Office papers (in the Public Records Office, London)

H.O. 103.8
H.O. 103.9 }(Scottish Letter Books, 1836–42).

H.O. 40.53
H.O. 40.56 }(Chartist disturbances and intercepted letters).
H.O. 40.57

H.O.79.4 (Secret and Confidential Despatch Book).

Parliamentary papers

Report from Select Committee on Inquiry into Drunkenness (1834 VIII).

Report from Select Committee on Handloom Weavers' Petitions (1834 X).

Report from Select Committee on Combinations of Workmen (1837–8 VIII).

Report from Assistant Handloom Weavers Commissioners (1839 XLII).

Reports from Handloom Weavers Commission (1840 XIII, XIV).

Report from Select Committee on Payment of Wages, 1842.

Report from Select Committee on Distress (Paisley), 1843.

Report from Midland Mining Commission (1843 XIII).

Report from Select Committee on the National Land Company (1847–8 XIX).

Report on the Sanitary Condition of the Labouring Classes of Great Britain, 1842 (Poor Law Commission).

Report on the General Sanitary Condition of the Working Classes and the Poor in the City of Glasgow. Sanitary Inquiry (Scotland), 1842.

Report from Royal Commission on the State of Large Towns and Populous Districts (1844 XVII).

Reports of the Commissioners appointed to enquire into the Organisation and Rules of Trades Unions and other Associations, 1867–69 (Royal Commission on Trades Unions).

Accounts and Papers (Finance), 1836–53 (for newspaper stamp returns).

Place collection (in the British Museum)
Add. Mss 27,819 (London Working Men's Association).

27,820
27,821 }(Historical narratives of 1838–9 by Francis Place).
27,822

34,245A }(Correspondence of the General Convention of
34,245B }the Industrious Classes, 1839).

27,789–97

Cole collection (in Nuffield College Library, Oxford).
Cowen collection (in Central Library, Newcastle upon Tyne).
Howell collection (in the Bishopsgate Institute, London).
Lovett collection (in Birmingham Public Library).
Moir collection (in Mitchell Library, Glasgow).
Hovell collection (in Manchester University Library).

2. SCOTTISH NEWSPAPERS (in order of usefulness)

The True Scotsman (Chartist, 1838–41, 1842–3) (Paisley Burgh Library).
The Scottish Patriot (Chartist, 1839–41) (Mitchell Library, Glasgow).
The Glasgow Argus (Liberal, 1833–47) (Mitchell Library, Glasgow).
The Glasgow Sentinel (Radical, 1850–77) (Mitchell Library, Glasgow).
The Glasgow Chronicle (Liberal, 1811–57) (Mitchell Library, Glasgow).
The Glasgow Examiner (Radical, 1844–64) (Mitchell Library, Glasgow).
The Glasgow Saturday Post and Paisley and Renfrewshire Reformer (Radical, 1828–1875) (Mitchell Library, Glasgow).
The Chartist Circular (Chartist, 1839–42) (National Library, Edinburgh).
The Scotsman (Liberal, 1817–) (National Library, Edinburgh).
The (Loyal) Reformers' Gazette (Radical/Liberal, 1831–7) (Mitchell Library, Glasgow).
The Scotch Reformers' Gazette (Radical/Liberal, 1837–54) (Mitchell Library, Glasgow).
The Glasgow Herald (Conservative, 1802–) (Mitchell Library, Glasgow).
The Edinburgh Monthly Democrat and Total Abstinence Advocate (Chartist, 1838) (National Library, Edinburgh).
The Scots Times (Radical/Chartist, 1825–41) (Mitchell Library, Glasgow).
The Herald to the Trades Advocate (Radical/trade union, 1830–1) (Mitchell Library, Glasgow).
The Monthly Liberator (Chartist 1838) (Goldsmith's Library, University of London).
The Aberdeen Herald (Radical, 1832–60) (British Museum newspaper repository).

The Weavers' Journal (Radical/Trade Union, 1835–7) (Mitchell Library, Glasgow).
The Liberator (*Radical trade union,* 1832–38) (British Museum newspaper repository).
The Workman (Radical, 1855–8) (Mitchell Library, Glasgow).
The Perth Chronicle (Chartist, 1839–42) (British Museum newspaper repository).

Other files of some of these papers are available in the National Library of Scotland, the Advocates' Library, Edinburgh, and the British Museum newspaper repository, Colindale.

3. ENGLISH NEWSPAPERS (in order of usefulness)

The Northern Star (Chartist, 1837–52) (British Museum newspaper repository).
The Birmingham Journal (Radical/Chartist, 1825–) (Birmingham Public Library).
The Leeds Times (Liberal) (Leeds Central Library).
The Northern Liberator (Chartist, 1837–40) (Manchester Central Library).
The Champion (Radical/Chartist, 1836–40) (Manchester Central Library).
The Chartist (Chartist, 1839) (Nuffield College Library).
The Charter (Chartist, 1839–40) (Nuffield College Library).
The English Chartist Circular (Chartist, 1841–2) (Nuffield College Library).
The New Moral World (Owenite Socialist, 1833–45) (Nuffield College Library).
The Nonconformist (Sturgeite Radical, 1841–5) (Nuffield College Library).
McDouall's Chartist and Republican Journal (Chartist, 1841) (Nuffield College Library).
The Leader (Chartist, 1850–9) (Nuffield College Library).
The Democratic Review (Chartist, 1849–51) (Nuffield College Library).
The English Republic (Chartist, 1851–5) (Nuffield College Library).
The People's Paper (Chartist, 1852–8) (British Museum newspaper repository).
Cooper's Journal (Chartist, 1850) (Nuffield College Library).
Reynold's Weekly Newspaper (Chartist/Co-operative, 1850–) (British Museum newspaper repository).

Other files of some of these papers are available in the British Museum newspaper repository, the Leeds Central Library, the library of the London School of Economics, the Rylands Library, Manchester and the Bishopsgate Institute, London.

BIBLIOGRAPHY

4. CONTEMPORARY PAMPHLETS, MEMOIRS AND HISTORIES

Alfred (Samuel Kydd), *History of the factory movement*, London, 1857.

A. Alison, *Essays*, Edinburgh, 1850.

— *Some account of my life and writings*, Edinburgh, 1883.

W. P. Alison, *Observations on the management of the poor in Scotland and its effects on the health of the great towns*, Edinburgh, 1840.

P. Brewster, *Essay on passive obedience*, Paisley, 1836 (Mitchell Library, Glasgow).

— *Seven Chartist and military discourses*, Glasgow, 1843.

J. Cleland, *Annals of Glasgow*, Glasgow, 1816.

— *The former and present state of Glasgow*, Glasgow, 1840.

W. Cobbett, *Tour in Scotland*, London, 1833.

H. Cockburn, *Memorials of his own times*, Edinburgh, 1856.

— *Journal of Henry Cockburn*, Edinburgh, 1874.

— *Sedition trials*, Edinburgh, 1888.

T. Cooper, *Life of Thomas Cooper*, London, 1872.

H. Craig, *The spirit of persecution displayed against Hugh Craig, etc.*, Kilmarnock, 1834 (Bodleian, Oxford).

A. Duncanson, *The political rights of the people*, Falkirk, 1843.

J. Dunlop, *Autobiography* (published privately, 1932).

J. R. Fraser, *Memoir of John Fraser*, Paisley, 1879.

A. Gray, *The present conflict*, n.d. (Mitchell Library, Glasgow).

London Working Men's Association, *The rotten House of Commons* (British Museum).

— *The People's Charter*, 1838 (British Museum).

W. Lovett, *The life and struggles of William Lovett*, London, 1876.

P. MacKenzie, *Reminiscences of Glasgow*, Glasgow, 1865-68.

R. Malcolm, *Literary gleanings*, Glasgow, 1850.

E. Mein, *Through four reigns* (life of Robert Cranston), Edinburgh, 1948.

Memoranda of the Chartist agitation in Dundee, n.d. (Dundee Central Library).

J. Myles, *The Charter examined in its Six Points*, Dundee, 1848.

G. H. Nicholls, *A history of the Scotch poor laws*, London, 1856.

W. Norrie, *Edinburgh Newspapers: Past and present*, Earlston, 1891.

J. Pagan, *Glasgow past and present*, Glasgow, 1856.

J. Parkhill, *History of Paisley*, Paisley, 1857.

— *Life and opinions of Arthur Sneddon*, Paisley, 1860.

The People's Charter, 1848 (Mitchell Library, Glasgow).

Political Almanac of J. R. Richardson (1839), 1840 (Mitchell Library, Glasgow).

Report of the trial of Thomas Hunter, Peter Hacket, Richard McNeil, James Gibb, and William McLean (edited by A. Swinton), Edinburgh, 1838.

Report of the trial of Thomas Hunter, etc. (edited by J. Marshall), Edinburgh, 1838.

Reports of the National Reform Conferences, 1862, 1864, 1865.

Reports of the trials for treason, 1817, 1820.

A. B. Richmond, *Narrative of the condition of the manufacturing population and the proceedings of Government, etc.,* Glasgow, 1825.

W. S. Villiers Sankey, *Popular control over hasty legislation,* Edinburgh, 1838 (British Museum).

— *The rights of the operatives asserted,* Edinburgh, 1838 (British Museum).

Sheffield Free Press Serials No. 13, *The Chartist Correspondence,* Sheffield, 1856.

J. Smith, *The grievances of the working classes,* Glasgow, 1846.

A. Somerville, *The autobiography of a working man,* London, 1848.

— *The whistler at the plough,* London, 1852.

J. C. Symons, *Arts and artizans at home and abroad,* London, 1839.

J. Taylor, *Case of duel and statement of the conduct of T. F. Kennedy Esq. of Dunure, M.P., etc.,* 1833 (Bodleian, Oxford).

— *The coming revolution,* Carlisle, 1840 (British Museum).

— *Christian lyrics,* Dublin, 1851 (British Museum).

— *Letters on the ballot,* Glasgow, 1838 (Bodleian, Oxford).

G. E. Troup, *Life of George Troup, journalist,* Edinburgh, 1881.

J. Turner, *Recollections,* Glasgow, 1854.

5. CHARTIST STUDIES

A. Briggs (ed.), *Chartist studies,* London, 1959.

G. D. H. Cole, *Chartist portraits,* London, 1941.

E. Dolléans, *Le Chartisme,* Paris, 1912–13.

H. U. Faulkner, *Chartism and the Churches,* New York, 1916.

H. T. N. Gaitskell, *Chartism,* London, 1929.

R. G. Gammage, *History of the Chartist movement,* London and Newcastle, 1854.

R. Groves, *But we shall rise again,* London, 1938.

M. Hovell, *The Chartist movement,* Manchester, 1918.

F. C. Mather, *Public order in the age of the Chartists,* Manchester, 1959.

D. Read and E. Glasgow, *Feargus O'Connor,* London, 1961.

F. F. Rosenblatt, *The Chartist movement and its social and economic consequences,* New York, 1916.

T. H. Rothstein, *From Chartism to Labourism,* London, 1929.

J. Saville, *Ernest Jones, Chartist*, London, 1952.
A. R. Schoyen, *The Chartist challenge*, London, 1958.
P. W. Slosson, *The decline of the Chartist movement*, New York, 1916.
N. Stewart, *The struggle for the Charter*, London, 1937.
G. C. Thorne, *Chartism: a short history*, London, 1966.
J. West, *History of the Chartist movement*, London, 1920.
D. Williams, *John Frost*, Wales, 1939.
A. Wilson, *The Chartist movement in Scotland*, Wakefield, 1964.
— *Scottish Chartist portraits*, Wakefield, 1965.
L. C. Wright, *Scottish Chartism*, Edinburgh, 1953.

6. SCOTTISH BACKGROUND

C. E. Adams, *The political state of Scotland in 1788*, Edinburgh, 1887.
A. Aird, *Reminiscences of editors, reporters, etc.*, Glasgow, 1890.
D. Bremner, *The industries of Scotland: their rise, progress and present condition*, Edinburgh, 1869.
R. Brown, *History of Paisley*, Paisley, 1886.
J. Cameron, *The parish of Campsie*, Kirkintilloch, 1892.
R. H. Campbell, *Scotland since 1707: the rise of an industrial society*, Oxford, 1965.
— and J. B. A. Dow, *Source book of Scottish economic and social history*, Oxford, 1968.
T. Chalmers, *On political economy*, Glasgow, 1832.
R. M. W. Cowan, *The newspaper in Scotland*, Glasgow, 1946.
H. Craik, *A century of Scottish history*, Edinburgh and London, 1911.
G. Donaldson, *The Scots overseas*, London, 1966.
T. Ferguson, *The dawn of Scottish welfare—to 1863*, Edinburgh and London, 1948.
H. G. Graham, *Social life in Scotland in the eighteenth century*, London, 1901.
I. F. Grant, *The economic history of Scotland*, London, 1934.
J. Grant, *Old and new Edinburgh*, Edinburgh, 1880.
E. S. Haldane, *The Scotland of our fathers*, London, 1933.
H. Hamilton, *The industrial revolution in Scotland*, Oxford, 1932.
— *The economic evolution of Scotland in the eighteenth and nineteenth centuries*, London, 1933.
T. W. Hamilton, *The temperance reformation in Scotland*, Greenock, 1929.
J. Handley, *The Irish in Scotland*, Cork, 1943.
— *The Irish in modern Scotland*, Cork and Oxford, 1947.
W. Hanna, *Memoirs of the life and writings of Thomas Chalmers* (4 vols.), 1850–52.

History of the Hawick Co-operative Store Coy. (Limited), Hawick, 1889.

T. Johnston, *The history of the working classes in Scotland*, Glasgow, 1920.

W. Logan, *Early heroes of the temperance reformation*, London, 1873.

D. F. MacDonald, *Scotland's shifting population, 1770–1850*, Glasgow, 1937.

I. McDougall (ed.), *An interim bibliography of the Scottish working class movement*, Edinburgh, 1965.

J. K. McDowall, *The people's history of Glasgow*, Glasgow, 1899.

G. McGeorge, *History of Glasgow*, Glasgow, 1881.

A. M. Mackenzie, *Scotland in modern times*, London and Edinburgh, 1941.

J. Mackinnon, *The social and industrial history of Scotland from the union to the present time*, London, 1921.

J. Maclaren, *History of Dundee*, Dundee, 1874.

J. Marwick, *The river Clyde and the Clyde burghs*, Glasgow, 1909.

W. H. Marwick, *Early trade unions in Scotland*, London, 1935.

— *Economic developments in Victorian Scotland*, London, 1936.

— *Labour in Scotland*, Glasgow, 1951.

W. L. Mathieson, *Church and reform in Scotland, 1797–1843*, Glasgow, 1916.

— *The awakening of Scotland, 1747–97*, Glasgow, 1910.

W. Maxwell, *The history of co-operation in Scotland*, Glasgow, 1910.

S. Mechie, *The Church and Scottish social development, 1780–1870*, Oxford, 1960.

H. W. Meikle, *Scotland and the French revolution*, Glasgow, 1912.

W. M. Metcalfe, *History of Paisley*, Paisley, 1909.

C. A. Oakley, *The second city*, London and Glasgow, 1946.

G. S. Pryde, *Social life in Scotland since 1707*, London, 1934.

R. S. Tait, *Scotland*, London, 1911.
    and G. S. Pryde, Scotland, 1934.

D. Ramsey, *Reminiscences of Scottish life and character*, Edinburgh and London, 1873.

W. Robbie, *History of Aberdeen*, Aberdeen, 1893.

J. B. Russell, *Public health administration in Glasgow*, Glasgow, 1905.

W. Sanderson, *Scottish life and character*, London, 1904.

L. J. Saunders, *Scottish democracy, 1815–40*, Edinburgh, 1950.

W. Stewart, *The Glasgow press in 1840*, Glasgow, 1921.

A. H. Stirling, *A sketch of Scottish industrial and social life in the nineteenth century*, London, 1906.

T. C. Smout, *A history of the Scottish people, 1560–1830*, London, 1969.

J. Thomson, *History of Dundee*, Dundee, 1874.

7. BRITISH WORKING CLASS MOVEMENT AND REFORM BACKGROUND

G. Armitage-Smith, *The free trade movement and its results*, London, 1903.
J. M. Baernreither *English associations of working men*, London, 1893.
S. Bamford, *Passages from the life of a Radical*, London, 1893.
D. G. Barnes, *The corn laws*, London, 1930.
H. L. Beales, *The early English Socialists*, London, 1933.
— *The industrial revolution*, London, 1958.
M. Beer, *History of British Socialism*, London, 1940.
A. Briggs, *The age of improvement*, London, 1959.
— and J. Saville (eds.), *Essays in labour history*, London, 1967.
T. Carlyle, *Sartor resartus, Heroes, Chartism, etc.* London, 1890.
— *Latter day pamphlets*, London, 1872.
J. H. Clapham, *Economic history of modern Britain. The early railway age*, Cambridge, 1926.
G. D. H. Cole, *British working class politics, 1832–1914*, London, 1941.
— *A short history of the British working class movement, 1789–1947*, London, 1948.
— *A century of co-operation*, London, 1945.
— *Robert Owen*, London, 1925.
— and A. Filson, *British working class movement documents*, London, 1951.
— and R. Postgate, *The common people*, London, 1948.
M. Cole, *Makers of the Labour movement*, London, 1948.
C. D. Collett, *History of the taxes on knowledge*, London, 1933.
B. Disraeli, *Sybil*, London, 1845.
A. E. Dobbs, *Educational and social movements, 1700–1850*, London, 1919.
E. Dolléans, *Histoire du mouvement ouvrier, 1830–71*, Paris, 1936.
M. Edwards, *Methodism and England*, London, 1943.
F. Engels, *Condition of the working classes in 1844*, London, 1892.
C. R. Fay, *Life and labour in the nineteenth century*, Cambridge, 1920.
— *Great Britain from Adam Smith to the present day*, London, 1928.
S. E. Finer, *The life and times of Sir Edwin Chadwick*, London, 1952.
F. E. Gillespie, *Labor and politics in England, 1850–67*, Durham, North Carolina, 1927.
E. Halèvy, *A short history of the English people, 1830–41*, London, 1941.
— *A short history of the English people, 1841–52*, London, 1947.
J. L. and B. Hammond, *The age of the Chartists*, London, 1930.
— *The town labourer*, London, 1917.
— *The skilled labourer*, London, 1919.

J. L. and B. Hammond, *The rise of modern industry*, London, 1930.

S. Hobhouse, *Life of Joseph Sturge*, London, 1919.

E. J. Hobsbawm, *The age of revolution*, London, 1962.

G. J. Holyoake, *History of co-operation*, London, 1906.

— *Sixty years of an agitator's life*, London, 1906.

G. Howell, *Labour legislation, labour movements and labour leaders*, London, 1902.

J. Irving, *Annals of our time, 1837-71*, London, 1876.

C. B. Kent, *The English Radicals*, London, 1899.

C. Kingsley, *Yeast*, London, 1851.

— *Alton Locke*, London, 1862.

F. E. Kingsley, *Charles Kingsley: letters and memories of his life*, London, 1883.

R. E. Leader, *Life and letters of J. A. Roebuck*, London, 1897.

J. M. Ludlow and L. Jones, *The progress of the working classes*, London, 1867.

J. McCarthy, *A short history of our time*, London, 1891.

S. Maccoby, *English Radicalism, 1832-52*, London, 1935.

— *English Radicalism, 1852-86*, London, 1938.

K. Marx, *Capital*, London, 1886.

J. Morley, *Life of Richard Cobden*, London, 1879.

M. Morris (ed.), *From Cobbett to the Chartists, 1815-48*, London, 1951.

A. L. Morton and G. Tate, *The British Labour movement, 1770-1920*, London, 1956.

W. Napier, *Life of Sir Charles J. Napier*, London, 1857.

E. Porritt, *The unreformed House of Commons*, London, 1903.

A. Prentice, *History of the Anti-Corn Law League*, London, 1853.

C. E. Raven, *Christian Socialism. 1848-54*, London, 1920.

D. Read, *Press and people, 1790-1850*, London, 1941.

H. Richard, *Memoirs of Joseph Sturge*, London, 1864.

J. H. Rose, *The rise of democracy*, London, 1897.

W. W. Rostow, *British economy of the nineteenth century*, Oxford, 1948.

— and A. J. Schwarz, *The growth and fluctuation of the British economy, 1790-1850*, Oxford, 1953.

G. Rudé, *The crowd in history*, New York, 1964.

W. Smart, *Economic annals of the nineteenth century, 1820-30*, London, 1917.

N. J. Smelser, *Social change in the industrial revolution*, London, 1959.

A. Somerville, *Free trade and the League*, London, 1853.

E. P. Thompson, *The making of the English working classes*, London, 1963.

BIBLIOGRAPHY

A. Toynbee, *The industrial revolution*, London, 1884.
D. Urquhart, *The progress of Russia*, London, 1853.
C. M. Wakefield, *The life of Thomas Attwood*, London, 1885.
G. Wallas, *Life of Francis Place*, London, 1898.
J. T. Ward, *The factory movement, 1830-55*, London, 1962.
— (ed.), *Popular movements, c. 1830-50*, London, 1970.
R. F. Wearmouth, *Some working class movements of the nineteenth century*, London, 1948.
— *Methodism and the history of working class movements*, London, 1937.
R. K. Webb, *The British working class reader, 1790-1848*, London, 1955.
S. and B. Webb, *The history of trade unionism*, London, 1894.
— *Industrial democracy*, London, 1897.
P. T. Winskill, *Rise and progress of the temperance reformation*, London, 1881.

Index

Principal references are given in *italic* figures

Newspapers, Chartist—*contd*
cratic Review, 246; *Dundee
Chronicle*, 124, 182, 184, 270;
Dundee Herald, 184, 194, 270;
Edinburgh Monthly Democrat, 57,
59, 132, 182; *Leader* 249; *Monthly
Liberator*, 52, 183; *New Liberator*,
34, 45, 54, 94, 181–2; *North British (Weekly) Express*, 216, 236,
239; *Northern Star*, 37, 54, 56, 70,
94, 99, 110, 124, 149, 152, 168–70,
173, 176, 181–2, 184, 199, 201,
203–4, 210–11, 216, 229–30, 232,
235, 270; *Perthshire Chronicle*,
124, 182–3, 270; *Red Republican*,
246; *Scots Times*, 54, 67, 70, 81,
120, 124, 181; *Scottish Patriot*, 81,
96, 99, 106, 109–10, 112, 120,
123–4, 134, 141–2, 151–2, 156–8,
164, 169–70, 181–5, 270; *Star of
Freedom*, 252; *True Scotsman*, 59,
62, 67, 70, 79, 81, 96, 110–11, 114,
120–1, 123–4, 129, 136, 147, 158,
161, 182–3, 185, 270

O'Brien, J. B. ('Bronterre'), 54, 72,
73, 76, 77, 78, 170, 212, 229, 231,
245, 248
O'Connell, Daniel, 37, 64–5, 105, 117,
157–61
O'Connor, Feargus, 34–5, 37, 54–6,
61, 64–7, 71, 76, 78–9, 83, 87–8,
103, 105, 117, 133, 152, 157,
160–1, 164, 167–75, 178, 184–8,
201, 205–7, 210, 212–13, 222, 225,
228–32, 235, 243–5, 247–50
O'Neill, Arthur George, 85, 104,
116–18, 124, 134, 144–5, 153,
161–2, 175

Paisley, 2, 5, 17–18, 36, 45–6, 51, 60,
64, 66 8, 74, 77, 85–6, 97, 102,
107, 109, 118, 120, 124, 127, 135,
140, 142, 144, 147, 154–5, 164,
169–71, 173, 175, 179, 183, 187–9,
201–3, 206, 212, 217–18, 220–3,
226, 229, 245, 247–50, 258, 260–1,

264, 274; R. Bissett, 155; S. Miller,
155; E. Polin, 94, 155
Pattison, William C., 50, 80–1, 90–5,
104, 112, 115, 122, 131, 134–5,
151, 153, 157, 163, 168, 173, 202,
204, 233, 252, 257–8, 272
Perth, 2, 47, 53, 68, 77, 88, 107,
135, 147–8, 156, 164, 170, 250,
273
Perthshire, 71–2, 152, 271, 273
Police: Edinburgh, 217, 230–2, 236;
Glasgow, 154, 169, 208, 218–21,
226, 233, 248; Captain Miller, 13–
14, 169, 227; Captain Pearce, 219–
220
Political background: Aberdeen
trades, 205; anti-corn law associations, 31, 34, 41; Bonnymuir, 27,
33; conservative operatives, 35;
disillusion with Reform Act, 22,
30–1, 50; early Radicalism, 19,
23–9; Edinburgh trades, 29, 32,
263; Friends of the People, 23–4;
Glasgow trades, 28–9, 31–2, 35–6,
39, 47, 54, 81, 97, 153, 230, 257,
263–5; London trades, 263; Operative Cotton Spinners, and cotton
spinners' trial, 17, 36–40, 43; parliamentary elections, 32–3, 74,
163–5, 208–9, 261; political unions,
28, 31–3, 41; Poor Law Amendment Act, 151, 172; riots, 22, 216,
218, 223; spy system, 25, 27, 95–6,
105, 108; trades unions, 19, 31,
35–6, 50, 53; Sir James Graham,
188–9; Sir Robert Peel, 35, 99;
Alexander Richmond, 25, 33; Lord
John Russell, 82, 232–3, 251

Renfrewshire, 53, 77, 83, 121, 194,
271
Ross, George, 41, 91, 123, 163, 167,
177, 183, 186, 196, 201, 206–7,
225, 233, 247, 251, 258, 265, 272

Sankey, W. S. Villers, 59, 72–3, 103,
117, 155–6